From Seed *to* Table

DIANE DEVEREAUX

The Canning Diva®

TEN PEAKS PRESS®
EUGENE, OR

Scripture verses marked KJV are taken from the King James Version of the Bible.

Verses marked NIV are taken from the Holy Bible, New International Version®, NIV®. Copyright © 1973, 1978, 1984, 2011 by Biblica, Inc.® Used with permission of Zondervan. All rights reserved worldwide. www.zondervan.com. The "NIV" and "New International Version" are trademarks registered in the United States Patent and Trademark Office by Biblica, Inc.®

Verses marked NLT are taken from the *Holy Bible*, New Living Translation, copyright © 1996, 2004, 2015 by Tyndale House Foundation. Used with permission of Tyndale House Publishers, Carol Stream, Illinois 60188. All rights reserved.

The author is represented by Tom Dean, Literary Agent with A Drop of Ink LLC, www.adropofink.pub.

Cover design by Faceout Studio, Addie Lutzo
Interior design by Faceout Studio, Paul Nielsen
Photography by Jeff Hage, Green Frog Photo
A special thank you to Paulson's Pumpkin Patch in Belding, Michigan

FROM SEED TO TABLE

Published by Ten Peaks Press, an imprint of Harvest House Publishers
Eugene, Oregon 97408

ISBN 978-0-7369-8909-1 (pbk.)
ISBN 978-0-7369-8910-7 (eBook)

Library of Congress Control Number: 2025940213

Printed in China

26 26 27 28 29 30 31 32 33 34 / DC / 10 9 8 7 6 5 4 3 2 1

To Vicki Neal, Joseph Westmoreland, and Jim Mowrey:

Your friendship, loyalty, and unwavering support have meant more to me than words can express. I am honored to walk this journey with you.

And to the nearly 100,000 members of our private canning group:

Thank you for turning a shared passion into something so much more—a family. You are the heart of this journey, and I am endlessly grateful.

Contents

Introduction

Make it your goal to live a quiet life, minding your own business and working with your hands, just as we instructed you before. Then people who are not believers will respect the way you live, and you will not need to depend on others.

1 THESSALONIANS 4:11-12 (NLT)

Let's face it. The dream of owning a huge homestead with acres of land, a large garden, and possibly some livestock is comforting—exciting, even. We watch popular homesteaders' reels on Instagram and TikTok that make it all look so inviting, wishing we could be just like them one day. Self-sustaining. Self-reliant. Happy.

The movement of "homesteading" has given us all hope and aspirations of a brighter, more simple future where the food is pure and working the land is therapy. But what about those of us who wish to eat and live well, to have food security and be self-reliant, but moving to the countryside is not an option?

The reality is that for most of us, throwing caution to the wind and selling everything to go buy a plot of land to live off simply isn't feasible. Many of us have full-time careers, or live in a city or an apartment or condo, or have no desire to live isolated in the countryside to become self-sufficient.

At the end of the day, though, we shouldn't have to be a homesteader to eat healthier, to adopt a healthier lifestyle. So how do we become food secure with limited land, smaller homes, and limited financial means?

We embrace seasonal living.

What Is Seasonal Living?

A natural cycle governs the changes in the environment and affects human activities, especially in relation to agriculture, food production, and cultural practices. As civilizations have evolved, they've learned to align their lifestyles with these rhythms, fostering a deeper connection with the land and its resources. Each season brings unique characteristics that influence the timing of planting, harvesting, and preserving food. Many refer to this as the *change in seasons.*

For instance, spring is often seen as a time of renewal and growth, when gardeners prepare their soil and sow seeds, anticipating the abundance of summer. Summer, with its long days and warm weather, is a period of vigorous growth and harvesting, filled with vibrant fruits and vegetables that require immediate attention and preservation for the months to come.

As autumn approaches, the focus shifts to gathering and storing the harvest. This season represents a time of reflection, gratitude, and preparation for the colder months ahead. Many cultures celebrate the harvest through festivals that honor the earth's bounty, highlighting the importance of community and shared sustenance. Finally, winter brings a period of rest and introspection. It's a time for utilizing stored foods, gathering around warm fires, and preserving traditions through storytelling and shared meals.

This cyclical nature of seasons not only impacts agricultural practices but shapes cultural identities, influencing everything from dietary habits to social structures. For instance, while the American tradition of Thanksgiving is often associated with the story of Pilgrims and Native Americans coming together, the origins of the holiday are deeply rooted in seasonal rhythms and the celebration of the harvest.

The convenience of modern grocery stores has distanced many people from the experience of growing their own food and the sense of fulfillment that comes with it. For countless generations, food wasn't simply something to be purchased; it was the product of hard work, patience, and a deep connection to the land. Each meal represented the culmination of planning, planting, tending, and harvesting, the example of a true labor of love. The rhythm of seasonal eating was woven into daily life, and people celebrated the fruits of their labor with a gratitude that came from knowing the effort required to bring food to the table.

Today, it's easy to lose sight of that effort. We've traded the satisfaction of growing, preserving, and preparing our food for convenience, often forgetting how miraculous it is to eat something we've nurtured from seed to table. And while convenience has benefits, it often comes at the cost of understanding where our food comes from and the value of eating seasonally and locally.

Reconnecting to Earth's Seasonal Rhythms

In today's fast-paced world, the rise of technology and the convenience it offers have led to a profound disconnection from the natural rhythms that once governed our lives. With the advent of global logistics, food has become available at our fingertips, transcending seasonal boundaries and eliminating the traditional cycles of planting, harvesting, and preserving.

This disconnection is compounded by our reliance on imported goods rather than on cultivating our own food sources. Much of our commercially grown produce is laden with pesticides and harmful chemicals that not only compromise our health but degrade the quality of our soil. The overuse of synthetic fertilizers and pesticides has created a vicious cycle, depleting the earth's natural nutrients and beneficial microorganisms. Further, the expansion of hybrid crops has stripped away essential nutrients, resulting in limited nourishment to our bodies.

Even more so, the reliance on external sources not only drastically impacts our health and well-being but compromises our food security. The fragility of the global supply chain is laid bare during times of crisis, revealing the vulnerabilities of our disconnected lifestyle. To reclaim our autonomy and resilience, it's essential to reintegrate the rhythms of each season into our daily lives.

The Importance of Food Security in Today's World

In the past five years, the world witnessed what happened when the entire supply chain came to an abrupt halt. In American grocery stores, shelves were left bare. Some state governments forbade purchasing certain items, even roping off whole store areas or shuttering businesses' doors altogether. In Great Britain, supermarkets rationed items to their patrons and even turned new customers away.

For the first time in the twenty-first century, much of society was caught off guard and struggled to procure basic consumables. Worse, when these everyday goods were again made available, their prices were exorbitant, leaving people in complete despair. This wake-up call catapulted many into a desire to get back to their roots—or the basics—so they would never again be unable to provide sustenance for themselves or their families.

While working on this book, I spent almost three weeks in Florence, Italy, learning more about the Italian way of life, their growing habits, and their seasonal food production. Italy's dedication to seasonal living and authentic food preparation is an inspiring model of how our connection to the land shapes our well-being.

During my time there, I was struck by how deeply ingrained the seasonal rhythms of nature are within their daily life. In every region, people embrace the seasons not only through their recipes but also in their commitment to sustainable practices like crop rotation, composting, and the preservation of traditional harvesting methods. This respect for the land goes hand in hand with their commitment to food as true nourishment. It's not just about filling a plate; it's about creating a true expression of nature and human skill in balanced harmony.

Italy's 2024 decision to ban lab-grown meat and insects from traditional foods like pasta reflects this ethos. They cherish the idea that food should be a product of honest labor, careful cultivation, and clean ingredients. In a culture where home gardens are common, cooking from scratch is the norm, and ingredients are chosen with care, food security becomes a community endeavor. It is the way of life.

How to Live Seasonally from Seed to Table

We can restore our connection to seasonal living and cultivate our own food security and self-reliance in many ways. While Italy provides one example we can mirror, it's my intent that *From Seed to Table* cultivates what we see God intended for us in 1 Thessalonians 4:11-12: that we live a quiet life, mind our own business, work with our hands, and no longer need to depend on others. The latter includes not depending on a broken system for daily nourishment.

It is my hope that this book gives you some valuable tools and inspiration to pursue the ten goals on the following pages.

1 Start a Seasonal Garden

Grow your own fruits, vegetables, and herbs in alignment with the seasons. Begin with a few plants and expand over time. Growing your own food provides not only fresh ingredients but an understanding of what foods thrive at different times of the year.

2 Preserve the Harvest

Embrace canning, dehydrating, and freezing to extend the shelf life of seasonal produce and proteins. This allows you to enjoy your garden's bounty year-round, reducing reliance on out-of-season, often imported, produce.

3 Cook from Scratch

Avoid processed foods by cooking with whole, fresh ingredients. Try to use local or homegrown ingredients whenever possible. Cooking from scratch allows you to control what goes into your food, avoiding additives, to make healthier meals.

4 Prioritize Farmers Markets and Local Producers

Support local farmers by shopping at farmers markets, where you'll find fresh, seasonal produce. Buying local means you are getting foods likely harvested at peak ripeness, which boosts flavor and nutritional content.

5 Compost to Build Soil Health

Start a compost pile or bin to recycle kitchen scraps and yard waste. This enriches your soil, reduces the need for chemical fertilizers, and promotes a closed-loop system in your gardening practice.

6 Practice Crop Rotation and Companion Planting

No matter the type of garden, learn to rotate your crops each season and consider companion planting to maximize plant health and yield. This reduces pest problems, builds soil fertility, and increases your garden's resilience over time.

7 Raise Backyard Chickens or Small Livestock

If space and local ordinances allow, consider raising chickens for eggs or small livestock for meat. This helps foster a direct connection to your food sources and reduces dependence on industrially produced animal products.

8 Forage for Wild Foods

Learn about edible wild plants in your area and try foraging for mushrooms, herbs, berries, and other local treasures. Foraging fosters a direct connection with nature, expands your understanding of local ecology, and adds variety to your diet.

9 Create a Food Community

Build relationships with neighbors and local farmers, and consider organizing food exchanges where you can trade what you grow or preserve with others. This builds community resilience, strengthens social bonds, and promotes local food security.

10 Embrace Seasonal Cooking

Cook and eat in sync with the seasons, focusing on lighter, refreshing dishes in the warmer months and heartier, warming foods in the cooler months. This practice helps keep meals fresh, exciting, and nutritionally aligned with what your body needs seasonally.

By taking even small steps toward these practices, we can become more self-reliant and gain a greater sense of security in our food sources. More importantly, we can nurture a deeper connection to the land and our food. Embracing seasonal living isn't merely a return to the past; it's a proactive step toward a more resilient and fulfilling future—just as God intended.

1

Establishing Food Security

Brothers and sisters, we urge you to warn those who are lazy. Encourage those who are timid. Take tender care of those who are weak. Be patient with everyone. See that no one pays back evil for evil, but always try to do good to each other and to all people. Always be joyful. Never stop praying. Be thankful in all circumstances, for this is God's will for you who belong to Christ Jesus.

1 THESSALONIANS 5:14-18 (NLT)

In 2020, the world stood still. People were locked down in their homes, prevented from roaming freely, from shopping, from attending church. Grocery store shelves were bare, and restaurants were closed. Many individuals were caught unaware with limited food in their homes, and necessities were unavailable for purchase.

While some people weathered this calamity with ease, others grappled with the fact that they'd been unprepared for tough times, caught without the nutrition they needed to stay healthy. Worse, in the midst of a global pandemic, we noticed our food supply chain was being dismantled. And most of us weren't prepared for what lay ahead while the world got "back on track," a process still ongoing. Fires have also killed a large portion of American poultry and livestock, making this so-called comeback even harder and more expensive for the everyday person and small business owner.

What Does This Mean for the Security of Our Food?

Most Americans rely on commercial farms for their key sources of protein. According to recent USDA data, average American consumption of poultry each year is 97 pounds per person, and beef consumption is approximately 58 pounds per person per year. Obviously, these averages can vary slightly based on dietary trends and so forth, but reliance on these sources of protein is clear.

Consider, then, the effect of something like a commercial barn fire. In a mere 14-month period of April 2021 to June 2022, there were 96 recorded barn fires in the United States alone, leading to the death of millions of farm animals. With demand high and availability scarce, this led to skyrocketing prices. To a nation still in pandemic recovery, the impact to our food resources was substantial.

Adding Insult to Injury

In addition to pandemic-related supply chain challenges and the destruction of millions of healthy animals, the use of harmful substances in commercial food production has reached an all-time high in America. This has raised significant concerns regarding public health. Regulatory bodies like the USDA and FDA have come under scrutiny for allowing the overuse of chemicals and additives in commercial agriculture and food processing. For example, pesticides such as glyphosate, a chemical that's been linked to health issues, are widely used in the cultivation of various crops. Despite mounting evidence of its potential carcinogenic effects, glyphosate continues to be permitted in food production across the United States, with residues commonly detected in grains and other staple foods.

Similarly, food additives such as artificial colorings and preservatives are permitted in processed foods in the US, even though studies have associated some of these substances with adverse health effects, including hyperactivity in children and increased risk of chronic diseases. This regulatory leniency has encouraged industrial agriculture practices to prioritize high yields and cost efficiency over consumer health.

Economic and Industry Influence on Regulations

In the United States, the FDA and USDA are heavily influenced by industry through lobbying efforts and the so-called "revolving door" phenomenon, where individuals move between roles in government regulatory bodies and the industries they regulate. This influence often leads to regulations that are more lenient in the US compared to other countries.

In the case of pesticides like glyphosate, the US regulatory stance has generally aligned with industry research and data that favor continued use. Independent studies, however, have associated glyphosate exposure with increased cancer risk, particularly non-Hodgkin's lymphoma, fueling legal battles and consumer concerns. The U.S. Environmental Protection Agency (EPA) has faced criticism for relying on industry-funded studies when assessing glyphosate's safety. The American regulatory bodies regulate using the proverbial analogy of the fox guarding the hen house.

The result: a high rate of chronic disease in America.

For this reason, society is beginning to see the value in prioritizing fresh, minimally processed foods and advocating for stronger regulations to counteract these systemic issues. And until there is a holistic change in how these agencies "regulate" our food and water supply, home-growing and preservation methods enable individuals to avoid these harmful chemicals, providing a cleaner and healthier alternative for themselves and their families.

Benefits of Growing and Preserving Your Own Food

Let's switch gears back to when governments and regulatory bodies encouraged their people to be self-sustaining. During World War II, the US government encouraged Americans to be self-sustaining in powerful ways, fostering resilience and community. At a time when rationing, scarcity, and sacrifice were the norm, citizens were urged to embrace what were called Victory Gardens, preserve food at home, and support local farmers. These efforts weren't just practical solutions to wartime challenges; they were a call to action that united people and strengthened communities. Advertisements were made promoting self-reliance.

Americans were also encouraged to keep a few chickens in their backyards, providing their families with a steady supply of fresh eggs and sometimes meat. This served as a reminder that even small efforts could make a big impact. Chickens offered self-sufficiency on a manageable scale and provided a tangible sense of security for families amid wartime uncertainties. Today, we can draw on this inspiration, as raising backyard chickens continues to be a rewarding way to participate in a sustainable lifestyle. It's why many residents in America are fighting local ordinances to return to chicken keeping instead of viewing these self-sustaining measures as "blight" within the community.

Home Canning and Food Preservation

Home canning became a staple in American households during WWII. Canning at home allowed families to store seasonal produce, stretching their food supplies through the winter and times when fresh produce was scarce. The government promoted canning as a vital skill, distributing pamphlets and holding community demonstrations on how to safely preserve food. Canning not only ensured a steady food supply but connected people to their food in a deeply meaningful way. The jars lining pantries and root cellars weren't "just food"; they were a testament to resourcefulness and shared knowledge passed down through generations.

Supporting Local Farmers and Buying Local

Buying local and supporting small farms were also priorities during WWII. With limited fuel and transportation resources, Americans were encouraged to source food from local farmers, fostering a community-based approach to food security. Farmers markets thrived as neighbors came together, shared their harvests, and made conscious choices to buy from within their own communities. This local-first approach kept money circulating in local economies, strengthened agricultural connections, and ensured that fresh, seasonal foods were always available.

This era showed that self-sufficiency wasn't about going it alone but rather about creating a network of support benefiting everyone in the community. People shared seeds, swapped gardening tips, and hosted canning parties where neighbors would come together, share equipment, and preserve the harvest as a collective effort. This shared work strengthened the sense of community and mutual support. By growing, preserving, and sharing food, Americans and their allies not only reduced the strain on the national food supply but created bonds that helped them weather the hardships of wartime.

The Movement Toward Self-Reliance and Seasonal Living

Creating food security in our homes starts with reconnecting with the most fundamental process: growing, preserving, and preparing our food. When you grow and preserve your own food, you take control over what you and your family consume. In an age when food sourcing is often removed from our immediate lives, the ability to grow and preserve is a form of self-empowerment.

Let's delve into some of the key benefits.

Nutritional Advantages

Homegrown and preserved foods retain the nutrients you need to thrive. By harvesting at peak ripeness and preserving promptly, you maximize the retention of vitamins, minerals, and antioxidants. When canned, fresh vegetables retain essential nutrients—and in some cases the process of canning actually enhances their benefits. For example, canned tomatoes are a rich source of lycopene, a powerful antioxidant that becomes more bioavailable through the heat of the canning process.

When you preserve food, you also maintain control over the ingredients and methods used. Without relying on preservatives, dyes, or excess sodium, you capture the true flavors and wholesome nutrients. Canning at home means each jar is a testament to your own care and commitment to health. In contrast, store-bought products often contain additives that you can easily avoid by preparing your own pantry essentials.

Preservation techniques further contribute to sustainability by allowing you to store food when it's abundant and avoid waste. In times of surplus, you can dehydrate, cold-store, or can excess produce, which ensures you have a supply of homegrown food all year long. This practice aligns your food consumption with the natural seasons, reducing the need for imported, out-of-season produce.

Understanding Your Local Ecosystem

Every region has its own unique ecosystem that supports certain types of plants. Learning about the soil, climate, and natural cycles where you live gives you an advantage in growing a healthy, productive garden. As you observe the ways plants interact with one another, attract pollinators, and respond to your local weather patterns, you gain insight into the delicate balance that supports sustainable food production.

We'll explore this knowledge further in chapter 2, which will help you choose crops well-suited to your environment, reducing the need for synthetic fertilizers or pesticides. You can plan your garden in harmony with the land by growing varieties that naturally thrive in your area. By cultivating a strong local ecosystem, you create a self-sustaining environment where plants, insects, and animals work together.

Further, eating with the seasons brings a sense of rhythm and satisfaction that's often missing in the modern diet. Seasonal eating encourages us to embrace the natural cycles of abundance, savoring foods at their peak of freshness. When you're enjoying a meal made with food from your own garden, each bite is a celebration of nature's bounty.

Building a Well-Rounded Food Supply

Throughout this book we'll dive into the various areas we can control within our own homes and on our land, no matter how small. While each chapter gives an in-depth look at how to do that, the goal is to have a well-rounded pantry supply. We must secure a lasting supply of ingredients needed to prepare balanced, nutritious meals throughout the year. I'll show you how, through incorporating various preservation methods, you can create a pantry that supports you through each season and supplies essential nutrients no matter what challenges arise.

So that you can relate the material in this book to your home, budget, lifestyle, and needs, it's important to have the foundational essentials ready. Your pantry should include a diverse array of items covering basic food groups and provide the foundation for meals. Dry goods like grains, legumes, and pasta offer shelf-stable sources of protein and carbohydrates. Cold-storage items, such as root vegetables, apples, and cabbages, can last for months in the right conditions. Dehydrated foods, including herbs, fruits, and vegetables, are nutrient-dense and lightweight, making them easy to store and use.

Canned foods are versatile and convenient, giving you ready-to-eat, fully cooked foods at the pop of a lid. With home-canned soups, stews, and sauces, you can prepare a hearty meal in minutes. These foods allow you to take advantage of seasonal abundance, preserving peak-season produce to enjoy year-round. Freeze-dried and dehydrated ingredients store beautifully and are lightweight and easy to transport. While they require reconstituting with fresh drinkable water, freeze-dried foods retain the most nutrients, giving your family sustenance when it's needed most.

The Must-Haves in a Seasonal Pantry

To create a seasonal pantry that serves you well, focus on a few key staples that provide essential nutrients and versatility in the kitchen.

- Whole grains like rice, oats, and barley form the base of many meals. Dried beans and lentils are rich in protein and fiber. Root vegetables, squash, garlic, and onions are flavorful and long-lasting. Include herbs and spices to elevate simple meals and provide variety. Canned tomatoes, homemade stocks and broths, and preserved meat and fish enhance your culinary options and allow you to cook with creativity and ease.
- Other pantry staples include fats and oils, flour, and baking supplies like baking soda, salt, baking powder, cornmeal, and sugars. Also include supplements like pasta, molasses, honey, and nut butter. Keeping homemade vanilla extract, apple cider vinegar, and herbal tinctures in your pantry are essential items for staying healthy and enhancing your meals and baking.
- Items to keep on hand so you can continue to both preserve and create include canning lids and rings, mason jars, pickling lime, canning and pickling salt, pink curing salt, and 40-proof alcohol (vodka or bourbon). Other essentials like instant yeast for bread making and mesophilic cultures for cheese making should be kept in cold storage or your refrigerator.

Throughout this book you'll learn a variety of food crafts so you can make your own butter, create your own apple cider vinegar, water glass eggs, and so much more. Having a well-rounded pantry of not only foods to consume but the agents to help you craft and preserve are essential to being well-rounded in your food security plan.

Seasonal Variations and Stocking Strategies

Your pantry needs to change with the seasons, so it's essential to adapt your storage practices to fit your current needs. In the summer you might focus on canning tomatoes, peppers, and stone fruits, while in the winter you might dehydrate herbs and make soup bases from stored root vegetables. By aligning your preservation activities with the seasonal harvest, you ensure a continuous supply of food that matches your culinary needs.

When stocking your pantry, think about how much you consume and then plan accordingly. And be sure to rotate your supply of essentials on hand, using the oldest items first to maintain freshness and reduce waste. The last thing you want is to forget you stored something and stumble upon it well after it's safe to consume. To help you rotate your pantry items efficiently and keep your pantry organized and prevent spoilage, label each container with the date it was preserved and follow a "first in, first out" system. The key is using the oldest items before newer ones. Last, store items in a cool, dark place to extend their shelf life.

Regularly review your pantry to see what needs to be restocked or used up. To do so, create an itemized list of your pantry contents and their use-by dates. Tally up how much you have of each item, and then when you shop in your pantry, be sure to notate what you've used on your list. By maintaining an organized and well-stocked pantry, you build a resilient food system that supports you through each season and ensures food security for your household.

Food Security Starts at Home

In a time when food supply chains are more vulnerable than ever, building personal food security is a crucial safeguard. I've highlighted the immense scale of food lost due to fires, production failures, and regulatory shortcomings, underscoring how critical it is to establish a steady, reliable food supply at home. Just as Americans did during World War II, we can fortify our pantries, preserve what we grow, and build a foundation of self-reliance. By maintaining a 3-month, 6-month, 9-month, or even a year's worth of food, we're not only protecting ourselves against shortages but gaining peace of mind and resilience only self-sufficiency can provide.

Creating a robust food reserve doesn't have to be overwhelming. You can start small and feel confident knowing each step brings you closer to security. Begin by incorporating a few extra shelf-stable items into each shopping trip: an extra bag of rice here, a couple boxes of canning lids there. Plan your canning calendar annually to ensure you're preserving foods at the height of harvest. If this is a new endeavor for you, start by focusing on building a 3-month food supply.

3-Month Food Supply Plan (Family of 4)

This plan incorporates a variety of shelf-stable items, preserved foods, and fresh storage items to create balanced and nutritious meals. It also provides tips on building and maintaining your reserve items throughout the year.

Grains and Legumes

RICE: 50 pounds (versatile for side dishes, casseroles, stir-fries)

PASTA: 30 pounds (include a variety of types for meal variety)

OATS: 15 pounds (great for breakfasts, baking, and snacks)

DRIED BEANS AND LENTILS: 40 pounds (mix of black beans, lentils, chickpeas, etc. for soups, stews, and salads)

FLOUR: 25 pounds (useful for baking bread, pancakes, and other staples)

Proteins

HOME-CANNED MEAT: 30 quarts or 60 pints mason jars (mix of chicken, tuna, and salmon; about 3 quarts per week for protein additions)

HOME-CANNED BEANS: 15 quarts or 30 pints mason jars (supplement additional protein with canned beans if you don't have access to fresh water to cook dried beans)

NUT BUTTERS: 6 jars (variety of peanut, almond, and sunflower butter for easy snacks and meal additions)

EGG SUBSTITUTES: 12 containers of powdered eggs or equivalent substitutes (for baking and meal prep when fresh eggs aren't available)

SHELF-STABLE TOFU OR TEMPEH: 10 packs (alternative plant-based protein option)

Fruits and Vegetables

CANNED VEGETABLES: 60 cans (variety of tomatoes, green beans, corn, peas, etc.)

CANNED FRUITS: 30 cans (mix of peaches, pineapple, and pears; packed in water or juice)

DRIED FRUITS: 10 pounds (such as raisins, cranberries, and apples; great for snacks and adding to cereals or baking)

POTATOES: 50 pounds (these will last a few months if properly stored, in a cool, dry place)

ONIONS AND GARLIC: 10 pounds (essential for flavoring meals; also store well in a cool, dark place)

CANNED SOUPS AND STEWS: 24 cans (for easy, quick meals on busy days)

Dairy and Alternatives

POWDERED MILK: 6 cans or boxes (useful for cooking, baking, and as a milk substitute)

SHELF-STABLE MILK ALTERNATIVES: 12 quarts (such as almond, oat, or soy milk; good for those with dairy allergies)

CHEESE POWDER OR CANNED CHEESE: 6 cans (use for flavoring dishes or as an ingredient in sauces and casseroles)

Oils and Fats

COOKING OIL: 3 gallons (olive, vegetable, or coconut oil; essential for cooking and baking)

GHEE OR SHELF-STABLE BUTTER SUBSTITUTE: 6 jars or containers (useful for sautéing, frying, and as a fresh butter substitute)

SHORTENING OR LARD: 2 pounds (useful for baking and cooking needs)

Seasonings and Condiments

SALT: 3 pounds (for cooking, preserving, and adding flavor)

HERBS AND SPICES: variety pack (include essentials like basil, oregano, cinnamon, black pepper, and garlic powder)

HONEY OR MAPLE SYRUP: 2 quarts (natural sweeteners that also store well)

VINEGAR: 2 gallons (apple cider and white vinegar; useful for cooking, cleaning, and preserving)

SOY SAUCE, HOT SAUCE, OR OTHER FLAVOR ENHANCERS: 3 bottles (helps add variety to meals)

Other Essentials

TEA OR COFFEE: 5 pounds (whatever your family drinks daily for comfort and routine)

CANNED OR DRY SOUPS: 12 cans (for quick meals when cooking isn't an option)

BAKING SUPPLIES: baking powder, baking soda, yeast (for making bread and baked goods)

FREEZE-DRIED SNACKS AND COMFORT FOODS: crackers, granola bars, dried fruit, and nuts (2 to 3 pounds each for snacking and to boost morale)

These items are what you will keep on "reserve" in your pantry to use in the event of a natural or man-made disaster. And a disaster is relative to you and your family. It could be a job loss, a death in the family, caring for a sick spouse or family member. Or it could be something catastrophic like a wildfire, hurricane, tornado, or winter ice storm.

The key is having a well-rounded pantry with fully cooked, ready-to-eat items, dried food items, and baked goods, as well as fresh foods in cold storage and freeze-dried foods—all with the longest shelf life and highest nutritional value.

Tips for Building Your 3-Month Food Supply

1 Start Small

Begin by buying one or two extra items on each shopping trip. Focus on shelf-stable foods your family already enjoys, gradually building a stock of items you know will get used.

2 Focus on One Food Category at a Time

For example, spend a month adding canned proteins to your stockpile, then switch to grains or home-canned vegetables. Over time, this helps you build variety without overwhelming your budget.

3 Rotate and Replace Regularly

Use a "first-in, first-out" system, especially for canned goods, and replace items as you use them to maintain freshness.

4 Leverage Sales and Bulk Buys

Look for sales on staple items like rice, pasta, dried beans, and coffee, or consider buying in bulk at warehouse stores to save on cost.

5 Shop Thrift Stores and Estate/Yard Sales

At thrift stores and estate or yard sales, various food-crafting items—like water bathers, pressure canners, jars, food-grade storage buckets, crocks, and brining containers—are often available at steep discounts. Purchasing used items helps stretch your budget so more can be spent on quality ingredients.

As you add more items to your food supply, be sure to plan meals around your reserves, using and replenishing them on a consistent basis. By gradually working toward a full year's supply, you develop both a resource and a system.

This approach is not just about having enough food stocked up. It's also about learning how to live in harmony with every change in season and find joy in preserving your harvest. In doing so, you're not only building personal food security but creating a community-centered approach to food resilience for a time when it is needed the most.

In an era when we've been coaxed into believing that health and wellness can be found in pills, lab-developed ingredients, and overly processed foods, it's more important than ever to remember the true foundation of health: our soil.

Ball
MASON

2

Planting and Growing

This constant lying is not aimed at making the people believe a lie, but at ensuring that no one believes anything anymore. A people that can no longer distinguish between truth and lies cannot distinguish between right and wrong. And such a people, deprived of the power to think and judge, is, without knowing and willing it, completely subjected to the rule of lies. With such a people, you can do whatever you want.

HANNAH ARENDT

German historian and philosopher, October 14, 1906–December 4, 1975

Just as Hannah Arendt poignantly observed in her quote above, when people are deprived of the ability to distinguish truth from lies, they become vulnerable to forces that care little about their well-being. For decades, Big Pharma and Big Agriculture have influenced our understanding of health and food, leading many to believe convenience equates to nourishment and synthetically enhanced products are as good as—if not better than—what nature has to offer. This detachment from our seasonal rhythms has left us unhealthy, malnourished, and disconnected from the very source of our vitality: the earth.

Let's begin our focus with reconnecting to the soil and its vital role in nurturing our bodies. By cultivating our food and adopting sustainable gardening practices, we regain control over what we consume and how it's produced. The health of the soil is inseparable from our own; it breathes life into the plants we eat, and these plants in turn offer the nutrition that sustains us.

Health begins in the ground beneath our feet. So let's dig in and reclaim our connection to what defines true wellness.

Understanding Soil Composition

Soil varies drastically across the world, shaped by climate, geological history, and even cultural agricultural practices. From the sandy soils of arid deserts to the rich, dark loams of river valleys, each type of soil offers unique challenges and benefits for growing food. Recognizing and working with the specific soil composition in your area is the first step to successful gardening or farming.

By understanding the basic components of soil, you'll be able to evaluate and amend it to support healthy plant growth no matter where you are in the world.

Organic Matter

Organic matter is the decomposed remains of plants, animals, and other organisms, and it's critical to soil health. This component is often referred to as humus and serves as a reservoir of nutrients. Organic matter also improves soil structure, which enhances root penetration and boosts water retention. It fosters an environment where beneficial microbes and earthworms can thrive, further enriching the soil ecosystem. No matter where you live, adding organic matter like compost can significantly boost your soil's productivity.

Sand

Sand particles are the largest of the three mineral components and feel gritty to the touch. While sandy soils often drain well and allow roots to spread easily, they struggle to retain water and nutrients. This can be particularly challenging in areas with low rainfall, as sandy soils tend to dry out quickly. Because sandy soils are often well-aerated, however, they're excellent for crops that require good drainage, such as carrots and asparagus. Adding organic matter to sandy soil can help improve water and nutrient retention, making it more versatile for a broader range of plants.

Silt

Silt particles are smaller than sand particles and feel smooth when rubbed between your fingers. This soil type is often found near rivers, as water transports and deposits silt along riverbanks and floodplains. Silt has moderate water retention and nutrient-holding capacity, making it quite fertile and easier to work with than sand or clay. Its fine particles contribute to a smooth soil texture, which can compact over time, reducing aeration. Incorporating organic matter into silt-heavy soils can help improve structure, promoting better drainage and root development.

Clay

Clay particles are the smallest and are known for their ability to hold water and nutrients effectively. Clay-heavy soils are found in many parts of Asia and Eastern Europe, and although they can be difficult to manage, they're commonly associated with high fertility. While clay soil is rich in essential nutrients, it tends to become compacted, leading to poor drainage and root penetration. This means that in wet conditions, clay soil can become waterlogged, depriving plants of oxygen. By adding organic matter or sand, however, you can help break up the clay, improving drainage and creating a more balanced soil for a range of crops.

Putting It All Together

Healthy soil is the cornerstone of productive gardening, so investing time in understanding and amending your soil can lead to robust plants, nutritious produce, and a more resilient growing environment regardless of where you live.

As you can clearly see from the various soils listed above, organic matter is the key to amending soil, no matter which type of soil makes up your land. But each of these components contributes to the overall structure, fertility, and productivity of soil. For example, if your soil is primarily sandy, adding organic matter and a small amount of clay can improve water retention and nutrient availability. If your soil is clay-heavy,

SOIL COMPOSITION GUIDE WITH AMENDMENTS

Soil Type	Characteristics	Amendments Needed	Recommended Crops
SAND	Drains quickly, low in nutrients, poor water retention	Add organic matter (compost, manure), clay to improve water retention, mulching to prevent evaporation	Carrots, lettuce, peppers, strawberries, tomatoes
SILT	Smooth texture, moderate water retention, moderate nutrient holding	Add compost to enhance structure and drainage, cover crops to prevent compaction, use organic fertilizers for nutrients	Beans, peas, herbs, root vegetables, greens
CLAY	High water retention, nutrient-dense, poor drainage, compacts easily	Incorporate organic matter (compost), gypsum, sand to improve drainage, aerate regularly	Broccoli, cabbage, spinach, kale, berries
LOAM	Balanced mix of sand, silt, clay; good drainage and nutrient retention	Generally well-balanced; maintain with compost, rotate crops to replenish nutrients	Most vegetables and herbs, including tomatoes, squash, cucumbers, peppers

incorporating organic matter, sand, or even gypsum can help break up compaction and enhance root growth.

Benefits of Raised Container Beds for Small Spaces and Challenging Soils

It's often assumed that, as The Canning Diva, I have a huge farm with an acre garden. The reality is I don't—not anymore. When I was a teenager, we had a huge hog farm, worked over 80 acres of crops for our livestock, and had a 2-acre garden for our personal consumption. And while I've always had a garden, later in life I transitioned to raised container beds after working hard to keep a 40 × 40-foot garden amended. But now, with two adult children and having downsized my home and outdoor space, I grow produce in in-ground beds in my yard and raised container beds on my back deck. I also use grow bags throughout my landscaping. For gardeners like me, working with limited space or dealing with problematic soil types, raised container beds offer a practical and highly effective solution.

Raised and in-ground beds allow you to bypass the limitations of your native soil by giving you complete control over soil composition, drainage, and even the structure and height of your growing area. Whether you have a small backyard, a patio,

or even just a rooftop, these beds can turn otherwise unusable space into a thriving garden.

Here are some important reasons to consider using raised or in-ground garden beds:

Control Over Soil Composition

Gardeners are no longer at the mercy of their existing soil. You can fill the beds with a balanced mix of organic matter, compost, and topsoil, creating the ideal growing medium tailored specifically to your plants' needs. This will give you healthier plants and higher yields.

Improved Drainage and Aeration

Raised and in-ground beds naturally enhance drainage, which is essential for most plants to thrive. Elevation of the beds prevents water from pooling around the roots and promotes healthier, more oxygen-rich soil. For raised beds not connected to the earth, most are self-watering with drain plugs to avoid drowning the roots of the plants.

Efficient Use of Space

Raised beds allow gardeners short on space to make the most of their area. Not limited to in-ground plots, you can build raised beds in various shapes and sizes, adjusting them to fit around walkways, patios, or other landscaping features. Vertical gardening techniques, such as trellising and stacking, can also be incorporated into raised beds to further maximize your growing area.

Easier Maintenance

Raised and in-ground beds reduce the amount of weeding required by elevating your plants above ground level, which helps keep out unwanted weeds and grasses. They also allow for easier maintenance, as you can work at a comfortable height, reducing strain on your back and knees.

Aesthetics and Accessibility

The beauty of green leaves and produce adorns my deck, giving life and ambiance to my outdoor living space. It truly is beautiful and peaceful, my favorite place to sit and relax while sipping a cup of coffee or a glass of wine. Raised beds also improve accessibility. When I'm making dinner, there's nothing better than stepping onto my deck to pick a handful of green beans to create a side dish or cut a bunch of lettuce to make a salad.

Whether you're facing poor soil, limited space, or mobility concerns, raised and in-ground beds make it possible to grow abundant, healthy plants in nearly any environment. By investing in them, you can cultivate a productive garden supporting fresh, healthy produce.

Companion Planting and Crop Rotation

Companion planting offers continual nutrients back into the soil during growth and keeps pests away naturally. When I toured Dalle Nostre Mani, a vineyard and ancient olive grove in Fucecchio, Tuscany, Italy, the people there shared their pride in remaining true to the old ways of companion planting. Alongside their rows of grape vines, they

Instructions for Erecting an In-Ground Garden Bed

Those of us who want to stay connected to the earth and keep our garden beds connected to the soil may opt for in-ground garden beds. After carefully selecting a location in your yard, you must take these five important steps prior to filling your in-ground bed with soil.

1. Cut down large cardboard boxes and remove any adhesive tape, staples, or clamps.
2. Place the cardboard on the ground inside the in-ground bed and be sure to cover the ground (or grass) completely. It's okay to double up the cardboard layer to fully cover the ground.
3. Next, place sticks and small branches on top of the cardboard, ensuring they lay as flat as possible and don't poke upward into the garden bed.
4. Add a layer of topsoil, then a layer of compost or organic matter, then a layer of raised garden bed soil, and then a layer of loam or sandy loam. Repeat this process until the bed is filled, then mix well.
5. Mix in an all-purpose organic and natural plant fertilizer such as Trifecta+ (5-10-4), according to the directions. The 5-10-4 represents a safe blend of nitrogen, phosphate, and potash, aiding in root and plant growth as well as boosting a plant's immunity.

purposefully grow fava beans. They do this because the beans give the soil a constant supply of nitrogen. After the beans are harvested and the plants quit producing, they till the bean plants into the soil so they decompose, creating organic matter, which gives further nutrients back to the grape vines.

Many organic farmers in America do the same. Earlier, I mentioned that those 80 acres we had when I was growing up in northern Michigan grew crops for our livestock. Corn is a common crop grown in my home state, but it robs the soil of nitrogen. So every other season we grew green beans where we'd just grown corn, then returned to growing corn. Using this natural method of soil amendment, we were able to keep our soil organic without the need for synthetic fertilizers.

Rotating corn with nitrogen-fixing plants like green beans is a time-tested method that benefits soil health and enhances crop productivity. If you grow corn in your garden, container bed, or otherwise, be sure to rotate the corn's location each year and grow green beans in its place. In addition to providing nutrients to the soil, companion plants work to keep pests at bay, whether insects or vermin like deer, rabbits, and squirrels.

Here are ten easy-to-grow vegetables along with two companion plants each—one to enrich the soil and one to help deter pests:

Lettuce +

SOIL ENRICHER: **Radishes**—grow quickly and loosen the soil, which can help air and water reach lettuce roots.

PEST DETERRENT: **Chives**—help repel aphids and other common lettuce pests because of their scent.

Spinach +

SOIL ENRICHER: **Peas**—are nitrogen-fixing plants that enhance soil fertility.

PEST DETERRENT: **Garlic**—repels aphids and other pests with its strong aroma.

Carrots +

SOIL ENRICHER: **Bush Beans**—fix nitrogen in the soil and enhance soil structure for future carrot crops.

PEST DETERRENT: **Rosemary**—deters carrot flies and other root pests with its scent.

Radishes +

SOIL ENRICHER: **Legumes** (such as peas or beans)—fix nitrogen in the soil.

PEST DETERRENT: **Nasturtiums**—attract aphids away from radishes and act as a natural pest trap.

Beets +

SOIL ENRICHER: **Lettuce**—helps cover the soil, reducing moisture loss, and helps beets grow.

PEST DETERRENT: **Mint**—repels pests like aphids and flea beetles with its scent.

Peppers +

SOIL ENRICHER: **Clover**—is a ground cover that provides nitrogen and helps with soil health.

PEST DETERRENT: **Basil**—repels aphids, spider mites, and mosquitoes while enhancing pepper flavor.

Tomatoes +

SOIL ENRICHER: **Borage**—adds trace minerals back to the soil and is known to improve tomato flavor.

PEST DETERRENT: **Marigolds**—repel nematodes, aphids, and other harmful insects.

Cucumbers +

SOIL ENRICHER: **Peas**—are nitrogen-fixing plants that help the soil, especially in early spring.

PEST DETERRENT: **Dill**—attracts beneficial insects that prey on cucumber pests like aphids and squash bugs.

Bush Beans +

SOIL ENRICHER: **Thyme**—helps improve soil quality over time and releases beneficial compounds.

PEST DETERRENT: **Marigolds**—help deter beetles and other pests that could damage beans.

Zucchini +

SOIL ENRICHER: **Nasturtiums**—grow as a ground cover that adds nutrients and keeps soil healthy.

PEST DETERRENT: **Catnip**—naturally deters aphids, squash bugs, and flea beetles.

These vegetables and their companion plants are easy to manage in raised and in-ground beds, as well as planted directly in the ground, supporting healthy soil and offering natural pest control. Even if you've already started your vegetable garden, you can still find areas to add these helpful companion plants. Use the sides of the garden beds or the start and end of each row, and feel free to pepper these plants throughout the rows even if your garden is already growing. Doing so will give your vegetables and the soil exactly what they need.

Companion Herb Planting for Culinary Use and Pest Control

When it comes to gardening, herbs offer so much more than just fresh flavors for your cooking. These powerful plants can boost soil health, repel pests, and make your garden more productive overall. By incorporating herbs as companion plants, you'll improve your garden's ecosystem and have a steady supply of fresh ingredients to dehydrate, can, and cook with all year long.

Let's take a closer look at how some key herbs can work alongside your vegetables to keep your garden healthy and your pantry well-stocked.

Basil

SOIL BENEFITS: Improves the flavor of tomatoes and peppers when planted nearby and helps with soil fertility by attracting pollinators.

PEST CONTROL: Repels aphids, asparagus beetles, and tomato hornworms.

CULINARY USE: Is a versatile herb, perfect for pesto, salads, and tomato dishes. Dehydrate or can basil-infused oils for year-round use.

Thyme

SOIL BENEFITS: Thrives in a variety of soil types, and its ground-covering properties help reduce soil erosion.

PEST CONTROL: Wards off cabbage worms, whiteflies, and corn earworms.

CULINARY USE: Is excellent for roasting meats and vegetables. Dry thyme sprigs or add them to vinegar for flavorful homemade marinades.

Sage

SOIL BENEFITS: Acts as a living mulch, retaining moisture and suppressing weeds.

PEST CONTROL: Repels cabbage moths, carrot flies, and flea beetles.

CULINARY USE: Adds a savory touch to soups and roasted dishes. Dries well and retains its pungent flavor for rubs and seasoning blends.

Rosemary

SOIL BENEFITS: Is great for loose, sandy soils and can be used in areas where soil compaction is an issue.

PEST CONTROL: Deters mosquitoes, carrot flies, and slugs.

CULINARY USE: Is ideal for roasting meats and making herbed salts. Can be dehydrated and stored or added to infused oils for a culinary treat.

Mint

SOIL BENEFITS: Helps aerate soil with its spreading root system; however, it's best planted in containers to avoid taking over the garden.

PEST CONTROL: Repels ants, aphids, and flea beetles.

CULINARY USE: Is a refreshing addition to teas, desserts, and salads. Can be dried for teas or blended into sauces.

Dill

SOIL BENEFITS: Is known to attract beneficial insects, like ladybugs and hoverflies, which improve soil health by reducing harmful pests.

PEST CONTROL: Is effective against aphids and spider mites, while also attracting pollinators.

CULINARY USE: Is ideal for pickling, adding to seafood dishes, and flavoring dips. Can be dried for use in spice blends or added to pickling jars for extra zing.

Chives

SOIL BENEFITS: Helps improve soil health by repelling pests and growing back quickly after harvesting.

PEST CONTROL: Repels aphids, carrot rust flies, and Japanese beetles.

CULINARY USE: Adds a mild onion flavor to dishes. Can be frozen or dried for use in soups, salads, and savory dishes.

Now let's have some fun looking at which herb works best with specific vegetables to give you the ultimate garden success—and a stocked pantry.

Basil + Tomatoes

WHY IT WORKS: Basil improves the flavor of tomatoes and supports healthy growth. Together, they deter pests like tomato hornworms and aphids.

CULINARY USE: The classic basil-tomato pairing is a favorite in sauces, salads, and pesto. Dehydrate or freeze the basil leaves to enjoy them well beyond the growing season.

Thyme + Cabbage Family (Broccoli, Cauliflower, Brussels Sprouts)

WHY IT WORKS: Thyme helps repel cabbage worms and other pests that often plague brassicas.

It also acts as a ground cover, keeping the soil moist and suppressing weeds.

CULINARY USE: Thyme adds a savory touch to roasted veggies and meats. Dry thyme or infuse it into oils for added flavor when cooking.

Sage + Carrots

WHY IT WORKS: Sage wards off carrot flies and other common pests, while also acting as a living mulch, keeping the soil around carrots cooler and moist.

CULINARY USE: Sage brings an earthy flavor to root vegetable dishes. You can dry sage leaves to make rubs or use them fresh for added flavor in soups and stews.

Rosemary + Beans

WHY IT WORKS: Rosemary's scent keeps bean beetles and other pests away. It also supports the soil's structure, making it easier for beans to thrive.

CULINARY USE: Rosemary is perfect for roasting and grilling. Dry it for use in herbed salts or to add to spice blends that work well with meats and vegetables alike.

Mint + Peppers

WHY IT WORKS: Mint repels aphids and ants, which are common pests of pepper plants. Plant mint in containers near peppers to control its spread.

CULINARY USE: Mint adds fresh flavor to salads, teas, and desserts. It's easy to dry mint for tea blends or to create syrups for drinks and marinades.

Dill + Cucumbers

WHY IT WORKS: Dill attracts beneficial insects that pollinate cucumbers, while also deterring pests like aphids and spider mites.

CULINARY USE: Dill is a perfect match for pickling cucumbers. Use fresh dill for canning, or dry it for seasoning in salad dressings, dips, and seafood dishes.

Chives + Tomatoes and Carrots

WHY IT WORKS: Chives help deter aphids and carrot flies, making them a great addition to any tomato or carrot bed. They also improve overall soil health with their frequent regrowth after harvesting.

CULINARY USE: Chives bring a mild onion flavor to soups, salads, and baked potatoes. Dry or freeze chives to use as a garnish or seasoning.

What *Not* to Plant Together

Companion planting is truly so much fun, and you'll reap countless rewards for pairing the right vegetables, herbs, and plants and rotating them to avoid soil nutrient depletion. But we should *never* introduce some pairings in our vegetable gardens. Poor unions sometimes result in a competition for nutrients, an attraction of pests sabotaging your food supply, or an off-putting flavor transmission.

Basil and Sage

WHY IT WORKS POORLY: Sage prefers drier soil, while basil needs more moisture. Their different water requirements can lead

to competition, making it harder for basil to thrive when planted near sage.

Carrots and Dill

WHY IT WORKS POORLY: As dill matures, it can stunt carrot growth and attract pests like carrot flies. These pests can damage the carrots, making dill a poor companion plant in the same bed.

Beans and Onions (including Garlic, Leeks, and Shallots)

WHY IT WORKS POORLY: Alliums (onions, garlic, leeks) release compounds that can inhibit the growth of beans and peas. Additionally, both plants are heavy feeders, leading to nutrient competition.

Cucumbers and Aromatic Herbs (like Basil, Sage, and Oregano)

WHY IT WORKS POORLY: Strong aromatic herbs can interfere with the growth of cucumbers. Cucumbers thrive in a calmer environment, so planting them with herbs like dill is a better choice.

Tomatoes and Corn

WHY IT WORKS POORLY: Corn attracts pests like tomato fruit worms and corn earworms, which can easily spread to tomatoes. Both plants also require similar nutrients, leading to competition that can stunt growth.

Potatoes and Tomatoes

WHY IT WORKS POORLY: Both potatoes and tomatoes are part of the nightshade family and are susceptible to similar diseases, such as blight. Planting them together increases the risk of disease and leads to competition for nutrients.

Asparagus and Garlic/Onions

WHY IT WORKS POORLY: Garlic and onions compete heavily with asparagus for soil nutrients. Planting them together can reduce the yield for both, as they each pull essential nutrients.

Carrots and Parsnips

WHY IT WORKS POORLY: Carrots and parsnips attract similar pests, like carrot flies, which can damage both crops. Planting them together also increases the likelihood of pest infestations and competition for nutrients.

Cabbage Family (Brussels Sprouts, Kale, Broccoli) and Strawberries

WHY IT WORKS POORLY: Strawberries attract pests that can also harm cabbage family plants, like slugs. Additionally, the roots of strawberries can inhibit the growth of brassicas, so keeping them apart promotes healthier growth.

Peppers and Fennel

WHY IT WORKS POORLY: Fennel releases chemicals that can stunt the growth of many vegetables, especially peppers. It's best to plant fennel separately, as it generally doesn't benefit any neighboring vegetable in the garden.

Radishes and Hyssop

WHY IT WORKS POORLY: Hyssop can interfere with the growth of radishes, reducing yields. They don't benefit each other in any way, so it's best to plant them in different areas altogether.

Sunflowers and Potatoes

WHY IT WORKS POORLY: Sunflowers release allelopathic chemicals that inhibit potato growth. This can lead to reduced potato yields and poor development. Additionally, both plants compete for sunlight and space.

Pumpkins (or Squash) and Potatoes

WHY IT WORKS POORLY: Both plants are heavy feeders, meaning they'll compete for the same nutrients in the soil. They're also susceptible to similar pests, so planting them together increases pest risk.

Basil and Rue

WHY IT WORKS POORLY: Rue can inhibit the growth of basil, leading to poor flavor and weaker plants. It's best to keep them separated in the garden for optimal growth.

Cucumbers and Tomatoes

WHY IT WORKS POORLY: Cucumbers and tomatoes are heavy feeders and will compete for essential nutrients. They're also susceptible to similar diseases like blight and powdery mildew, which can spread quickly between them. Cucumbers' sprawling vines can crowd tomatoes, limiting airflow and increasing the risk of fungal issues.

Nurturing Seeds, Transplanting, and Caring for Young Plants

From only a tiny seed, we can grow a plant that will produce food for our family. And the pride we feel as a seed grows, flourishes, and ultimately provides nourishment for our loved ones is unmatched. Nurturing a seed into a thriving plant bearing food requires a delicate balance of preparation, patience, and knowledge. Whether you're starting your seedlings in soil or embracing a hydroponic approach, the techniques you employ during these early stages are vital.

Starting Seedlings in Soil

Starting seeds in soil is an intuitive and rewarding method, giving you the chance to witness the earliest stages of plant life firsthand. Begin by selecting containers that aren't too large but still have enough space for young roots to stretch out. Seed trays, small pots, and biodegradable containers all work well and make the transition to the garden easier.

Choosing the right soil mix is crucial for successful germination. Avoid garden soil, which may harbor pests or diseases, and instead opt for a sterile, lightweight, seed-starting mix. This type of mix is designed to retain moisture while providing essential nutrients for early growth.

Moisten your soil mixture and fill each container almost full. Then plant your seeds at a depth about twice their diameter, covering them lightly with soil and gently pressing down to secure them. A light misting of water is all that's needed at this stage; you don't want to displace the seeds with too much force.

Once the seeds are planted, place the containers in a warm area to encourage germination. A temperature of 70°F (21°C) to 75°F (24°C) is ideal for most vegetable seeds, and you may consider using a heat mat if you're growing indoors during cooler months. After they sprout, seedlings need plenty

of light to grow strong and avoid becoming leggy. Place them on a sunny windowsill or set up a grow light system. Keep the light source close to the plants, about 2 to 3 inches above the tallest seedling, and be sure they receive light for upwards of 16 hours a day.

I start some of my seeds during the winter months in my basement. To heighten the temperature around them, I often run a space heater. I set it on the floor beneath the TV trays that hold my hydroponic growing systems and soil seedling trays. Keeping the ambient temperature a bit warmer gives my seedlings the security they need to sprout.

Starting Seedlings Hydroponically

The process of starting seedlings hydroponically offers a unique and efficient approach to growing food. Hydroponics allows you to grow seedlings without soil, immersing them instead in nutrient-rich water. For this method, you'll need a suitable growing medium, such as Rockwool, coir (made from coconuts), or peat pellets. These materials provide a stable base for seedlings while allowing the roots to absorb nutrients directly from the water. Start by soaking the growing medium to ensure it's thoroughly moistened, then place it in a net pot or seed tray ready for the seeds.

Plant the seeds by pressing them gently into the moistened medium, making sure they're securely nestled. Keep the medium damp by misting water with a spray bottle and cover the tray with a humidity dome or plastic wrap to maintain a consistent moisture level.

Like soil-based seedlings, hydroponic seedlings need light to grow properly. Position a grow light above the tray, keeping it just a few inches away and gradually adjusting it as the seedlings grow. Hydroponic systems thrive on oxygenated water, so make sure the roots have access to fresh air. This is essential for developing strong, healthy plants. Most systems will come with a small air pump to keep the water oxygenated and circulating. If you created your own hydroponic growing system, any fish tank air pump system will work.

Feeding Seedlings for Optimal Root Growth

Nourishing your seedlings is key to establishing strong roots and resilient stems. For soil-grown seedlings, it's best to wait until they have their first true leaves before feeding. Start with a balanced liquid fertilizer, diluted to a quarter of the recommended strength. This diluted solution provides essential nutrients without overwhelming the delicate root systems. Feed the seedlings once every 2 weeks, gradually increasing the concentration as they mature.

Hydroponic seedlings benefit from nutrient solutions specifically designed for young plants. Once the seeds have germinated and sprouted their first true leaves, introduce a nutrient solution to the water, starting with a quarter-strength mix. Keep an eye on the pH levels, as most vegetables thrive in a range of 5.5 to 6.5. Adjust the nutrient concentration based on the plant's growth and ensure that the water is oxygenated. Properly feeding your seedlings at this stage will help them establish strong roots, which form the foundation of a productive plant.

Transplanting Seedlings to the Garden or Hydroponic System

Transplanting is a delicate process that requires a little planning and care to ensure that your young plants continue to thrive. For soil-based seedlings, the transition to the garden can be a bit of a shock. To prepare them, start by "hardening off" the plants, gradually exposing them to outdoor conditions. Over the course of 5 to 7 days, place the seedlings outside in a shaded spot for a few hours, gradually increasing their exposure to sunlight, wind, and varying temperatures. This process strengthens the plants and reduces transplant shock, making for a smoother transition.

Choose a cool, cloudy day or late afternoon for transplanting. This helps reduce stress on the plants. Carefully remove each seedling from its container, keeping the root ball intact, and place it in its new home in the garden. After planting, water well, then apply a light mulch around the base to retain moisture.

For hydroponic seedlings moving to soil, the process requires an additional step. Hydroponic plants need to adapt to the new environment, and this includes adjusting their roots. To "harden off" the roots, expose them to air for 15 to 30 minutes a few times over several days. This process allows the roots to develop a tougher outer layer, which helps them adjust to soil conditions.

When you're ready to transplant, gently rinse the growing medium from the roots, and plant in moist, well-draining soil. Be sure to water thoroughly and monitor the seedlings for a few days, keeping an eye out for any signs of stress as they settle into their new environment.

Caring for Young Plants After Transplanting

Once your seedlings are in their new location, they'll need consistent care to grow strong and robust. Watering is essential, as young plants are especially vulnerable to drying out. Keep the soil consistently moist, checking frequently and watering when the top inch feels dry. Hydroponic plants transitioning to soil may need slightly more attention at first, so avoid letting them dry out. But be cautious of overwatering, which can lead to root rot.

Feeding should continue as the plants grow. For soil-grown plants, use a water-soluble fertilizer every 2 to 3 weeks, or consider an organic compost tea to boost nutrients naturally. Hydroponic plants can return to their nutrient solutions, but maintain a lighter concentration for the first few weeks to avoid overwhelming the roots.

Mulching around soil-based plants helps conserve moisture and minimize weeds, providing an extra layer of protection for your young plants. Watch out for pests, which can quickly damage tender seedlings, and use natural deterrents like neem-oil or diatomaceous earth to keep them at bay.

Growing seedlings, whether in soil or hydroponically, is an incredibly fulfilling experience. By giving your plants the care and attention they need during these early stages, you're setting them up for a healthy, productive life. Before you know it, those tiny seedlings will grow into flourishing plants, ready to provide your family with fresh, nourishing food.

There's no greater reward than knowing you've cultivated a source of sustenance from a tiny seed.

Year-Round Seasonal Gardening Guide

Achieving year-round gardening success involves understanding the natural cycles of plants, your local climate, and the value of crop rotation. By aligning your planting, growing, and harvesting with the seasons, you can ensure a constant flow of fresh produce.

Here are a few of the best practices for each season:

Spring: Preparation and Early Planting

Spring is a time of renewal in the garden, ideal for preparing soil and planting crops that thrive in mild temperatures. Start by clearing away winter debris, composting, and adding organic matter to rejuvenate your soil. Raised beds, which allow for better drainage and warming, are especially advantageous during this season.

- **Cool-Weather Crops:** Early spring is perfect for planting cool-weather crops like lettuce, spinach, peas, and radishes. These plants flourish in cooler soil temperatures and can be sown directly outdoors as soon as the soil is workable.
- **Transplants:** For a jump start on warm-season crops like tomatoes, peppers, and cucumbers, start seeds indoors 6 to 8 weeks before the last predicted frost date. By the time they're ready for transplanting, they'll be strong and well-rooted, ready to thrive once the risk of frost has passed.
- **Crop Rotation Strategy:** Use spring to start your first rotation. Begin by planting nitrogen-fixing crops like peas and beans. These plants not only provide an early harvest but help replenish nitrogen levels, making them a great first crop to kick-start your rotation.

Summer: Growing and Harvesting

As temperatures rise, warm-weather crops take center stage. Summer is the peak growing season, and your garden will require consistent watering, mulching, and pest management to thrive. Consider placing taller plants like tomatoes and corn where they won't shade smaller plants that require full sun, such as peppers and eggplants.

- **Warm-Weather Crops:** In early summer, plant crops that thrive in heat, such as tomatoes, peppers, squash, and cucumbers. By staggering planting dates for crops like zucchini and bush beans, you can enjoy continuous harvests throughout the season.
- **Succession Planting:** As fast-growing crops like lettuce and radishes reach the end of their cycle, replant the empty spaces with other quick growers, like carrots, beets, or green beans. Succession planting makes efficient use of space, allowing you to maximize your summer harvest.
- **Crop Rotation Strategy:** Rotate warm-weather crops by placing heavy-feeding plants like tomatoes in soil where you grew legumes or leafy greens in the spring. Avoid planting the same family of crops (such as tomatoes and peppers) in the same space year after year, as this depletes nutrients and invites pests and diseases that target specific plants.

FOUR-BED CROP ROTATION BY SEASON

To give you an overview of how to rotate your crops over the seasons, here's an example of a four-bed rotation cycle that prevents nutrient depletion and minimizes pest issues.

Using this rotation pattern, nitrogen fixers help replenish soil nutrients for heavy-feeding plants that follow, while root crops aid in breaking up the soil and preventing it from compacting.

Bed	Spring	Summer	Fall	Winter
1	Peas (Nitrogen Fixers)	Tomatoes (Heavy Feeders)	Kale (Light Feeder)	Garlic
2	Spinach (Leafy Green)	Peppers (Heavy Feeders)	Carrots (Root Crops)	Clover (Cover Crop)
3	Radishes and Lettuce (Light Feeders)	Squash (Heavy Feeder)	Beets (Root Crops)	Mulch and Compost
4	Beans (Nitrogen Fixers)	Corn (Heavy Feeder)	Chard and Spinach (Leafy Greens)	Rye (Cover Crop)

Fall: Harvesting and Transitioning

Fall is a transitional period in the garden, a time for gathering the last of your summer harvests and preparing for winter. It's also a great time to plant cool-weather crops that benefit from the reduced sunlight and cooler temperatures.

- **Fall Crops:** Plant root vegetables like carrots, beets, and turnips, as well as leafy greens like kale, spinach, and Swiss chard. These plants can handle the cooler fall weather and often taste sweeter after a light frost.
- **Cover Crops:** After harvesting summer crops, consider planting cover crops such as clover or rye in empty garden beds. Cover crops reduce soil erosion, suppress weeds, and enhance soil fertility by fixing nitrogen

and adding organic matter when turned back into the soil.

- **Crop Rotation Strategy:** Rotate fall crops by placing root vegetables where heavy-feeding crops were planted in the summer. Root crops don't consume as many nutrients, allowing the soil to begin its natural regenerative process, and help aerate the soil.

Winter: Resting and Renewing Soil

While the garden rests, winter is a time for soil rejuvenation. For some gardeners, winter may mean preparing beds for next spring. But in milder climates, it could be an opportunity for them to grow hardy winter crops.

- **Winter Crops:** In milder climates, plant cold-hardy vegetables such as garlic, onions, and some varieties of kale. These crops will establish themselves during winter and be ready to grow once spring arrives.

- **Mulching and Composting:** Adding mulch to the garden beds insulates the soil, reduces erosion, and suppresses weeds. Add a layer of compost to introduce essential nutrients, enhancing soil fertility for the next growing season.

- **Crop Rotation Strategy:** Winter is the best time to plan your crop rotation for the following year. Consider the layout of your garden and identify the spaces where specific crops will be most effective. Remember the general rotation of nitrogen fixers, heavy feeders, and light feeders to maintain healthy soil and balanced nutrients.

Additional Tips for Year-Round Success

- Test soil pH and nutrient levels each year to understand the soil's current condition. Soil test kits are affordable and will guide your amendments throughout the seasons.

- Add compost or organic fertilizers regularly, particularly after the harvest in fall and before planting in spring. This boosts microbial life and supports healthy plants.

- Plan each season in advance. Knowing which crops you'll rotate and where to place them helps you make the most efficient use of space and keeps your soil healthier over the long term.

By following the rhythms of the seasons and implementing thoughtful crop rotation, you'll cultivate a garden that remains productive year-round. The journey through each season builds upon the previous one, fostering a regenerative cycle nourishing both your garden and your soul.

Winter Gardening with Cold Frames and Greenhouse Attachments

Winter gardening isn't limited to hardy crops. With the help of cold frames and small greenhouse-style attachments, you can transform your raised beds into cozy mini-greenhouses, giving your plants the protection they need to thrive during colder months. These structures capture and retain heat, allowing you to grow a variety of vegetables throughout winter, even in regions with harsher climates.

Cold Frames for Winter Gardening

Cold frames are simple, box-like structures with transparent lids that harness the sun's warmth. By shielding them from frost and cold winds, they're ideal for growing cool-season crops like lettuce, spinach, kale, and Swiss chard.

Here's how to set up and use a cold frame for your raised beds:

1 Build or Buy a Cold Frame

You can easily make your own cold frame using repurposed materials like old windows or by buying a pre-made model. The frame should be sturdy and fit snugly over your raised bed.

2 Prepare Your Bed

Before setting up the cold frame, clear the bed of any weeds or old plant material, then add a layer of compost to enrich the soil.

3 Position the Frame

Place the frame in a sunny spot, ideally on a slight south-facing slope to maximize sunlight and warmth.

4 Maintain Ideal Conditions

Monitor the temperature inside the frame, especially on sunny days. If the temperature inside the frame climbs above 55°F (13°C), open the lid slightly for ventilation, as excessive heat can stress winter crops. Closing the lid at night helps retain warmth and keeps plants safe from frost.

3

Harvesting and Preserving

Let us not become weary in doing good, for at the proper time we will reap a harvest if we do not give up.

GALATIANS 6:9 (NIV)

There's something truly magical about reaching harvest time in your garden. All the months of planting, watering, and tending have led to this moment when you finally get to gather the fruits of your labor. Yet just as planting requires skill and patience, so does the process of harvesting.

Picking at the right time not only ensures you're getting peak flavor and nutrition but lays the groundwork for preserving the harvest so you can enjoy it well into the colder months. Harvesting isn't simply the end of the gardening season; it's an integral part of the seasonal cycle, allowing you to extend your garden's gifts by saving seeds, drying herbs, and organizing your preserved foods for long-term storage.

Proper Harvesting Techniques for Peak Freshness

Despite the vast technological advances in agriculture, modern home gardeners often find themselves using techniques surprisingly like those practiced by ancient farmers. Like their ancient counterparts, today's gardeners watch the seasons closely, learning to recognize signs of ripeness and timing their harvests to capture peak freshness. Many gardeners still use hand tools for harvesting. Simple shears, clippers, and small sickles reminiscent of ancient tools allow us to gently gather crops without damaging the plants.

Tips for a Successful Harvest

The key to a great harvest lies in timing and technique. Each crop has its own signs of ripeness. For tomatoes, look for deep, consistent color and a slight yield when gently squeezed. If frost is coming, green tomatoes can be ripened indoors. Peppers can be picked green or left on the plant to fully mature and sweeten. They'll even change colors, like to red. Harvest herbs like basil and cilantro before flowering for the best flavor, and for garlic and onions, wait until the tops dry out and turn brown.

Here are some essential harvesting tips:

- **Harvest at the Right Time.** Pick fruits and vegetables at their peak ripeness to capture the best flavor and nutrient content.

- **Use the Right Tools.** Ensure you have sharp shears, a harvesting knife, or pruners to make clean cuts and avoid damaging the plant.
- **Harvest in the Morning.** Early morning, when temperatures are cooler and moisture levels are higher, is the ideal time to gather fresh produce.
- **Handle with Care.** Avoid bruising fruits and vegetables by handling them gently during harvest and transport.
- **Harvest Regularly.** Pick produce frequently to encourage continuous growth and prevent overripening or waste.
- **Know When to Stop.** Don't overharvest, especially with perennials or plants that require some fruit to mature for seed production.

Quick Tomato Gardening and Preserving Tip

Many of us who grow our own tomatoes will experience untimely ripening. We'll have several tomatoes ripen at once, but not enough to complete a canning recipe. To prevent your fresh tomatoes from going to waste while you wait for more to ripen, simply rinse and core them, then place them whole inside a large freezer bag or container. As more tomatoes ripen, repeat these steps until multiple freezer bags are full and you have enough tomatoes to create your canning recipe.

And the best part? When you thaw the tomatoes, their skins will slip right off, saving you time spent blanching and peeling them. The freezing and thawing do it for you.

Introduction to Seed Saving for Future Gardens

Ancient cultures developed various methods to store seeds, ensuring they had a reliable supply for future planting seasons. These early farmers understood that careful seed preservation was crucial for sustaining their crops and, ultimately, their communities.

In ancient Mesopotamia, seeds were stored in clay pots or woven baskets kept in cool, dry places to protect them from humidity, pests, and extreme temperatures. The Sumerians, one of the earliest agricultural societies in this region, likely stored seeds in temple granaries or communal storage areas, often elevated or sealed to deter rodents and insects. The Egyptians, too, took seed preservation seriously, storing seeds in clay jars sealed with wax or resin to keep out moisture. They even buried some seeds with the deceased as part of burial rites, symbolizing sustenance in the afterlife and further showing the importance of seeds in their culture.

Similarly, Native Americans developed sophisticated seed-saving techniques that aligned with the unique climates of their regions. They often stored seeds in animal skins or earthenware containers, which were then buried underground or kept in caves to maintain consistent, cool temperatures. In Mesoamerica, the Maya and Aztecs stored maize, beans, and squash seeds in underground pits lined with straw or ash to repel pests and absorb any excess moisture.

To this day, saving seeds is one of the most fulfilling aspects of gardening. It's a way to connect with the legacy of your plants, preserving the unique traits thriving in your soil and climate. Heirloom seeds are highly treasured for their robust genetics and rich diversity. By saving and planting them, you're not only ensuring the continuation of your garden each year but enhancing the biodiversity and resilience of plant life in your local environment.

Seed Saving Tips

When it comes to seed saving, choosing the right plants is crucial. Heirlooms are the best choice because they're open-pollinated, meaning they reproduce true to type. Hybrid plants, on the other hand, often will not produce offspring identical to the parent plant, so they aren't ideal for seed saving. Focus on well-performing plants in your garden, showing disease resistance, high yields, and flavors you enjoy.

Timing is everything in seed saving. Let the seeds mature fully on the plant before harvesting. For tomatoes, this means allowing the fruit to ripen beyond the typical eating stage. The seeds are encased in a gel that contains natural growth inhibitors, so once you scoop them out, they need a good rinse. Some gardeners prefer to let them sit in water for a couple of days, which helps break down the gel. Once clean, spread the seeds out on a paper towel to dry. Properly dried seeds should feel hard and snap cleanly if you try to break them.

Beans and peas have some of the easiest seeds to save. Let the pods dry on the plant until they're brittle, then shell them and store the seeds. With squash, cucumbers, and melons, the seeds should be rinsed and then dried thoroughly. It's important to keep saved seeds in a dark, cool, and dry place, as temperature and humidity can affect their viability. Using a mason jar with a lid is a simple and effective way to store seeds, and placing the jar in a refrigerator can further extend their lifespan.

Labeling your seeds is a small but essential step. Write the plant name, the variety, and the year harvested on each packet. This not only helps with organization but allows you to track which seeds have the highest germination rates over time. Seed saving is an ongoing experiment, a way to fine-tune your gardening practices from season to season.

Time-Honored Food Preservation Methods

Drying is one of the most rewarding ways to preserve food, and humans have been practicing it for centuries. There's satisfaction in knowing that the same drying techniques used by ancient cultures are still effective today. Drying doesn't require complicated equipment; it can be as simple as tying a bundle of herbs together and hanging them in your kitchen. While each drying method has its own intricacies, understanding these methods can make a significant difference in the outcome.

Air-drying is perhaps the simplest and most traditional method. For hardy herbs like rosemary, thyme, and sage, gather small bunches and remove any damaged leaves. Once tied together, hang them in a dry, well-ventilated place, ideally out of

SEED COLLECTING & DRYING

Vegetable / Herb	Seed Collection Timing	Seed Preparation
Tomatoes	Allow fruit to ripen fully on the vine until soft, then collect seeds.	Ferment seeds in water to remove the gel coating, then rinse.
Cucumbers	Let fruit grow beyond edible stage until fully mature and yellow, then collect seeds.	Scoop out seeds, then rinse to remove any pulp.
Peppers	Allow peppers to reach full color (red, yellow, etc.) and soften slightly.	Scoop seeds; no fermentation needed.
Beans	Leave pods on the plant until they turn brown and dry out, then collect seeds.	Shell the pods, then remove the seed and discard the pods.
Peas	Wait until pods are fully dry and brittle on the plant before collecting seeds.	Remove the seeds from the dried pods.
Squash	Harvest once fruit is overripe, then scoop seeds and clean thoroughly.	Rinse seeds thoroughly, then pat dry to remove excess water to avoid mold.
Corn	Allow corn to dry on the stalk until kernels are hard, then harvest.	Remove kernels from the cob by hand, keeping them fully intact.
Brussels Sprouts	Wait until seed pods turn brown and dry on the plant before collecting seeds.	Break open the dried pods to release seeds, then use a paper bag to capture the seeds (they're tiny and hard to see).
Cabbage	Let seed heads mature and dry on the plant, then harvest seeds.	Cut seed heads and place in a paper bag, then shake gently to release seeds.
Lettuce	Allow plants to bolt and form flower heads, then collect seeds once flowers are dry.	Remove flower heads, then place in a paper bag and shake out seeds.
Spinach	Wait until seeds form on the stalk and begin to dry; collect before they fall.	Cut stalks, then place seeds in a paper bag and shake to release.
Tomatillos	Wait until fruit ripens and skin begins to dry, then scoop out seeds.	Scoop seeds, then rinse to clean and place them on a drying rack.
Basil	Wait until flowers form seed heads, then allow seeds to dry on the plant.	Clip seed heads, then place in a paper bag and shake to collect the seeds.
Cilantro	Harvest seeds after flowers have gone to seed and dried out on the plant.	Cut seed heads, then place in a paper bag and shake.
Dill	Allow seed heads to fully dry on the plant before collecting seeds.	Clip seed heads and place in a bag, then shake to release the seeds.
Parsley	Wait until the plant has flowered and the seed heads have dried.	Clip seed heads, then place in a paper bag and shake to release the seeds.
Sage	Collect seeds after flowers turn brown and dry out on the plant.	Harvest seed heads, then place in a bag and shake out seeds.
Marigold Flowers	Allow flowers to dry and brown on the stem, then collect seeds from the center.	Shake flower heads over a tray to release seeds.

Drying Tip	Storage Tips
Spread seeds on a paper towel or mesh screen for even drying; avoid stacking.	Store in a cool, dark place; refrigeration extends viability.
Use a fine mesh rack, ensuring seeds are in a single layer for airflow.	Keep in a dry, airtight container; avoid humidity.
Lay seeds on parchment paper, placing in a dry, well-ventilated area.	Store in a dark, cool space; label with year and variety.
Dry seeds on a cloth or mesh rack; avoid direct sunlight to prevent overheating.	Use an airtight container in a cool, dry place; label with date.
Use a tray lined with parchment paper; keep seeds in a shaded, dry spot.	Store in paper envelopes in a cool, dry place.
Spread seeds on a towel, turning them occasionally for even drying.	Place in an airtight container in a cool, dark location.
Lay kernels on a tray lined with cloth; allow for airflow and turn occasionally.	Store kernels in a paper bag in a cool, dry place; avoid humidity.
Use a mesh rack for even drying; avoid direct sunlight to prevent overheating.	Place seeds in an airtight container in a dark, cool area.
Spread seeds on parchment paper placed in a shaded, dry spot with good airflow.	Store seeds in a dry, dark place; use paper envelopes for air circulation.
Dry seeds on a cloth-lined tray in a cool, dry place away from direct sunlight.	Keep seeds in paper envelopes or small jars, then store in a dry location.
Spread seeds on a paper towel and let them air-dry in a well-ventilated area.	Store in a cool, dark space; paper envelopes work well for airflow.
Dry seeds on a paper towel–lined tray or drying rack; store in a dry, well-ventilated space to air-dry.	Place seeds in a labeled envelope or jar, then store in a cool, dry area.
Dry seeds on a paper towel–lined tray in a cool, dark place.	Store seeds in an airtight container in a cool, dark place.
Place seeds on parchment paper in a dry area with good airflow.	Keep seeds in a paper envelope or airtight container and store in a dry area.
Use a cloth-lined tray, then store in a well-ventilated, shaded area.	Store seeds in a cool, dark area in an airtight container or envelope.
Spread seeds on a paper towel, then let them air-dry in a cool space.	Store in paper envelopes or small containers; label with date and variety.
Place seeds on a rack or parchment paper; avoid high humidity areas.	Place seeds in an airtight container in a dark, cool area.
Use a paper towel–lined tray in a cool, dark place for even drying.	Store in paper packets or small containers; label with variety and date.

Step-by-Step Drying Techniques

Air-Drying Herbs: Choose bundles of herbs like rosemary, thyme, and sage. Remove any damaged leaves, then tie small bunches with string. Hang them in a dry, well-ventilated area out of direct sunlight.

Sun-Drying: Sun-drying can be effective for produce like tomatoes—as long as there's ample sunlight and low humidity. Spread slices on a mesh screen, then cover them with a net to keep pests away and let the sun do its work.

direct sunlight, which can cause the herbs to lose their color and flavor. You'll know they're ready when they crumble easily between your fingers, a sure sign that they're completely dried. This process can take anywhere from a few days to a couple of weeks, depending on the humidity in your area.

Sun-drying is another traditional method, ideal for tomatoes and fruits like apples or apricots. The key here is choosing a dry, sunny location with a steady breeze. Slice the tomatoes, arrange them on a mesh screen, and then cover them with a lightweight net to keep pests away. As the sun works its magic, you'll need to turn the slices every day or so to ensure even drying. With this method, you'll get chewy, concentrated flavors of summer in every bite.

Long-Term Storage Conditions for Harvested Foods and Seeds

Preserving your harvest is about setting up your pantry for success. A well-organized storage area can make all the difference, extending the life of your preserved foods and making it easy to access them when you need them. Creating the right storage conditions is like giving your garden bounty a cozy home, ensuring that it remains fresh and delicious for as long as possible.

The golden rule of food storage is to keep things cool, dark, and dry. Light, heat, and humidity are the enemies of stored foods. Find a space in your home that meets these conditions, often a basement or pantry. If you live in a humid climate, a dehumidifier can help maintain the right environment. Herbs, for example, are best stored in airtight containers, like mason jars. Keep these in a dark cupboard, and they'll retain their fragrance for months, even years.

For long-term storage, keeping dried foods in optimal conditions is essential. Herbs, for instance, are best stored in airtight glass jars, which protect them from moisture and light. If possible, keep them in a dark cabinet, as sunlight can fade both color and flavor. Once dried, onions and garlic can be kept in mesh bags in a cool, dry area with good airflow. And for dehydrated vegetables or fruits, airtight containers with a small silica pack to help absorb any residual moisture and an oxygen absorber extend shelf life.

Organizational Tips and Strategies

Organizing your pantry by category is another great habit. Grouping similar items together, such as herbs in one section and dried vegetables in another, makes it easy to find what you need. Rotating your food supply is essential too. Place newer items at the back and use older items first. This simple practice reduces waste and ensures you're always enjoying foods at their peak.

Optimal Storage Conditions

- 50°F (10°C) to 70°F (21°C) for best quality retention
- Below 95°F (35°C) and above 45°F (7°C) to avoid spoilage or freezing
- Low to no humidity
- No direct or indirect sunlight
- Never above appliances or near any appliances that kick off heat
- Limited storage space? These make excellent locations:
  - Linen and coat closets
  - Under beds
  - Rarely accessed kitchen cupboards
  - Under stairways
  - Spare bedrooms

QUICK PANT RY ORGANIZATION TIPS

Category	Tips
Use Clear Containers	Store dry goods like flour, sugar, rice, and pasta in clear, airtight containers to easily see contents.
Label Everything	Label jars, bins, and containers with the product name and expiration date for quick identification.
Group Similar Items	Arrange by category: grains, canned goods, spices, baking supplies, snacks, etc.
Maximize Vertical Space	Use tiered shelving, stackable bins, or hanging racks to make the most of pantry height.
First In, First Out	Place new items behind older ones to ensure you use the oldest products first.
Create Zones	Designate specific areas for snacks, canned goods, spices, or bulk items to keep things organized.
Use Lazy Susans	For small jars, spices, or condiments, a lazy Susan keeps items accessible and prevents clutter.
Adjustable Shelving	Install adjustable shelves to accommodate taller items or to change up your pantry layout as needed.
Use Baskets and Bins	Store loose items like onions, potatoes, or packets in baskets or bins for easy access and a cleaner look.
Utilize Doors and Walls	Hang spice racks, storage pockets, or hooks on pantry doors to save shelf space.

Long-Term Storage for Dried Foods

- **Herbs:** Store in airtight containers, ideally in a dark, cool place. Glass jars or opaque containers work best to keep herbs fragrant.
- **Onions and Garlic:** Once dried, onions and garlic can be stored in mesh bags or braids in a well-ventilated area. Check every few weeks for any signs of sprouting.
- **Dried Vegetables and Fruits:** These are best stored in airtight containers with silica packs to absorb moisture, preserving freshness for months.

The Aftermath of Harvesting and Seed Collecting

Once you've harvested your garden's bounty and collected seeds, it's time to consider what to do with the remaining plants. Rather than leaving them in the ground or simply discarding them, you can turn these leftover plant materials into valuable organic matter for your soil.

Two main methods ensure these plants contribute to your soil's fertility for the next season, and both will create organic matter for your soil.

Composting Leftover Plant Material

Composting is an excellent way to recycle your garden's plants and transform them into rich, fertile compost. This process not only reduces waste but provides nutrients that will improve soil structure and fertility.

- Start by pulling up the plants, roots and all. If they're large, chop them into smaller pieces. Smaller pieces break down faster, so cutting stems and leaves can speed up the composting process.
- Add the chopped plant material to your compost pile or bin, mixing it with other green materials (like kitchen scraps) and brown materials (like leaves, straw, or

cardboard) to maintain a balanced carbon-to-nitrogen ratio. This balance is key for a fast and effective composting process.

- To keep your compost pile active, make sure it stays moist but not soggy, and turn it every week or so. Aerating the compost adds oxygen, which helps beneficial microbes break down the plant matter.

Composting in this way not only helps with nutrient recycling but also encourages the growth of beneficial microorganisms that are essential for healthy soil.

Tilling Plant Material into the Soil

Another option is to till the plant material directly into your garden beds. This is often referred to as green manuring and is especially beneficial if you're planning to leave your beds fallow over the winter or are preparing the soil for a cover crop.

- Start by cutting the plants at the base, leaving the roots in the soil. Then use pruning shears or a spade to chop the remaining leaves and stems into smaller pieces. These can be left in place or lightly spread across the soil surface.

- Use a rototiller or garden fork to turn the chopped plant material into the top 4 to 6 inches of soil. This will help it decompose faster, as it becomes more accessible to soil microbes. Tilling the plants into the soil allows them to break down directly in the garden bed, adding organic matter and nutrients.

- It's important to give the plant material time to decompose, especially if you're adding high-carbon materials like cornstalks or woody stems. If possible, allow a few weeks between tilling and your next planting to ensure the organic matter has begun to break down and won't interfere with new seeds or seedlings.

Both composting and tilling plants back into the soil provide valuable benefits to enrich it with natural, sustainable amendments. Composting gives you the flexibility to manage your plant materials away from the garden, while tilling adds organic matter directly to your soil, improving its structure. You can even combine these methods: compost some of the material while tilling in the rest.

Preparing Your Garden Bed for Winter

As the gardening season draws to a close, taking steps to prepare your beds for winter can set the stage for a healthier, more productive garden next year. Even if you're not planning to grow during the winter months, caring for your soil and making a few strategic choices before the snow falls will ensure that your garden is ready to thrive in the spring.

One of the simplest yet most effective steps you can take is to mulch your garden beds. By adding a thick layer of mulch—about 2 to 4 inches thick and made from organic materials like straw, shredded leaves, or wood chips—you create a protective barrier over the soil. This layer acts as a natural insulator, regulating soil temperatures and preventing erosion from winter winds and heavy snow. Mulch also suppresses weeds, which means fewer unwanted plants in the spring. And as it decomposes, it enriches the soil with organic matter, setting your beds up for a nutrient-rich start next season.

Another excellent winter strategy is to plant cover crops. Varieties like winter rye, clover, and vetch provide a protective blanket for your soil while also contributing valuable nutrients. As these crops grow, they reduce soil compaction and prevent erosion. When spring arrives, you can turn them back into the soil, where they'll break down and add organic matter. This green manure boosts soil fertility and helps create a healthier environment for next year's crops.

While it may be tempting to leave your garden as-is after harvest, it's essential to clean up any garden debris. Removing dead plants, weeds, and leftover plant material prevents diseases and pests from overwintering. Composting healthy plant material and discarding anything diseased keeps your garden beds clean and ready for spring. Be sure to pull weeds carefully, including the roots, so they won't reappear when temperatures warm up. A thorough fall weeding session can make all the difference when it's time to plant again.

Winter is also an ideal time to amend your soil's pH, as certain amendments require time to work their way into the soil. Conduct a simple soil test to determine if yours is too acidic or alkaline, then add lime or sulfur as needed. By applying these amendments in fall, you give them several months to activate, ensuring a balanced soil pH come spring. This can improve nutrient uptake for your plants and create an environment where they can thrive.

As you prepare your garden for winter, take time to reflect on what worked well this year and what could be improved. Planning your garden layout now will help you make better crop rotation choices and ensure that you're building on past successes. Mapping out your beds and noting which crops were planted where allows you to rotate crop families effectively, reducing the risk of disease and promoting balanced soil health. Then as the snow begins to fall, you can rest easy knowing your garden beds are tucked in for winter, ready to come alive again when spring arrives.

4

Home Canning

In the fields of observation, chance favors only the prepared mind.

LOUIS PASTEUR

pioneering microbiologist

Louis Pasteur, known as a pioneering microbiologist, emphasized that discoveries often come to those who are ready to recognize and understand them. His quote above highlights the importance of preparation and knowledge in taking advantage of opportunities, aligning well with the meticulousness and readiness needed for home canning. His statement sets the tone of diligence and readiness, underscoring how well-prepared individuals can harness the benefits when learning the craft of home canning food.

Modern-Day Canning

We've expanded upon these discoveries in the twenty-first century. Advancements in technology allow us to get both water and air hotter than boiling water temperature, known as pressure canning. And this—combined with standardized safety methods using time, temperature, acidic value, and density—gives people across the globe the ability to preserve a sustainable food source for years.

Many home canners have also made the leap into digital canning, giving them the freedom to process food in jars without being chained to the stovetop. Digital canners offer precise temperature control without the fluctuations often experienced on a stovetop. In many cases, this precision helps decrease liquid siphoning from jars, therefore decreasing lid failures.

As an educator and recipe creator, I make it a point to teach the necessity of both thermal processing methods—water bathing and pressure canning. Every recipe I create will indicate which method of thermal processing is required to safely preserve the food in jars. Many times, the method of processing can be interchangeable. For instance, many water bath recipes, like salsa, can be processed in less time when using a pressure canner.

- **Water Bathing**—The most common form of home canning. Foods high in acid (with a pH between 1.0 and 4.6), like strawberries or apples, can be processed in a water bath using the temperature of boiling water, 212° F (100°C), to kill harmful microorganisms and foodborne pathogens.

- **Pressure Canning**—The best way to preserve low-acid ingredients like meat, soups, broths and stocks, and vegetables. Without the presence of acid (with a pH between 4.6 and 14.0) in foods like root crops or meat, we must process at 240°F (116°C) or higher to kill harmful microorganisms and foodborne pathogens.

In the end, it's the recipe's overall acidic pH value and the food's density that dictate how long the jars must process and at what temperature, therefore warranting the use of either a water bath canner or a pressure canner.

Incorporate Home Canning into Everyday Life

Home canning is more than just a seasonal task; it's a way to bring wholesome, handmade foods into your daily routine, no matter the time of year. By incorporating home canning into your life year-round, you're connecting with your food, saving money, and always having quality ingredients on hand. This section is about finding small, manageable ways to bring canning into your week without it feeling like a chore.

From setting aside a few hours each week for small-batch canning to hosting a canning party with a goal of cranking out as many jars as possible, with a little planning and a few modern tools, home canning can become a seamless part of your daily or weekly routine. This is especially true if your garden is in harvest or you find great deals at your local grocer. Capitalizing on seasonally available foods is the perfect way to stock your pantry and feed your family without breaking the budget.

The main reason I stress incorporating home canning into our everyday lives is that when we do, we preserve foods we enjoy eating rather than merely plunking anything into a jar just because it's "in season." There's nothing worse than putting a lot of your time and energy into preserving something that sits in your pantry for years uneaten, taking up valuable real estate. We must look at every inch of our pantry as space reserved only for the foods that (1) we enjoy eating, (2) provide us nutrition, and (3) permit us to create additional food crafts so we can continue to safely and securely preserve the foods that sustain us.

My advice: If you won't eat it, don't can it! Resist purchasing a "good deal" at your local grocer unless it's something you and your family enjoy eating and it provides valuable nutrition and sustenance.

Here are some ways to incorporate home canning into your everyday life:

1 Regularly clean out your freezer.

It's important that we circulate the food stored in our freezer (or freezers) every 3 to 4 months. As frozen foods approach their expiration dates, thawing and using them in canning recipes will both prevent the foods from spoiling and move them into a ready-to-eat, fully cooked and stored state. Rotating frozen foods out of the freezer is especially important when your garden harvest is on the horizon or at the start of hunting or fishing season in anticipation of securing fresh meat or fish. You'll need the freezer space.

2 Regularly clean out your pantry.

Just as we rotate the food out of our freezer, so must we rotate the food out of our pantry. For example, while storing dried beans is important, if stored for longer than the beans can handle, they won't soften no matter how long they're cooked, making them harder to digest. For this reason, the ideal storage time for dried beans is 12 months from date of purchase. If you grow, harvest, and dry your own beans, the ideal storage time is 18 months from date of drying. To extend the life of your dried beans, you can pressure can them to create jars of ready-to-eat beans to create meals or use the dried beans when creating and preserving meals in a jar, like Ham and Bean Soup.

3 Take advantage of fall hunting and butchering season.

In the Northern Hemisphere during the fall months, it's common for hunters to kill wildlife such as deer, elk, moose, pheasant, turkey, and rabbit. It's also time for farmers to slaughter their beef, pork, and chicken to support the local market. In the fall months, set aside time each week to preserve meat-based recipes such as Rabbit Cacciatore, Beef Stew, and Elk Chili with Beans.

4 Take advantage of spring berry and vegetable season.

Spring is often the time juicy berries are ripe for picking. Use your springtime to water bath preserves, jellies, chutneys, and fruit spreads. This is also the perfect season for asparagus and rhubarb in many areas of the world. Not only are they in abundance, but typically they're available at discounted prices. Freezing what you can't home can will give you seasonal variety in the meals you cook and can later in the year.

5 Take advantage of local advertisements and coupons.

Keep an eye out for special discounts hosted by your local grocer or butcher. Stay up-to-date using their newsletters, flyers, or digital communications. These sales are typically advertised for a specified period, allowing you time to plan and budget. Use these seasonal advertisements and coupons to plan your home-canning recipes. And if you happen across a great deal while out shopping, don't hesitate to take advantage of it if it's something your family loves to eat. Unexpected ingredient deals often result in impromptu canning sessions, giving us added value in our pantry and helping us chip away at our 3-month food supply plan.

6 Use digital canners for countertop use.

One of the most convenient ways to incorporate home canning into your everyday life is using a digital pressure canner—a frequently used appliance that will remain on your countertop throughout the year. In doing so, you can easily preserve those surprise deals with ease, make small batches of items as you harvest, or preserve leftovers with great ease, preventing you from taking up freezer space. For example, a leftover chicken carcass can easily become chicken broth. Using your digital pressure canner to preserve three quarts of broth before bed is three more jars for the pantry. And the best part? You're not chained to your stovetop during processing. Feel free to watch a movie with your family while the digital canner processes and cools down all on its own.

Time Management Tips

Time management is essential when you want to integrate canning into your schedule regularly. It helps break the process down into manageable steps you can complete incrementally.

Early Food Prep

For example, you might set aside one evening a week to prepare your produce—like chopping, seasoning, and preparing your ingredients—then can everything over the weekend. By dividing your tasks, you'll avoid feeling overwhelmed and will have a constant rotation of canned goods without devoting entire days to the process.

Organization

In addition to working in short sessions, keep all your canning supplies in one location. From the required utensils to the weighted gauge for a pressure canner, having everything necessary for home canning at your fingertips will save you valuable time hunting down these items mid-session.

The Right-Size Canner

Additionally, selecting the right canner for a recipe is crucial to saving you time. Size matters in home canning, and when you want to triple a standard batch, you must use a larger canning vessel to accommodate all the jars. While using a digital canner has many benefits, size isn't one of them. You can really increase your yield when using a tall 23-quart or large 41-quart pressure canner. Then you can double stack your pint jars, and in some instances your quart jars, increasing the output in one processing session. A larger vessel saves you so much time you would otherwise wrap up into processing (and cooling) when using a smaller canner.

Canning as a Community

Last, host or attend a canning party. You know the saying: Many hands make light work. Gather several friends, family members, or neighbors, then decide what two recipes your group would like to preserve. I recommend preserving one pressure canning recipe (like stew) and one water bath recipe (like apple pie filling) based on your season's availability.

The goal is for each person to leave the party with a full batch of each recipe, all while having worked together. Ask everyone to bring not only enough of a single ingredient for all the jars to be processed, but also their own jars, lids, and rings. And if you each pitch in a canner, there should be enough to keep processing each recipe's jars down to a single batch time versus using a single canner to process each recipe's jars multiple times.

If your home isn't large enough to throw a canning party, look within your community for a shared kitchen space. Some locations with ample space to host a group of canners might be a local church or community center, a hybrid commercial kitchen rented by the hour, or a local American Legion Post or Moose lodge. You can even get creative and host a canning party outdoors using a propane fueled Camp Chef dual burner stovetop or an outdoor gas kitchen.

Enjoy canning together, regaling in storytelling, laughter, food, and fellowship all the while filling your pantry.

Kerr
MASON

Preserving Potable Drinking Water

In the seasonal pantry, food security extends beyond meals; it also includes access to clean, safe drinking water. While many focus on preserving foods, canning potable water is often overlooked. Yet it's a crucial aspect of preparedness by way of a well-rounded pantry. Having a supply of potable drinking water ensures you and your family are ready for any emergency, be it a natural disaster, a power outage, or simply access to clean water when for some reason none is available.

Yes, boiling water can remove many harmful microorganisms, but pressure canning water allows you to store sterile water for extended periods of time without contamination. By sealing water in jars and processing it under pressure, you ensure that the water remains safe for consumption and free from bacteria, viruses, and fungi.

How to Preserve Safe Drinking Water

Preserving potable drinking water can be easily accomplished in one of two ways. One, by canning jars of water on their own, processing as many as possible in a single session. Or two, by adding one to two jars of water when processing a separate recipe. Many will do this to fill the canner to capacity. Either way, integrating jars of canned drinking water into your everyday canning cycles will quickly provide a solid supply of potable drinking water in your pantry.

To pressure can water, you'll need a pressure canner, jars, lids and rings, and clean drinking water to start. This 6-step process is simple and aligns with general pressure canning practices:

1. Fill each jar with clean, potable water, leaving a 1-inch headspace.
2. Wipe the rims of the jars with a washcloth dipped in vinegar.
3. Place the lids and rings on the jars and hand tighten.
4. Process the jars at 10 PSI for 10 minutes at zero elevation. For higher elevations, adjust the PSI according to your altitude (see the Altitude Guide on page 68).
5. After processing, allow the pressure canner to cool naturally and release pressure. Once safe to open, carefully remove the jars and set them on a cutting board covered with a dishtowel. After 3 hours, the lids should have sealed.
6. Label the jars with the date, then store them in a cool, dark place.

Canning for Your Season

Growing seasons are not the same worldwide, and the timing of seasonal produce can vary significantly depending on the region and climate. Take, for instance, asparagus. While asparagus is common in spring in many temperate regions, the actual months when it's in season can differ depending on where you live.

The local climate and agricultural practices also affect when crops are harvested. In temperate climates, spring and summer are typically the peak growing seasons for most fruits and vegetables. But tropical regions with year-round warm temperatures may grow certain produce continuously or during the rainy seasons. Winter is a recognized season worldwide, but its

Here's a quick list of seasonal produce for each hemisphere to help you preserve ingredients tailored to your region's changing seasons. Notice how we grow the same types of foods, just at different times of the year. This is why I share seasonally specific recipes—so you can create and preserve them when the timing is right for your area, not necessarily during a specific month.

Northern Hemisphere

SPRING (MARCH–MAY)

- Vegetables: Asparagus, peas, radishes, spinach, artichokes, leeks, spring onions
- Fruits: Strawberries, rhubarb, apricots

SUMMER (JUNE–AUGUST)

- Vegetables: Zucchini, cucumbers, tomatoes, bell peppers, eggplant, corn
- Fruits: Peaches, cherries, blueberries, raspberries, melons

FALL (SEPTEMBER–NOVEMBER)

- Vegetables: Pumpkins, sweet potatoes, carrots, Brussels sprouts, cauliflower, beets
- Fruits: Apples, pears, grapes, figs, cranberries

WINTER (DECEMBER–FEBRUARY)

- Vegetables: Cabbage, kale, winter squash, Brussels sprouts, turnips
- Fruits: Oranges, grapefruits, pomegranates, persimmons, kiwifruit

Southern Hemisphere

SPRING (SEPTEMBER–NOVEMBER)

- Vegetables: Asparagus, peas, radishes, spinach, artichokes, spring onions
- Fruits: Strawberries, rhubarb, apricots, loquats

SUMMER (DECEMBER–FEBRUARY)

- Vegetables: Zucchini, cucumbers, tomatoes, bell peppers, eggplant, corn
- Fruits: Peaches, cherries, blueberries, raspberries, melons, mangos

FALL (MARCH–MAY)

- Vegetables: Pumpkins, sweet potatoes, carrots, Brussels sprouts, cauliflower, beets
- Fruits: Apples, pears, grapes, figs, pomegranates

WINTER (JUNE–AUGUST)

- Vegetables: Cabbage, kale, winter squash, Brussels sprouts, turnips
- Fruits: Oranges, grapefruits, kiwifruit, persimmons, mandarins

timing and impact vary significantly based on your location.

More specifically, the timing of each season depends on which hemisphere you live in—the Northern Hemisphere or the Southern Hemisphere.

- **Northern Hemisphere:** Winter occurs from December to February. This includes regions like North America, Europe, parts of Asia, and most African countries. These temperate regions experience cold weather, snow, or frosty conditions in winter.

- **Southern Hemisphere:** Winter occurs from June to August. Countries like Australia, New Zealand, parts of South America, and some African countries experience winter during these months. Tropical regions closer to the equator may not have a traditional winter with cold weather. Instead, they might experience a dry season or cooler temperatures relative to their usual climate.

Seasonal Canning Recipes

As we dive into the next section, get ready to explore deliciously fun seasonal canning recipes tailored to both hemispheres. Whether you're preserving the flavors of a summer harvest or capturing the essence of fall, these recipes are designed to highlight the unique bounty of each season. Before we jump into the recipes, you'll find a handy guide on altitude adjustments and detailed charts to help you adjust for your region.

Let's get started bringing these vibrant seasonal flavors into your pantry!

Addressing Altitude

In home canning, we adjust the processing time based on altitude, because the higher up you are, the lower the boiling point of water is. This means at higher altitudes, water boils at a temperature that's not yet hot enough to kill all the harmful bacteria. To make sure the food is safe to eat, you'll need to increase the processing time or pressure (for pressure canning) to reach the correct temperature.

Use this handy guide to help you safely increase the processing time or PSI when you're home canning.

ALTITUDE GUIDE

Water Bathing Altitude Chart

Altitude in Feet	Increase Processing Time
1,001 to 3,000	5 minutes
3,001 to 6,000	10 minutes
6,001 to 8,000	15 minutes
8,001 to 10,000	20 minutes

Pressure Canning Altitude Chart

Altitude in Feet	Weighted Gauge Canner	Dial Gauge Canner
0 to 1,000	10	11
1,001 to 2,000	15	11
2,001 to 4,000	15	12
4,001 to 6,000	15	13
6,001 to 8,000	15	14
8,001 to 10,000	15	15

SPRING SEASON CANNING RECIPES

Pickled Fiddlehead Ferns

These young, coiled fern fronds are harvested early in the season and have a delicate, earthy flavor similar to asparagus or spinach. They make an excellent side dish or garnish, adding a bright, tangy note to meals. Feel free to adjust the spice level according to your taste!

YIELD: 6 pints or 12 half-pints

INGREDIENTS

3½ lbs. fresh fiddlehead ferns
4 cups white vinegar
4 cups water
⅓ cup canning salt
3 T. sugar
6 garlic cloves, peeled
6 tsp. mustard seeds
6 tsp. whole black peppercorns
6 sprigs fresh dill (optional)
3 tsp. red pepper flakes (optional)

DIRECTIONS

1. Rinse the fiddlehead ferns thoroughly under cold water, removing any brown husks and dirt. Trim the stems as needed.
2. Blanch the fiddlehead ferns in a stockpot of boiling water for 2 to 3 minutes. Using a slotted spoon, immediately transfer the fiddleheads to a bowl of ice water to stop the cooking process. Drain and set aside.
3. In a large stainless steel stockpot, combine the vinegar, water, salt, and sugar. Bring to a boil, stirring to dissolve the salt and sugar, then reduce the heat to a simmer.
4. Place 1 garlic clove, 1 teaspoon mustard seeds, and 1 teaspoon peppercorns (and a sprig of dill or ½ teaspoon red pepper flakes, if using) into each hot, sterilized pint-size jar. Pack the blanched fiddlehead ferns tightly into the jars, leaving ½ inch of headspace. If using half-pints, you may keep the same amount of seasonings or cut each ingredient in half.
5. Using a funnel, ladle the hot brine over the fiddleheads, maintaining the ½ inch of headspace. Remove any trapped air pockets and add additional brine if necessary to maintain the ½-inch headspace.
6. Wipe the rims with a washcloth dipped in vinegar. Place the lid and ring on each jar and hand tighten.
7. Place the jars in a boiling water bath canner, ensuring that the water covers the jars by at least 1 inch. Bring to a full rolling boil, then process both pint and half-pint jars for 10 minutes.

Mixed Berry Compote

This compote is a sweet mixture of seasonal berries cooked down with a hint of sugar and lemon. It is delicious on pancakes, when stirred into yogurt, or as a topping for desserts. It's a versatile treat that captures the flavor of summer berries to enjoy year-round.

YIELD: 6 pints or 12 half-pints

INGREDIENTS

7 lbs. mixed berries (strawberries, raspberries, blueberries, blackberries)

3 cups granulated sugar

⅓ cup lemon juice

2 tsp. lemon zest

DIRECTIONS

1. Rinse and hull the berries, removing any stems and leaves. Cut strawberries into quarters if they are large.
2. In a large stainless steel stockpot, combine the berries, sugar, lemon juice, and lemon zest. Stir well to coat the berries.
3. Bring the mixture to a boil over medium heat, stirring frequently to prevent sticking. Once it reaches a boil, reduce the heat to a simmer and cook for 15 to 20 minutes until the berries have broken down and the compote has thickened slightly.
4. Using a funnel, ladle the hot compote into hot, sterilized jars, leaving ¼ inch of headspace. Remove any trapped air pockets and add additional compote if necessary to maintain the ¼-inch headspace.
5. Wipe the rims with a washcloth dipped in vinegar. Place the lid and ring on each jar and hand tighten.
6. Place the jars in a boiling water bath canner, ensuring that the water covers the jars by at least 1 inch. Bring to a full rolling boil, then process both pint and half-pint jars for 10 minutes.

Asian-Style Pickled Radishes

This recipe of crisp radishes pickled with rice vinegar, ginger, and a hint of sesame creates a bold, tangy flavor with a touch of umami. It is perfect as a side dish or topping for salads, rice bowls, and sandwiches.

YIELD: 6 pints or 12 half-pints

INGREDIENTS

4 lbs. radishes
4 cups rice vinegar
1½ cups water
⅓ cup granulated sugar
⅓ cup canning salt
6 T. minced or finely chopped fresh ginger
6 tsp. sesame oil

DIRECTIONS

1. Rinse the radishes thoroughly and thinly slice them using a mandolin or sharp knife.
2. In a large stainless steel stockpot, combine the rice vinegar, water, sugar, and salt. Bring to a boil, stirring to dissolve the sugar and salt, then reduce the heat to a simmer.
3. Place 1 tablespoon of ginger and 1 teaspoon of sesame oil into each hot, sterilized jar. Pack the sliced radishes tightly into the jars, leaving ½ inch of headspace. If using half-pints, you may keep the same amount of ginger and sesame oil or cut each ingredient in half.
4. Using a funnel, ladle the pickling brine over the radishes, maintaining the ½ inch of headspace. Remove any trapped air pockets and add additional brine if necessary to maintain the ½-inch headspace.
5. Wipe the rims with a washcloth dipped in vinegar. Place the lid and ring on each jar and hand tighten.
6. Place the jars in a boiling water bath canner, ensuring that the water covers the jars by at least 1 inch. Bring to a full rolling boil, then process both pint and half-pint jars for 10 minutes.

Spring Pea and Mint Soup

This is a light and refreshing soup made with early spring sweet peas and fresh mint. This soup is perfect for a quick, healthy meal straight from the jar.

YIELD: 4 quarts or 8 pints

INGREDIENTS

6 lbs. fresh or frozen sweet peas

8 cups vegetable broth

4 cups water

2 cups finely chopped yellow onion

4 garlic cloves, minced

1 cup finely chopped fresh mint leaves

2 tsp. salt (optional)

1 tsp. black pepper

DIRECTIONS

1. In a large stainless steel stockpot, combine the peas, vegetable broth, water, onion, garlic, mint, salt (if using), and pepper. Bring to a boil over medium heat, then reduce to a simmer. Cook for 10 to 15 minutes, until the peas are tender.
2. Using a handheld immersion blender, or working in batches using a food processor, puree the soup, keeping liquidity yet ensuring everything is well blended.
3. Using a funnel, ladle the soup into jars, leaving a 1-inch headspace.
4. Wipe the rims with a washcloth dipped in vinegar. Place the lid and ring on each jar and hand tighten.
5. Process in a pressure canner at 10 PSI or according to your elevation and canner type. Process quart jars for 75 minutes and pint jars for 60 minutes.

Turkey and Vegetable Soup

Here is a light yet filling soup made with tender turkey and spring vegetables. This nutritious meal is perfect for a quick and hearty dinner after a busy day, capturing the freshness of seasonal ingredients in every jar.

YIELD: 7 quarts or 14 pints

INGREDIENTS

3 lbs. cooked turkey, shredded or cubed
8 cups turkey or chicken broth
3 cups water
4 cups peeled and diced carrots
4 cups diced celery
3 cups finely chopped yellow onion
2 cups diced zucchini
2 cups trimmed and cut green beans, 1-inch pieces
2 cups peas, fresh or frozen
1 T. salt (optional)
2 tsp. black pepper
2 tsp. dried thyme
1 tsp. dried rosemary
1 tsp. garlic powder

DIRECTIONS

1. In a large stainless steel stockpot, combine the turkey, broth, water, carrots, celery, onion, zucchini, green beans, peas, salt (if using), pepper, thyme, rosemary, and garlic powder. Bring to a boil over medium heat, then reduce to a simmer and cook for 10 minutes.
2. Using a funnel, ladle the soup into jars, leaving a 1-inch headspace.
3. Wipe the rims with a washcloth dipped in vinegar. Place the lid and ring on each jar and hand tighten.
4. Process in a pressure canner at 10 PSI or according to your elevation and canner type. Process quart jars for 75 minutes and pint jars for 60 minutes.

Clam Chowder

This classic New England–style chowder has a rich and hearty soup base, perfect for a cozy winter meal or to warm your body from the inside out on a dreary wet day. It captures the essence of the sea with its deep, savory clam flavor.

YIELD: 9 pints or 18 half-pints

INGREDIENTS

2 lbs. peeled and diced russet potatoes (4 cups)
2 cups diced celery
2 cups finely chopped yellow onion
4 garlic cloves, minced
6 cups clam juice
3 cups water
1 T. salt (optional)
2 tsp. black pepper
1 tsp. dried thyme
1 tsp. dried oregano
2 bay leaves
4 (6.5 oz) cans chopped clams, with juice

DIRECTIONS

1. In a large stainless steel stockpot, combine the potatoes, celery, onion, garlic, clam juice, water, salt (if using), pepper, thyme, oregano, and bay leaves. Bring to a boil over medium heat, then reduce to a simmer and cook for 10 to 15 minutes, until the vegetables are tender.
2. Add the chopped clams with their juice and continue to simmer for 5 more minutes. Remove the bay leaves and discard.
3. Using a funnel, ladle the soup into jars, leaving a 1-inch headspace.
4. Wipe the rims with a washcloth dipped in vinegar. Place the lid and ring on each jar and hand tighten.
5. Process in a pressure canner at 10 PSI or according to your elevation and canner type. Process pint jars for 70 minutes and half-pint jars for 60 minutes.

RECIPE TIP: When you're ready to enjoy the chowder, simply open a jar, pour it into a saucepan, and bring it to a simmer. Add ½ to 1 cup of heavy cream (or your preferred dairy or nondairy alternative) per pint for a creamy finish. Adjust seasoning if needed and enjoy!

SUMMER SEASON CANNING RECIPES

Pineapple Salsa

This is a bright and tropical salsa made with fresh pineapple, bell peppers, and cilantro. The apple cider vinegar adds depth and richness to the salsa with a slightly sweet, mellow finish that complements the tropical fruit and peppers. The sweet and zesty topping is perfect for tacos or nachos and excellent with grilled meats and fish.

YIELD: 4 quarts or 8 pints

INGREDIENTS

4 lbs. fresh pineapple, diced (14 cups)
2 cups diced red bell pepper
2 cups diced green bell pepper
1 cup finely chopped red onion
2 jalapeños, seeded and minced (optional, for heat)
1 cup chopped fresh cilantro
¾ cup lime juice
¼ cup apple cider vinegar
3 T. granulated sugar
1 T. salt (optional)

DIRECTIONS

1. In a large stainless steel stockpot, combine the pineapple, red bell pepper, green bell pepper, red onion, and jalapeños (if using). Add the cilantro, lime juice, apple cider vinegar, sugar, and salt (if using) to the pot. Stir well to combine all ingredients.
2. Bring the mixture to a boil over medium heat, stirring frequently to dissolve the sugar and salt. Once at a boil, reduce the heat to a simmer and cook for 10 to 15 minutes, allowing the flavors to meld and the salsa to slightly thicken. Stir often to avoid scorching.
3. Using a funnel, ladle the salsa into jars, leaving ½ inch of headspace. Remove any trapped air pockets and add additional salsa if necessary to maintain the ½-inch headspace.
4. Wipe the rims with a washcloth dipped in vinegar. Place the lid and ring on each jar and hand tighten.
5. Place the jars in a boiling water bath canner, ensuring that the water covers the jars by at least 1 inch. Bring to a full rolling boil, then process both quart and pint jars for 15 minutes.

Ground Cherries

Encased in papery husks, these small, golden fruits, also known as Cape gooseberries, have a sweet-tart taste ideal for jams, pies, and even fresh snacking. Their unique flavor makes them a favorite in both sweet and savory dishes, bringing a burst of brightness to every bite.

YIELD: 4 pints or 8 half-pints

INGREDIENTS

6 cups ground cherries, husked and rinsed
2 cups granulated sugar
1 cup water
½ cup lemon juice
1 tsp. vanilla extract

DIRECTIONS

1. In a large stainless steel stockpot, combine the ground cherries, sugar, water, lemon juice, and vanilla. Stir well to coat the cherries.
2. Bring the mixture to a boil over medium heat, stirring occasionally to dissolve the sugar. Once it reaches a boil, reduce the heat to a simmer and cook for 10 minutes, allowing the cherries to soften and release their juices.
3. Using a funnel, ladle the ground cherry mixture into jars, leaving ½ inch of headspace.
4. Wipe the rims with a washcloth dipped in vinegar. Place the lid and ring on each jar and hand tighten.
5. Place the jars in a boiling water bath canner, ensuring that the water covers the jars by at least 1 inch. Bring to a full rolling boil, then process pint and half-pint jars for 15 minutes.

Salsa Verde

A tangy, vibrant salsa made with tomatillos, green chiles, garlic, and fresh cilantro. Salsa Verde is a versatile staple in Mexican cuisine, bringing a burst of bright, zesty flavor to tacos, enchiladas, soups, or even as a fresh dip.

YIELD: 6 pints or 12 half-pints

INGREDIENTS

5 lbs. tomatillos, husked and rinsed
2 raw green chiles (such as Anaheim or poblano)
2 cups finely chopped onion
6 garlic cloves, minced
1 cup chopped fresh cilantro
1 cup lime juice
1 T. ground cumin
2 tsp. salt (optional)
1 tsp. black pepper

DIRECTIONS

1. Preheat your broiler. Place the tomatillos on a rimmed baking sheet. Place the green chiles on a separate baking sheet. Position the baking rack 5 to 8 inches from the broiler. Start with the green chiles and broil for 2 to 5 minutes, until the skin is blistered and blackened. Remove the peppers from the oven and let cool for about 30 minutes. Then peel the charred skin from the chiles, remove the seeds, and chop the chiles.
2. While the peppers are cooling, broil the tomatillos for 2 to 5 minutes or until the skin is blistered and darkening, but not charred. Remove the tomatillos from the oven, let cool, then chop the roasted tomatillos as well.
3. In a large stainless steel stockpot, combine the roasted tomatillos and green chiles, onion, garlic, cilantro, lime juice, cumin, salt (if using), and pepper. Mix well and bring to a boil over medium-high heat, stirring frequently. Once it reaches a boil, reduce the heat and simmer for 10 minutes, allowing the flavors to blend.
4. Using a funnel, ladle the salsa into jars, leaving ½ inch of headspace. Remove any trapped air pockets and add additional salsa if necessary to maintain the ½-inch headspace.
5. Wipe the rims with a washcloth dipped in vinegar. Place the lid and ring on each jar and hand tighten.
6. Place the jars in a boiling water bath canner, ensuring that the water covers the jars by at least 1 inch. Bring to a full rolling boil, then process both pint and half-pint jars for 15 minutes.

Spiced Plum and Star Anise Compote

Juicy plums when gently simmered with star anise, cloves, and a hint of brown sugar create an exotic, spiced compote. This flavorful combination adds a sweet yet complex touch to roasted meats, cheeses, or even desserts, making it a versatile companion for both savory and sweet dishes.

YIELD: 6 pints or 12 half-pints

INGREDIENTS

4 lbs. ripe plums, pitted and quartered
2 cups light brown sugar, packed
2 cups water
4 whole star anise
6 whole cloves
1 cinnamon stick
¼ cup fresh lemon juice

DIRECTIONS

1. In a large stainless steel stockpot, combine the plums, brown sugar, and water. Stir gently to dissolve the sugar.
2. Prepare a spice sachet by placing the star anise, cloves, and cinnamon stick in a piece of cheesecloth. Tie it securely with kitchen twine. Add the spice sachet to the pot. Slowly bring the mixture to a boil over medium heat, stirring often. Once at a boil, reduce the heat to a simmer and cook for 25 minutes, allowing the plums to soften and the spices to infuse their flavor. Stir often to avoid scorching.
3. Remove the spice sachet from the pot and discard. Stir in the fresh lemon juice. Remove compote from heat.
4. Using a funnel, ladle the compote into jars, leaving ½ inch of headspace. Remove any trapped air pockets and add additional compote if necessary to maintain the ½-inch headspace.
5. Wipe the rims with a washcloth dipped in vinegar. Place the lid and ring on each jar and hand tighten.
6. Place the jars in a boiling water bath canner, ensuring that the water covers the jars by at least 1 inch. Bring to a full rolling boil, then process both pint and half-pint jars for 15 minutes.

INGREDIENT TIP: For an extra layer of flavor, you can substitute the water with red wine or port, adding richness and depth to the compote. Serve with roasted pork, duck, or cheese boards for a delicious, aromatic pairing.

Spicy Zucchini Relish

This zesty, spicy relish made from fresh summer zucchini, jalapeños, and mustard seeds brings a bold kick to any dish. It's the perfect condiment for burgers, sausages, and sandwiches, or it can even be mixed into grain bowls for an extra punch of flavor.

YIELD: 9 pints or 18 half-pints

INGREDIENTS

5 lbs. zucchini, finely diced
2 cups finely chopped onion
1½ cups finely chopped red bell pepper
1 cup seeded and minced jalapeños
2 T. salt (optional)
2 cups apple cider vinegar
1 cup granulated sugar
2 T. mustard seeds
1½ T. celery seeds
1 tsp. turmeric
½ tsp. black pepper

DIRECTIONS

1. In a large stainless steel bowl, combine the zucchini, onion, red bell pepper, jalapeños, and salt (if using). Mix well and allow to sit for 1 to 2 hours. This will draw out excess moisture from the vegetables.
2. After 1 to 2 hours, drain the vegetable mixture in a colander and rinse it under cold water to remove excess salt. Drain well and set aside.
3. In a large stainless steel stockpot, combine the apple cider vinegar, sugar, mustard seeds, celery seeds, turmeric, and pepper. Bring the mixture to a boil over medium heat, stirring occasionally to dissolve the sugar.
4. Add the drained zucchini mixture to the pot, stirring well to combine. Reduce the heat and simmer for 20 minutes, stirring occasionally.
5. Using a funnel, ladle the hot relish into hot, sterilized jars, leaving ½ inch of headspace. Remove any trapped air pockets and add additional relish if necessary to maintain the ½-inch headspace.
6. Wipe the rims with a washcloth dipped in vinegar. Place the lid and ring on each jar and hand tighten.
7. Place the jars in a boiling water bath canner, ensuring that the water covers the jars by at least 1 inch. Bring to a full rolling boil, then process pint and half-pint jars for 10 minutes.

Chili with Beans

This rich and comforting chili is made with ground beef, kidney beans, tomatoes, and warm spices. It makes a perfect dinner on its own or served with cornbread for an extra touch of comfort. Adjust the level of heat by increasing or decreasing the cayenne pepper.

YIELD: 7 quarts or 14 pints

INGREDIENTS

2 cups dried kidney beans or 3 (15 oz.) cans kidney beans
4 lbs. ground beef
1 lb. ground Italian sausage
8 cups diced tomatoes
6 cups tomato sauce
4 cups beef broth
2 cups chopped green bell pepper
1 cup finely chopped onion
6 garlic cloves, minced
¾ cup chili powder
¼ cup ground cumin
2 tsp. salt (optional)
1 tsp. black pepper
1 to 3 tsp. cayenne pepper (optional)

DIRECTIONS

1. Place the dried kidney beans (if using) in a large pot and cover with water. Bring to a boil over medium-high heat, then cover and remove from heat. Let the beans soak for 1 hour, then drain and set aside.
2. In a large stainless steel stockpot, brown the ground beef and ground Italian sausage over medium-high heat until fully cooked. Drain any excess fat.
3. Stir in the diced tomatoes, tomato sauce, beef broth, green bell pepper, onion, garlic, chili powder, cumin, salt (if using), black pepper, and cayenne pepper (if using). Bring the mixture to a boil, then reduce the heat and simmer for 20 minutes, stirring occasionally.
4. Add the kidney beans to the chili, mix well to combine, and simmer for an additional 5 minutes.
5. Using a funnel, ladle the chili into jars, leaving 1 inch of headspace. Remove any trapped air pockets and add additional chili if necessary to maintain the 1-inch headspace.
6. Wipe the rims with a washcloth dipped in vinegar. Place the lid and ring on each jar and hand tighten.
7. Process in a pressure canner at 10 PSI or according to your elevation and canner type. Process quart jars for 90 minutes and pint jars for 75 minutes.

Vegetable Scrap Broth

This rich and flavorful broth has been a kitchen staple for centuries, providing a versatile base for soups, stews, risottos, and more. While traditionally made with fresh vegetables, this recipe is a sustainable and economical way to reduce food waste in the home. You can easily save your vegetable scraps in gallon freezer bags and store them in the freezer prior to use. Scraps from carrots, celery, onions, beets, green beans, leeks, tomatoes, and cauliflower are among many great options.

YIELD: 7 quarts or 14 pints

INGREDIENTS

8 cups vegetable scraps
2 heads garlic, top sliced off to expose the garlic cloves
4 cups mushrooms (optional)
2 T. avocado oil
1 T. salt (optional)
2 tsp. black peppercorns
6 bay leaves
1 bunch fresh parsley
1 bunch fresh thyme
12 quarts water

DIRECTIONS

1. Preheat the oven to 400°F (200°C). Toss the vegetable scraps, garlic heads, and mushrooms (if using) with avocado oil and spread them onto a baking sheet. Roast for 30 minutes, or until the vegetables are caramelized and golden brown.
2. In a large stockpot, add the roasted vegetables, salt (if using), peppercorns, bay leaves, parsley, and thyme. Pour the water over the ingredients. Bring to a boil over medium-high heat. Once boiling, reduce the heat to low and simmer uncovered for a minimum of 2 hours, reducing the volume by almost half.
3. Strain the broth through a fine mesh strainer or cheesecloth, discarding the solids.
4. Using a funnel, ladle the strained broth into jars, leaving 1 inch of headspace.
5. Wipe the rims with a washcloth dipped in vinegar. Place the lid and ring on each jar and hand tighten.
6. Process in a pressure canner at 10 PSI or according to your elevation and canner type. Process quart jars for 25 minutes and pint jars for 20 minutes.

INGREDIENT TIP: Certain vegetables have an overwhelming flavor that may change the outcome of the broth. Use the following scraps sparingly or avoid them altogether: asparagus, potato peels, broccoli, turnips, Brussels sprouts, and cabbage.

Canning Greens: Amaranth, Collard, or Mustard

These nutritious, spinach-like greens offer a slightly sweet, earthy taste and can be cooked like any other leafy green. In this recipe, ham hocks and chicken broth add depth and richness, giving the canned greens more flavor compared to the traditional method of canning them in water.

YIELD: 4 quarts or 8 pints

INGREDIENTS

2 ham hocks
8 cups chicken broth
4 cups water
18 lbs. fresh amaranth, collard, or mustard greens
1 medium onion, chopped
4 garlic cloves, minced
1 T. salt (optional)
1 tsp. black pepper

DIRECTIONS

1. In a large stockpot, add the ham hocks, chicken broth, and water. Bring to a boil, then reduce the heat and simmer for 45 minutes to 1 hour to allow the ham hocks to flavor the broth.
2. While the ham hocks are simmering, wash and chop the greens, removing any tough stems.
3. After the broth has simmered, remove the ham hocks and set them aside to cool slightly. Add the onion, garlic, salt (if using), and pepper to the pot and bring the mixture back to a boil.
4. Stir the greens into the boiling broth in batches, allowing them to wilt before adding more. Simmer the greens for 5 to 10 minutes until they are just tender. Shred any meat from the cooled ham hocks and stir it into the greens.
5. Using a funnel, ladle the greens into jars, leaving 1 inch of headspace. Tightly pack the greens, removing any trapped air pockets. Add additional broth if necessary to maintain the 1-inch headspace.
6. Wipe the rims with a washcloth dipped in vinegar. Place the lid and ring on each jar and hand tighten.
7. Process in a pressure canner at 10 PSI or according to your elevation and canner type. Process quart jars for 90 minutes and pint jars for 75 minutes.

Roasted Butternut Squash Soup

A cozy and warming soup made with roasted butternut squash is perfect for crisp autumn days. This recipe ensures the right balance of smoothness and liquidity when pureed, making it an ideal comfort food for any season.

YIELD: 7 quarts or 14 pints

INGREDIENTS

9 lbs. butternut squash, peeled, seeded, and cubed (13½ cups)

4 T. avocado oil, divided

3 cups finely chopped onion

6 garlic cloves, minced

10 cups chicken or vegetable broth

4 cups water

2 tsp. ground nutmeg

2 tsp. ground ginger

1 tsp. salt (optional)

1 tsp. black pepper

DIRECTIONS

1. Preheat the oven to 400°F (200°C). Toss the butternut squash in 2 tablespoons of avocado oil and spread it on a baking sheet. Roast for 40 minutes until tender and slightly caramelized.
2. In a large stainless steel stockpot, heat the remaining 2 tablespoons of oil over medium heat. Add the onion and garlic, sautéing until softened and translucent, about 5 to 7 minutes. Add the roasted butternut squash to the pot, along with the broth, water, nutmeg, ginger, salt (if using), and pepper. Stir to combine.
3. Bring the mixture to a boil, then reduce the heat and simmer for 20 minutes, allowing the flavors to meld and the squash to soften. Using a handheld immersion blender, carefully puree the soup until smooth, but not thick. If needed, adjust the consistency by adding additional water or broth.
4. Using a funnel, ladle the soup into jars, leaving 1 inch of headspace.
5. Wipe the rims with a washcloth dipped in vinegar. Place the lid and ring on each jar and hand tighten.
6. Process in a pressure canner at 10 PSI or according to your elevation and canner type. Process quart jars for 90 minutes and pint jars for 75 minutes.

Curried Cauliflower Pickles

A vibrant and flavorful twist on pickled cauliflower, these pickles are infused with curry powder, turmeric, and garlic for a bold and aromatic bite. The bright yellow hue from the spices makes these pickles stand out as a perfect addition to salads or grain bowls, or as a flavorful side to any meal.

YIELD: 9 pints or 18 half-pints

INGREDIENTS

8 cups white vinegar

3 cups water

1 cup granulated sugar

4 T. curry powder

2 T. canning and pickling salt

2 T. ground turmeric

18 garlic cloves, peeled

9 tsp. mustard seeds

4½ tsp. black peppercorns

5 medium heads cauliflower, cut into bite-size florets (18 cups)

DIRECTIONS

1. In a large stainless steel stockpot, combine the vinegar, water, sugar, curry powder, salt, and turmeric. Bring the mixture to a boil over medium heat, stirring until the sugar and salt are fully dissolved.
2. While the brine is heating, prepare your pint jars by adding 2 garlic cloves, 1 teaspoon mustard seeds, and ½ teaspoon black peppercorns to each. If using half-pints, add 1 garlic clove, ½ teaspoon mustard seeds, and ¼ teaspoon black peppercorns to each jar.
3. Pack the cauliflower florets into the hot, sterilized jars, leaving ½ inch of headspace. Using a funnel, ladle the hot brine over the cauliflower, ensuring the florets are fully submerged. Remove any trapped air pockets and add additional brine if necessary to maintain the ½-inch headspace.
4. Wipe the rims with a washcloth dipped in vinegar. Place the lid and ring on each jar and hand tighten.
5. Place the jars in a boiling water bath canner, ensuring that the water covers the jars by at least 1 inch. Bring to a full rolling boil, then process pint and half-pint jars for 10 minutes.

INGREDIENT TIP: For extra variety, feel free to experiment by adding other vegetables, like carrot sticks or sliced bell peppers, into the mix. These pickles are fantastic when paired with grilled meats, added to charcuterie boards, or simply served as a vibrant snack.

Apple and Fennel Chutney

This savory-sweet chutney combines the natural sweetness of apples with the subtle licorice-like flavor of fennel and the tang of balsamic vinegar. This chutney pairs beautifully with roasted meats or can be served alongside a cheese platter, adding a touch of sophistication to any meal.

YIELD: 9 pints or 18 half-pints

INGREDIENTS

6 lbs. apples, peeled, cored, and chopped (12 cups)
6 cups thinly sliced fennel bulbs
4 cups sugar
3 cups finely chopped onion
2 cups balsamic vinegar
2 T. mustard seeds
2 T. grated fresh ginger
2 tsp. ground cinnamon
1 tsp. ground cloves
1 tsp. black pepper
1 T. salt (optional)

DIRECTIONS

1. In a large stainless steel stockpot, combine the apples, fennel, sugar, onion, balsamic vinegar, mustard seeds, ginger, cinnamon, cloves, pepper, and salt (if using).
2. Bring the mixture to a boil over medium-high heat, stirring frequently to dissolve the sugar and blend the flavors. Reduce the heat and simmer the mixture for 45 minutes, stirring occasionally, until the chutney thickens and the flavors have melded together.
3. Using a funnel, ladle the chutney into jars, leaving ½ inch of headspace. Remove any trapped air pockets and add additional chutney to maintain the ½-inch headspace.
4. Wipe the rims with a washcloth dipped in vinegar. Place the lid and ring on each jar and hand tighten.
5. Place the jars in a boiling water bath canner, ensuring that the water covers the jars by at least 1 inch. Bring to a full rolling boil, then process pint and half-pint jars for 15 minutes.

INGREDIENT TIP: For a richer flavor, you can substitute pears for half of the apples or use red wine vinegar in place of balsamic vinegar. This chutney is perfect for pairing with pork, lamb, or sharp cheeses.

WINTER SEASON CANNING RECIPES

Ham and Bean Soup

A hearty and warming soup made with tender ham, creamy white beans, and earthy root vegetables, this dish is perfect for cold winter days, offering a nourishing, ready-made meal that's filling and flavorful.

YIELD: 7 quarts or 14 pints

INGREDIENTS

3 cups dried white beans (great northern or navy beans)
2 T. olive oil
2 cups chopped celery
1 cup finely chopped onion
4 garlic cloves, minced
2 lbs. diced cooked or uncooked ham
4 cups peeled and chopped carrots
10 cups chicken broth
4 cups water
2 tsp. salt (optional)
2 tsp. black pepper
2 tsp. dried thyme
2 bay leaves

DIRECTIONS

1. Place the dried beans in a large pot and cover with water. Bring to a boil over medium-high heat, then cover and remove from heat. Let the beans soak for 1 hour, then drain and set aside.
2. In a large stainless steel stockpot, add the oil, celery, onion, and garlic. Over medium-high heat, sauté until softened, about 8 to 10 minutes.
3. Add the diced ham, carrots, chicken broth, water, soaked beans, salt (if using), pepper, thyme, and bay leaves to the pot. Mix well and bring the soup to a boil, then reduce the heat and simmer for 15 minutes, stirring occasionally.
4. Using a funnel and slotted spoon, fill each jar halfway with the ham and bean mixture. Next, ladle the soup broth into each jar, leaving 1 inch of headspace.
5. Wipe the rims with a washcloth dipped in vinegar. Place the lid and ring on each jar and hand tighten.
6. Process in a pressure canner at 10 PSI or according to your elevation and canner type. Process quart jars for 90 minutes and pint jars for 75 minutes.

INGREDIENT TIP: If you don't wish to use dried beans or prefer commercially canned beans, use 4 (15 oz.) cans of great northern or navy beans to create this recipe.

Sausage and White Bean Cassoulet

A comforting, French-inspired dish featuring smoked sausage, creamy white beans, carrots, and fragrant herbs. This hearty cassoulet is perfect for canning, making it a convenient, rich meal for cold winter days or when sustenance is a must.

YIELD: 7 quarts or 14 pints

INGREDIENTS

3 cups dried white beans (great northern or cannellini beans)

1 T. avocado oil

½ lb. pancetta

2 lbs. smoked sausage links (such as pork or chicken sausage), cut into 2-inch pieces

4 cups peeled and chopped carrots

2 cups finely chopped onion

1 cup chopped celery

6 garlic cloves, minced

8 cups chicken broth

4 cups water

2 tsp. salt (optional)

2 tsp. black pepper

2 tsp. dried thyme

1 tsp. dried rosemary

DIRECTIONS

1. Place the dried beans in a large pot and cover with water. Bring to a boil over medium-high heat, then cover and remove from heat. Let the beans soak for 1 hour, then drain and set aside.
2. In a large stainless steel stockpot, heat the oil over medium-high heat and add the pancetta. Cook until lightly brown, about 5 minutes. Next, add the sausage pieces and heat until lightly browned. Remove the meat and set aside.
3. In the same pot, add the carrots, onion, celery, and garlic and cook until onion is translucent, about 8 to 10 minutes. Return the meat to the stockpot and add the broth, water, soaked beans, salt (if using), pepper, thyme, and rosemary to the pot. Mix well and bring to a boil, then reduce the heat and simmer for 10 minutes, stirring occasionally.
4. Using a funnel, ladle the cassoulet into jars, leaving 1 inch of headspace. Remove any trapped air pockets and add additional cassoulet if necessary to maintain the 1-inch headspace.
5. Wipe the rims with a washcloth dipped in vinegar. Place the lid and ring on each jar and hand tighten.
6. Process in a pressure canner at 10 PSI or according to your elevation and canner type. Process quart jars for 90 minutes and pint jars for 75 minutes.

Lemon Curd

A creamy and tangy spread made from fresh winter lemons, this lemon curd is perfect for spreading on pastries, filling cakes, or adding a zesty touch to desserts. Its smooth texture and bright flavor make it a versatile addition to any kitchen.

YIELD: 4 pints or 8 half-pints

INGREDIENTS

10 to 12 lemons, juiced and zested (2 cups juice, ½ cup lemon zest)

14 large egg yolks

8 whole eggs

4 cups granulated sugar

1½ cups cubed unsalted butter

DIRECTIONS

1. Zest your whole lemons first, then set aside. Next, slice each zested lemon in half and juice. If your lemons don't yield 2 cups of juice, you can make up the difference with bottled lemon juice. Set each aside.
2. Using a large double boiler, start water simmering in the bottom of the double boiler using low heat. In the top saucepan away from the heat, whisk together the egg yolks, whole eggs, sugar, and lemon zest until smooth.
3. Slowly whisk in the fresh lemon juice until fully combined. Next, add the butter and place the top saucepan onto the base of the double boiler. Stirring constantly, whisk until the butter has fully melted and blended.
4. Measure the temperature of the lemon curd using a candy thermometer or similar device. Do not let the curd exceed 180°F (82°C). Once the butter has been fully integrated into the mixture, remove the top saucepan from the double boiler and whisk for an additional 8 to 10 minutes, or until the lemon curd has thickened and set.
5. Using a funnel, ladle the lemon curd into jars, leaving ½ inch of headspace. Remove any trapped air pockets and add additional curd if necessary to maintain the ½-inch headspace.
6. Wipe the rims with a washcloth dipped in vinegar. Place the lid and ring on each jar and hand tighten.
7. Be sure the canner water has been simmering. Place the jars into the water bath canner, ensuring that the water covers the jars by at least 1 inch. Increase heat to high and bring to a full rolling boil, then process pints and half-pints for 15 minutes.

Marinated Mushrooms

Tender mushrooms preserved with garlic, herbs, and vinegar create a flavorful and versatile ingredient. These marinated mushrooms are perfect for serving as an appetizer, tossed in salads, or as a savory addition to a charcuterie board.

YIELD: 9 pints or 18 half-pints

INGREDIENTS

6 cups white vinegar (5% acidity)
6 cups water
2 cups red wine vinegar
1½ cups olive oil
1 head garlic, peeled and minced (¼ cup)
3 T. salt
6 tsp. dried oregano
6 tsp. dried thyme
2 to 3 tsp. red pepper flakes (optional)
6 lbs. button or cremini mushrooms, cleaned and trimmed
9 bay leaves

DIRECTIONS

1. In a large stainless steel stockpot, bring the white vinegar, water, red wine vinegar, olive oil, garlic, salt, oregano, thyme, and red pepper flakes (if using) to a boil over medium-high heat. Add the mushrooms, mix well, reduce heat, and simmer for 15 minutes to allow the flavors to blend and the mushrooms to reduce in size by half. Stir occasionally.
2. Place 1 bay leaf into each pint jar, and a half bay leaf into each half-pint jar. Using a funnel and slotted spoon, fill each hot, sterilized jar with mushrooms, leaving ½ inch of headspace. Pack them in tightly without destroying their shape. Be sure the herbs, seasonings, and garlic are evenly distributed between the jars as well.
3. Next, ladle the brine into each jar, leaving ½ inch of headspace. Remove any trapped air pockets and add additional brine if necessary to maintain the ½-inch headspace.
4. Wipe the rims with a washcloth dipped in vinegar. Place the lid and ring on each jar and hand tighten.
5. Place the jars in a boiling water bath canner, ensuring that the water covers the jars by at least 1 inch. Bring to a full rolling boil and process pint and half-pint jars for 20 minutes.

Beet and Orange Marmalade

Earthy beets blend beautifully with the bright sweetness of fresh oranges and a hint of ginger, creating a vibrant marmalade with unique flavor. Perfect for spreading on sandwiches or adding a bold twist to desserts, it pairs wonderfully with goat cheese, sharp cheddar, or brie, and is a fantastic addition to any cheese platter or sandwich.

YIELD: 7 pints or 14 half-pints

INGREDIENTS

- 2 lbs. beets, peeled and finely grated
- 4 large oranges, thinly sliced including peel, seeds removed
- 2 T. fresh grated ginger
- 1 cup water
- 3 T. lemon juice
- 4 cups granulated sugar

DIRECTIONS

1. In a large stainless steel stockpot, combine the beets, oranges, ginger, water, and lemon juice. Bring the mixture to a boil over medium heat. Stir in the sugar and continue stirring until the sugar is fully dissolved.
2. Reduce the heat to low and simmer the mixture for 45 minutes, stirring occasionally, until the marmalade thickens and reaches a gel-like consistency.
3. Using a funnel, ladle the marmalade into jars, leaving ¼ inch of headspace. Remove any trapped air pockets and add additional marmalade if necessary to maintain the ¼-inch headspace.
4. Wipe the rims with a washcloth dipped in vinegar. Place the lid and ring on each jar and hand tighten.
5. Place the jars in a boiling water bath canner, ensuring that the water covers the jars by at least 1 inch. Bring to a full rolling boil, then process pint and half-pint jars for 20 minutes.

Lemon Herb Roasted Chicken

This light and flavorful roast chicken infused with fresh lemon and herbs celebrates the freshness of spring. This meal in a jar features a beautiful mix of white and dark meat with no need for added liquid, just its natural juices from the chicken, lemons, and herbs.

YIELD: 7 quarts or 14 pints

INGREDIENTS

2 T. olive oil

5 lbs. chicken (a mix of white and dark meat), cut into 3-inch pieces

1 T. salt (optional)

2 tsp. black pepper

2 tsp. dried oregano

2 tsp. dried thyme

14 garlic cloves, peeled

7 sprigs fresh rosemary

7 sprigs fresh thyme

4 lemons, thinly sliced

DIRECTIONS

1. In a large stainless steel skillet, heat the olive oil over medium-high heat. Lightly brown the chicken pieces on all sides, working in batches. Be sure not to cook the chicken. Place the browned chicken pieces into a large bowl. Add the salt (if using), pepper, oregano, and thyme and toss to thoroughly coat. Set aside.
2. In each quart jar, add 2 garlic cloves, 1 sprig of rosemary, and 1 sprig of thyme. If using pint jars, add 1 garlic clove, ½ sprig of rosemary, and ½ sprig of thyme.
3. Packing the jars in layers, add several pieces of the browned chicken pieces, then 2 slices of lemon. Pack tightly into the jars, layering until there is 1 inch of headspace. Work to distribute the chicken pieces, spices, and lemon slices evenly among the jars.
4. Wipe the rims with a washcloth dipped in vinegar. Place the lid and ring on each jar and hand tighten.
5. Process in a pressure canner at 10 PSI or according to your elevation and canner type. Process quart jars for 90 minutes and pint jars for 75 minutes.

Handy Canning Charts

For many home canners, preserving a single ingredient per jar offers flexibility and convenience when it comes time to cook. It allows you to use just what you need without altering the flavor of a recipe, while also streamlining the canning process—keeping your kitchen cleaner and the task simpler. To help you get started, I've created easy-to-follow canning charts that detail the preparation, quantities, and processing times for various ingredients. Whether you're canning beans, vegetables, meats, or fruits, these charts will guide you step by step, ensuring your jars are packed safely and efficiently.

DRIED BEANS PRESSURE CANNING CHART

There are many benefits to having fully cooked beans in your pantry, especially if you need alternative protein. Using a pressure canner is the ultimate way to store cooked beans for a long term. After cleaning and rinsing your dried beans in a colander, the following chart gives you the amount of dried beans per jar size. You then cover the beans with water, filling to a 1-inch headspace, then process at 10 PSI or according to your elevation and canner type. Processing time for quarts is 90 minutes, pints is 75 minutes.

Type of Bean	Amount Needed for 7 Quarts or 14 Pints	Cups per Quart Jar	Cups per Pint Jar
Black	4½ lbs. (72 oz.)	1½	¾
Kidney	3 lbs. (46 oz.)	1	½
Cannellini	3¼ lbs. (50 oz.)	1	½
Pinto	3 lbs. (47 oz.)	1	½
Navy	5 lbs. (77 oz.)	1½	¾
Borlotti (Roman)	3 lbs. (48 oz.)	1	½
Great Northern	3 lbs. (46 oz.)	1	½
Black-Eyed Peas	2½ lbs. (41 oz.)	1	½
Garbanzo Beans	4¾ lbs. (74 oz.)	1½	¾
Lima	2¾ lbs. (44 oz.)	1	½
Lentils	1½ lbs. (22 oz.)	½	¼
Split Pea	2 lbs. (30 oz.)	⅔	⅓

For elevations above 1,000 feet, refer to the Altitude Guide on page 68.

VEGETABLES IN WATER PROCESSING CHART

Almost every vegetable is low in acidity, so when canned in water, the recommended means of preserving is pressure canning. The exceptions are tomatoes and tomatillos, which may be pressure canned or water bathed. Use this handy chart to preserve vegetables in water, filling each jar to a 1-inch headspace. Salt is not required when preserving vegetables; it is merely for flavor. If you wish to add canning salt to your vegetables, add 1 teaspoon to each quart and pint-and-a-half jar, ½ teaspoon to each pint, and ¼ teaspoon to each half-pint jar.

Type of Vegetable	Preparation Information	Amount Needed for 7 Quarts or 14 Pints
Asparagus	whole or pieces	25 lbs.
Beets	peeled and quartered or small beets whole	21 lbs.
Carrots	peeled, sticks or rounds	18 lbs.
Corn Kernels	whole	32 lbs. (husked)
Green Beans	whole or pieces	14 lbs.
Green Peas (shelled)	whole	32 lbs. (pods)
Mushrooms	whole or sliced	28 lbs.
Okra	whole or chopped; soak for 30 minutes in vinegar, then rinse and pat dry	11 lbs.
Parsnips	peeled and diced	14 lbs.
Peppers (Hot or Sweet)	broil at 500°F (260°C) then remove char; or core and deseed fresh, sliced or halved	14 lbs.
Potatoes	sliced, whole, quartered, or diced	20 lbs.
Pumpkin	cubed	16 lbs.
Spinach or Collard Greens	deveined, then coarsely chopped	28 lbs.
Sweet Potatoes	cubed	18 lbs.
Turnips	peeled, diced	14 lbs.
Winter Squash	peeled, cubed	16 lbs.

Jar Packing Method	Pressure Canning Time (Quarts and Pint-and-a-Half Jars)	Pressure Canning Time (Pints and Half-Pints)
Either	40 minutes	30 minutes
Hot Pack	35 minutes	30 minutes
Raw Pack	30 minutes	25 minutes
Raw Pack	85 minutes	55 minutes
Either	25 minutes	20 minutes
Either	40 minutes	40 minutes
Hot Pack	90 minutes	45 minutes
Hot Pack	40 minutes	25 minutes
Raw Pack	35 minutes	30 minutes
Hot Pack	70 minutes	35 minutes
Raw Pack	40 minutes	35 minutes
Raw Pack	90 minutes	55 minutes
Hot Pack	90 minutes	75 minutes
Raw Pack	90 minutes	65 minutes
Raw Pack	35 minutes	30 minutes
Raw Pack	90 minutes	55 minutes

Type of Vegetable	Preparation Information	Amount Needed for 7 Quarts or 14 Pints	Jar Packing Method	Pressure Canning Time (Quarts)	Pressure Canning Time (Pints)	Water Bath Time (Quarts)	Water Bath Time (Pints)
Tomatillos (whole)	halved, add 2 tablespoons bottled lemon juice per quart, 1 tablespoon per pint	9 lbs.	Either	10 minutes	10 minutes	45 minutes	40 minutes
Tomatoes (whole)	peeled, add 2 tablespoons bottled lemon juice per quart, 1 tablespoon per pint	21 lbs.	Either	10 minutes	10 minutes	45 minutes	40 minutes
Tomatoes (diced or crushed)	peeled, add 2 tablespoons bottled lemon juice per quart, 1 tablespoon per pint	21 lbs.	Either	10 minutes	10 minutes	45 minutes	40 minutes

For elevations above 1,000 feet, refer to the Altitude Guide on page 68.

SYRUP MAKING CHART

Type of Syrup	Granulated Sugar	Water	Syrup Yield
Light	1¼ cups	5½ cups	6 cups
Medium	3¼ cups	5 cups	7 cups
Heavy	4¼ cups	4¼ cups	7 cups
Honey	1 cup	4 cups	5 cups

For elevations above 1,000 feet, refer to the Altitude Guide on page 68.

A Note on Processing Fruit

Home-canned fruits and berries are a beautiful way to preserve the harvest and have versatility in your seasonal pantry. If you don't wish to add sugar to your fruit or berries, you can use any unsweetened juice, such as apple or pineapple. See the Syrup Making Chart (on page 100) if you wish to add a bit of sweetness that way.

If you choose to simply add water to fill your jars of fruit or berries, know their flavor after storage may be a bit bland. Many canners love to add bottled lemon juice to their home-canned fruit to heighten the acidity. If you wish to do that, add 2 tablespoons to each quart jar, 1 tablespoon for pint-and-a-half and pint jars, and ½ tablespoon for half-pint jars. Pack the fruit in jars, leaving a ¾-inch headspace. When ladling hot juice, water, or syrup over the top of the fruit, fill each jar to a ½-inch headspace.

FRUIT IN SYRUP OR JUICE PROCESSING CHART

Type of Fruit	Preparation Information	Amount Needed for 7 Quarts or 14 Pints	Jar Packing Method
Apples	peeled, cored, and sliced	21 lbs.	Hot Pack
Apricots	halved and pitted, peeling optional	16 lbs.	Either
Berries (Raspberry, Blackberry)*	destemmed	10½ lbs.	Raw Pack
Berries (Blue, Elder, Currants, Goose, and Huckle)*	destemmed	10½ lbs.	Raw Pack
Cherries (Sweet)*	destemmed and pitted	16 lbs.	Raw Pack
Cherries (Tart)*	destemmed and pitted	16 lbs.	Raw Pack
Crabapples	whole, unpeeled	21 lbs.	Hot Pack
Figs	whole	16 lbs.	Hot Pack
Grapefruit	peeled and sectioned	14 lbs.	Raw Pack
Grapes	destemmed	14 lbs.	Raw Pack
Guavas	peeled, seeded, and halved	14 lbs.	Hot Pack
Mangoes	peeled and sliced	14 lbs.	Hot Pack
Nectarines	halved and pitted	21 lbs.	Raw Pack
Papayas	peeled, seeded, and cubed	22 lbs.	Hot Pack
Peaches	pitted, halved or sliced	18 lbs.	Either
Pears	peeled, cored, halved	18 lbs.	Hot Pack
Pineapple	peeled, cored, and cubed or sliced	21 lbs.	Hot Pack
Plums	whole or halved and pitted; prick peel with fork	14 lbs.	Raw Pack
Rhubarb	leaf and end removed; chopped	10½ lbs.	Raw Pack
Strawberries	hulled, whole or halved	10½ lbs.	Raw Pack

For elevations above 1,000 feet, refer to the Altitude Guide on page 68.

**If preserving for baking, cooking down with sugar and water prior to filling jars is best. Reduce processing time by 5 minutes.*

Pre-Boil Time (if Hot Packing)	Preferred Syrup Type	Water Bath Canning Time (Quarts and Pint-and-a-Half Jars)	Water Bath Canning Time (Pints and Half-Pints)
5 minutes	Medium	20 minutes	20 minutes
5 minutes	Light	25 minutes	20 minutes
	Light	20 minutes	15 minutes
	Medium	20 minutes	15 minutes
	Light	25 minutes	25 minutes
	Heavy	25 minutes	25 minutes
5 minutes	Medium	20 minutes	20 minutes
5 minutes	Light	50 minutes	45 minutes
	Light	10 minutes	10 minutes
	Light	20 minutes	15 minutes
10 minutes	Light	20 minutes	15 minutes
5 minutes	Light	20 minutes	15 minutes
	Light	30 minutes	25 minutes
5 minutes	Heavy	20 minutes	15 minutes
5 minutes	Light	25 minutes	20 minutes
5 minutes	Medium	25 minutes	20 minutes
5 minutes	Light	20 minutes	15 minutes
	Medium	25 minutes	20 minutes
	Heavy	15 minutes	15 minutes
	Heavy	15 minutes	10 minutes

MEAT, POULTRY, AND FISH PRESSURE CANNING CHART

Having fully cooked, ready-to-eat meat, poultry, and fish in your pantry is vital for meeting the needs of your family throughout every season.

When canning these proteins, it's important to remember that no additional water needs to be added to the jars. Meat, poultry, and fish will naturally release their own juices during processing, ensuring full flavor and ideal texture. You're

Type	Preparation Information	Amount Needed for 7 Quarts or 14 Pints	Jar Packing Method
Boneless Skinless Poultry Breasts	whole or cut in pieces	10½ lbs.	Raw Pack
Boneless Skinless Poultry Thighs	whole or cut in pieces	17½ lbs.	Raw Pack
Bone-In Poultry Breasts	whole; keep or remove skin	17½ lbs.	Raw Pack
Bone-In Poultry Thighs	whole; keep or remove skin	9 lbs.	Raw Pack
Bone-In Poultry Legs	whole; keep or remove skin	10½ lbs.	Raw Pack
Ground Poultry	cooked	14 lbs.	Hot Pack
Pork Tenderloin	cut into 2-inch pieces	14 lbs.	Raw Pack
Pork Shoulder	slow cooked and shredded or cubed and seared	14 lbs.	Hot Pack
Pork Stew Meat	raw or seared	14 lbs.	Either
Pork Butt	slow cooked and shredded or cubed and seared	14 lbs.	Hot Pack

For elevations above 1,000 feet, refer to the Altitude Guide on page 68.

welcome to add water or broth to beef, pork, and poultry if you wish to have more broth available upon use; however, do not add water or broth to jars of fish.

Using wide-mouth jars for greater jar-packing ease is recommended. Always leave a generous inch of headspace in each jar to allow for safe expansion as the contents are processed.

Use this chart so you can easily incorporate reliable proteins into your seasonal living.

Approx. Amount per Quart	Approx. Amount per Pint	Pressure Canning Time (Quarts and Pint-and-a-Half Jars)	Pressure Canning Time (Pints and Half-Pints)
4	2	90 minutes	75 minutes
8	4	90 minutes	75 minutes
2	1	75 minutes	65 minutes
4	2	75 minutes	65 minutes
6	3	75 minutes	65 minutes
2 lbs.	1 lb.	90 minutes	75 minutes
2 lbs.	1 lb.	90 minutes	75 minutes
2 lbs.	1 lb.	90 minutes	75 minutes
2 lbs.	1 lb.	90 minutes	75 minutes
2 lbs.	1 lb.	90 minutes	75 minutes

MEAT, POULTRY, AND FISH PRESSURE CANNING CHART, CONTINUED

Type	Preparation Information	Amount Needed for 7 Quarts or 14 Pints	Jar Packing Method
Boneless Pork Chops	cut into 2-inch pieces, seared	14 lbs.	Hot Pack
Ground Pork	cooked	14 lbs.	Hot Pack
Bacon Slices	laid onto parchment paper, then covered with a second sheet, rolled	7 lbs.	Raw Pack
Ham (cooked or raw)	diced or cubed	12½ lbs.	Raw Pack in water
Beef Chuck Steak	slow cooked and shredded or cubed and seared	14 lbs.	Hot Pack
Beef Round Roast	cut into 2-inch pieces, seared	14 lbs.	Hot Pack
Beef Stew Meat	raw or seared	14 lbs.	Either
Ground Beef	cooked	14 lbs.	Hot Pack
Fish (Not Tuna)	cut into pieces to fit jar length less 1 inch for headspace	14 lbs.	Raw Pack
Halibut	cut into pieces to fit jar length less 1 inch for headspace; add 2 T. avocado oil per quart, 1 T. per pint	14 lbs.	Raw Pack
Smelt, Sardines, or Other Small Fish	whole with head/tail removed	14 lbs.	Raw Pack

For elevations above 1,000 feet, refer to the Altitude Guide on page 68.

Approx. Amount per Quart	Approx. Amount per Pint	Pressure Canning Time (Quarts and Pint-and-a-Half Jars)	Pressure Canning Time (Pints and Half-Pints)
2 lbs.	1 lb.	90 minutes	75 minutes
2 lbs.	1 lb.	90 minutes	75 minutes
1 lb.	N/A	90 minutes	N/A
2 lbs.	1 lb.	90 minutes	75 minutes
2 lbs.	1 lb.	90 minutes	75 minutes
2 lbs.	1 lb.	90 minutes	75 minutes
2 lbs.	1 lb.	90 minutes	75 minutes
2 lbs.	1 lb.	90 minutes	75 minutes
2 lbs.	1 lb.	160 minutes	100 minutes
2 lbs.	1 lb.	160 minutes	100 minutes
2 lbs.	1 lb.	160 minutes	100 minutes

5

Dehydrating and Freeze-Drying

Without tradition, art is a flock of sheep without a shepherd. Without innovation, it is a corpse.

WINSTON CHURCHILL

Winston Churchill, known for his steadfast leadership during World War II, once said, "He who fails to plan is planning to fail." His words resonate with the timeless importance of preparation, embodied in both the ancient art of drying food and the modern innovation of freeze-drying. Both methods ensure that abundance today becomes sustenance tomorrow, bridging tradition and progress. His belief in strategic foresight ties naturally to why I educate the masses on the many benefits and methods of food preservation as a means of preparing for both abundance and scarcity.

During World War II, Churchill encouraged citizens to conserve resources, grow their own food, and "make do and mend." These values resonate with the spirit of food preservation as a means of resourcefulness and self-reliance. His legacy is one of ingenuity and pragmatism, qualities reflected in the progression from drying as one of humanity's oldest preservation methods to freeze-drying as a marvel of modern science.

Benefits of Dehydrating Foods

Dehydrating is the process of preserving food by removing most of its moisture content. This inhibits the growth of bacteria, yeast, and mold, thereby extending shelf life. Dehydrating foods is also an excellent way to retain much of their nutritional value.

Unlike preservation methods that require the addition of salt, sugar, or preservatives, dehydrating often relies on nothing more than air and heat, maintaining the purity of the food. It's a safe and natural preservation technique. The process also concentrates the flavors, making fruits and vegetables taste sweeter and more intense, which enhances their appeal in snacks and recipes.

Dehydrated foods are incredibly lightweight and compact, making them ideal for storage, travel, or outdoor adventures like hiking and camping. Additionally, this method allows for minimal waste, as excess produce from a garden or bulk purchases can be preserved before they spoil. By dehydrating foods, you can create healthy, shelf-stable options ready to use whenever needed, reducing reliance on commercially processed items and contributing to food security and sustainability.

Benefits of Freeze-Drying Foods

Freeze-drying is a preservation method that removes moisture through freezing and sublimation under a vacuum. Sublimation is the process where a substance transitions directly from a solid to a gas phase without passing through the liquid phase. In freeze-drying, sublimation occurs when frozen water (ice) in the food is exposed to low pressure and heat, causing it to convert directly into water vapor. This process is key to freeze-drying, as it removes moisture while preserving the food's structure, flavor, and nutrients.

Freeze-drying foods offers exceptional benefits by preserving their taste, texture, original shape, color, and nutritional content with minimal alteration. This technique also preserves up to 97 percent of the nutrients, making it one of the most effective methods for maintaining the health benefits of fresh produce. Additionally, freeze-dried foods have a remarkably long shelf life, often decades when stored properly, making them a favorite for emergency preparedness and long-term storage.

Their lightweight nature and ability to rehydrate quickly also make them ideal for space-saving storage and convenient use during outdoor activities or travel. Unlike canned or dehydrated foods, freeze-dried products are versatile and can be rehydrated to closely resemble their fresh state, offering an unparalleled level of quality and convenience.

Method	Pros	Cons
Dehydrating	Affordable initial cost, simple process, and versatile for most foods. Compact and lightweight results, ideal for snacks and short-term storage.	Shorter shelf life, texture changes, and moderate nutrient loss. Some foods may require further preparation before consumption.
Freeze-Drying	Preserves nutrients and original food structure, long shelf life, and excellent for emergency preparedness. Can closely resemble fresh food when rehydrated.	High upfront cost and energy use. Specialized equipment required with significant initial investment.

Equipment Required to Dehydrate Food

To dehydrate food, you'll need a food dehydrator, the most common and efficient piece of equipment for this purpose. Dehydrators come in various sizes and models, ranging from basic units with stackable trays to advanced models with digital controls and temperature settings. Entry-level dehydrators start at around $40 to $60 and are suitable for beginners or those who occasionally dehydrate smaller batches of food. Mid-range models, which often include adjustable temperature controls, timers, and more even drying, range from $100 to $200. High-end dehydrators, used by enthusiasts or for larger-scale operations, can cost anywhere from $300 to $600, offering advanced features like stainless steel construction, larger drying capacities, and precision settings.

For those on a tighter budget, a conventional oven can also be used to dehydrate food, though it may not be as energy-efficient or consistent as a dehydrator. Solar dehydrators, which use natural sunlight, are another cost-effective option, though they are weather-dependent and less reliable in humid climates.

Time investment varies based on the food being dehydrated and the equipment used. Fruits and vegetables generally take 6 to 16 hours in a dehydrator, while meats for jerky can take 4 to 6 hours. Herbs and leafy greens dry faster, often within 2 to 4 hours. Solar dehydrators may take significantly longer, sometimes up to 2 days, depending on sunlight and humidity levels. Prep time for slicing and arranging food on trays is minimal, often 30 minutes or less, depending on the batch size.

The process also requires a small energy investment, particularly for electric dehydrators. But for many users, their efficiency and convenience outweigh these costs.

Equipment Required to Freeze-Dry Food

Freeze-drying requires specialized equipment designed to preserve food by removing moisture through sublimation, the process that transitions ice directly into vapor without passing through a liquid phase. The most efficient and reliable tool for this is a home freeze-dryer, which combines freezing and vacuum technology to achieve professional-grade results. These machines range in cost from $2,500 to $6,000 or more, depending on the size and features. Home freeze-dryers are capable of processing food batches in 20 to 48 hours, making them faster and more effective than traditional preservation methods.

While the upfront investment is substantial, freeze-dryers offer the advantage of preserving up to 97 percent of the food's nutrients and retaining its original flavor, texture, and color. Additionally, freeze-dried food has an exceptionally long shelf life, often lasting decades when stored properly. Though they require significant energy to operate, the convenience, efficiency, and superior quality of preservation make freeze-dryers an ideal choice for those who are serious about long-term food storage.

How to Create a Non-Electric Air Dehydrator

Creating a non-electric air dehydrator is a budget-friendly and sustainable option for preserving food. A simple, effective setup can be made using materials like screens, a wooden frame, and mesh.

Here's how you can make one:

Materials Needed:

- Use untreated, sturdy wood to construct a rectangular or square frame. Repurposed wood can work well for this project as long as it's free from chemicals or paint that could contaminate the food.
- Food-grade mesh or five-wire mesh (such as stainless steel or aluminum) is ideal for the drying surface. Avoid materials coated in plastic or paint, as these can release harmful chemicals when exposed to heat.
- Attach legs or create a simple stand to elevate the dehydrator off the ground, allowing air to circulate beneath it.
- A second piece of mesh or a breathable cloth like muslin or cheesecloth can protect the food from dust and insects while still allowing air to flow.
- An option to speed up drying is using a reflective material (like aluminum foil or a light-colored board) to direct sunlight toward the food.

Assembly:

1. **Build the Frame.** Assemble the wooden frame to create a flat surface for the mesh. Ensure the frame is sturdy and large enough to hold the quantity of food you want to dry.
2. **Attach the Mesh.** Secure the mesh tightly across the frame using staples or nails, ensuring no loose edges where food can fall through.
3. **Add Legs or Elevate.** Attach legs or place the frame on bricks, cinder blocks, or another stable structure to elevate it off the ground. This elevation helps improve air circulation.
4. **Create the Cover.** Use another frame or drape a breathable cloth over the top to keep insects and debris out while still allowing air and sunlight to pass through.
5. **Use an Optional Solar Reflector.** Place the dehydrator near a wall or surface that reflects sunlight or line the area around the frame with foil to increase heat exposure.

Most materials can be sourced affordably or repurposed, keeping the total cost under $50—especially if you already have some of the supplies on hand. While the drying process takes longer than with an electric dehydrator (up to 3 days), this method is energy-free, making it an excellent option for those looking to save money while preserving food sustainably.

DIY Freeze-Drying Process Using a Freezer

1. Slice food into small, uniform pieces to facilitate freezing and moisture removal.
2. Spread the food in a single layer on baking sheets or trays. Place the trays in the freezer or deep freeze for 24 to 48 hours until the food is completely frozen.
3. Leave the frozen food in the freezer and allow sublimation to occur naturally. This requires keeping the food frozen for 1 to 3 weeks and opening the freezer occasionally to release moisture. If using a frost-free freezer, the system may help remove some moisture automatically.
4. Check the food by breaking or biting into a piece. Properly freeze-dried food should be crisp and have no moisture inside.
5. Transfer the freeze-dried food to vacuum-sealed bags or airtight containers with desiccant (moisture absorber) packs for long-term storage.

Essential Accessories

Preparing food for dehydrating or freeze-drying is easier with a range of helpful tools and accessories. For dehydrating, items like citric acid or lemon juice are essential for soaking fruits to prevent browning, while mandolins or food slicers ensure uniform slices for even drying. Silicone mats or mesh tray liners keep smaller items or sticky foods like fruit leathers in place.

In preparation for freeze-drying, flat freezer trays or baking sheets allow foods to be prefrozen in a single layer, while stackable freezer racks maximize space for freezing large batches. Freezer-safe containers or molds are ideal for prefreezing liquids like soups or sauces. Silicone mats also come in handy to prevent sticking during prefreezing. Covering trays with plastic wrap or tray covers helps prevent freezer burn, and a freezer thermometer ensures the temperature stays at 0°F (-18°C) or lower for thorough freezing.

Dehydrating and freeze-drying processes share a need for essential accessories geared to make them efficient and ensure long-term storage success. Tools like airtight containers, vacuum sealers, and oxygen absorbers are critical for maintaining the freshness and quality of preserved foods, regardless of the method. Mylar bags and heat sealers are also useful for both, especially for long-term storage. Tray liners, such as parchment paper or silicone mats, simplify cleanup and prevent sticking, while digital kitchen scales and labels help with portioning and organization.

Although freeze-drying and dehydrating have unique tools, such as herb-drying trays for dehydrators or tray dividers for freeze-dryers, the shared focus on proper preparation, storage, and labeling highlights the similarities in accessories needed for both methods.

ACCESSORIES TO MAKE DRYING EASIER AND MORE EFFICIENT

Dehydrating	Freeze-Drying
Mandolin or Food Slicer	Freeze-Dryer Trays
Herb-Drying Trays	Parchment Paper
Mesh Tray Inserts	Silicone Mats
Dehydrator Liners	Vacuum Sealer and Heat Sealer
Citrus Juice	Airtight Storage Containers and Mylar Bags
Spray Bottle	Oxygen and Moister Absorbers
Jar Funnel	Digital Kitchen Scale
Airtight Storage Containers and Mylar Bags	Silicone Tray Dividers and/or Cubes
Oxygen and Moisture Absorbers	Stackable Freezer Racks
Vacuum Sealer and Heat Sealer	Freezer Thermometer

Textural Differences in Foods

Dehydrating significantly alters the texture of food by removing most of its moisture, which causes it to become dry and often chewy or leathery. For fruits like apples or bananas, this process results in a pliable, slightly sticky texture, while vegetables like zucchini or mushrooms may become more brittle or crisp. For meats, such as in jerky, dehydration creates a firm, chewy consistency.

The degree of texture change depends on the food type and the level of dehydration. For example, foods dehydrated to a very low moisture content, such as herbs, become crumbly and easy to powder, whereas foods that retain a small amount of moisture for preservation, like dried apricots, maintain some softness.

While the chewy or leathery texture can be ideal for snacks, some dehydrated foods require rehydration (soaking in water or cooking) to regain a texture closer to their fresh state for use in meals. However, dehydrating does not restore the original crispness or juiciness of most foods, as the structural changes caused by moisture removal are irreversible.

Freeze-drying preserves food texture exceptionally well compared to other preservation methods. Because the process involves freezing the food first and then removing moisture through sublimation (bypassing the liquid phase), it retains much of the food's original structure. This results in a light, airy, and crisp texture that closely resembles the fresh product in shape and appearance.

Fruits like strawberries or apples become crunchy and brittle, making them ideal for snacking. Vegetables maintain their firmness and structure, making them easy to rehydrate for use in cooking. Meats, on the other hand, may have a spongy or flaky texture when freeze-dried but return to their original texture after rehydration.

Unlike dehydrated foods, freeze-dried items can be rehydrated to nearly their fresh state with water, maintaining their integrity, flavor, and mouthfeel. This makes freeze-drying ideal for foods intended for long-term storage, emergency preparedness, or any application where preserving the natural texture is a priority.

Let's Talk Nutrition

The nutritional retention of dehydrated versus freeze-dried foods differs significantly due to the methods used. Dehydration uses heat to remove moisture, which can degrade certain heat-sensitive vitamins like vitamin C and some B vitamins. This process also results in some nutrient loss due to oxidation and prolonged exposure to heat. On average, dehydrated foods retain about 60 to 80 percent of their original nutrients, making them a viable option for preserving most foods but not ideal for maximizing vitamin and mineral content.

In contrast, freeze-drying occurs at very low temperatures, preserving up to 97 percent of the original nutrients. Since the primary process doesn't involve heat, freeze-dried foods maintain higher levels of heat-sensitive vitamins, including vitamin C and folate. Minerals, which are heat-stable, are largely unaffected by either method, but freeze-drying's ability to retain the food's structure also helps preserve nutrient density more effectively than dehydration.

Overall, while both methods are effective for preserving food for storage, freeze-drying is superior in maintaining the nutritional value of the food, making it a better choice for long-term storage when nutrient preservation is a priority. The nutritional loss in dehydrated foods is relatively modest, however, and it remains a practical option for shorter-term storage or cost-effective preservation.

Practical Tips for Successful Drying

Preparing foods for dehydrating and freeze-drying involves careful planning and proper techniques to ensure the best results. For both methods, starting with fresh, high-quality produce is essential, as spoilage or imperfections can compromise the preservation process. Thoroughly wash all fruits and vegetables to remove dirt and pesticides, then pat them dry to eliminate excess moisture.

Uniform slicing is crucial for both dehydrating and freeze-drying, because cutting food into even pieces ensures consistent results and prevents under- or over-drying. Tools like mandolins and food slicers can help achieve precision.

Blanching is a key preparatory step for many vegetables before dehydrating. Briefly boiling and then cooling the vegetables in ice water helps preserve their color, texture, and nutritional value during the drying process. This step is less critical for freeze-drying, as the process itself locks in nutrients and color. For fruits, dipping slices in a solution of water and lemon juice can

Important Tips for Dehydrating

1. Start with fresh ingredients and lean cuts of meat. Remove excessive fat for best results.
2. Produce: Wash and dry thoroughly. Meats & Poultry: Properly trim and slice.
3. Keep slices consistent in size for uniform drying, using a mandolin, food slicer, or sharp knife. For jerky, aim for ¼-inch-thick slices.
4. Blanch vegetables to stop the enzymes from darkening the food. Briefly boil them, then cool them in ice water to help maintain their color and texture.
5. Enhance the flavor of your jerky by marinating whole sliced meats for at least 4 hours before dehydrating. Add dried seasonings to jerky made with ground meat.
6. Avoid browning by dipping fruits like apples or bananas in a mixture of water and lemon juice to prevent oxidation.
7. Arrange items in a single layer on dehydrator trays with space for airflow. Place the thickest side of the food toward the airflow to help it dry evenly.
8. Set the correct temperature according to your instructions. If no drying time is listed, the rule of thumb is 135°F (57°C) for fruits, 125°F (52°C) for herbs, and 160°F (71°C) for jerky.
9. Rotate the trays if your dehydrator doesn't have even airflow. When doing so, check for desired texture (for example, chewy for jerky, crisp for veggies) to move the least dry tray closest to the airflow.
10. Before storing it, allow food ample time to thoroughly cool. This will avoid condensation within airtight containers that will cause the food to spoil.

prevent oxidation and browning during dehydration, though this isn't typically necessary for freeze-drying.

When arranging food for dehydrating, spread slices in a single layer on the dehydrator's trays without overlapping to allow proper airflow. Then set the dehydrator to the appropriate temperature based on the type of food. For instance, fruits often require a lower setting (around 135°F/57°C), while meats for jerky need a higher temperature (around 160°F/71°C). For freeze-drying, foods should be pre-frozen in a standard freezer before placing them in the freeze-dryer to expedite the process and reduce energy use.

Important Tips for Freeze-Drying

1. Choose fresh fruits, vegetables, fully cooked meals, or lean proteins like chicken or beef.
2. Properly clean fresh fruits and produce, then cut them into uniform pieces or portions.
3. Pierce the skins of thick-skinned fruits such as blueberries, grapes, and cherry tomatoes before freeze-drying. This step facilitates moisture release and will help cut drying time.
4. Trim excess fat from raw cuts of meat and drain excess fat from whole meals. While high-fat foods freeze-dry well, they require proper storage to maintain quality and prevent spoilage over time.
5. Spread whole meals, soups, stews, casseroles, and fully cooked meats like chicken breasts and ground beef evenly on the trays.
6. Acclerate the freeze-drying process by pre-freezing: place prepared foods on trays and set them inside a standard freezer or deep freezer. Pre-freeze foods with pungent odors—like garlic and onions—separately, avoiding flavor transfer onto other foods.
7. Consider that foods with high moisture content—like ice cream, soup, fresh pineapple, or peaches—may require longer freeze and dry times to ensure complete moisture removal. Increasing both will help you achieve optimal results.
8. Test for doneness by breaking or biting into foods to confirm they're completely dry. Meats should snap or crumble, with no residual moisture.
9. Thoroughly cool food before transferring it to vacuum-sealed bags—or Mylar bags with oxygen absorbers for long-term storage—and then store properly. This cannot be stressed enough.

Successful outcomes also depend on monitoring the process. For dehydrating, periodically check the progress and rotate trays if your equipment lacks even airflow. Over-drying can make food brittle, while under-drying leaves moisture that can cause spoilage. For freeze-drying, ensure the machine completes its cycle fully, as stopping early can leave residual moisture.

Finally, for both methods, allow the food to cool completely before transferring it to storage to prevent condensation, which could compromise the preservation effort. These practical tips will help ensure your dehydrated or freeze-dried foods are delicious, nutritious, and ready for long-term storage.

Proper Storage Techniques to Maintain Freshness and Nutritional Value

Storage tips for dehydrated and freeze-dried foods are largely the same because both methods aim to keep food dry and free from moisture and air that can compromise shelf life. Here are detailed storage tips:

1 Use Airtight Containers

Both dehydrated and freeze-dried foods must be stored in airtight containers to prevent exposure to air and moisture. Options include vacuum-sealed bags, mason jars with tight-fitting lids, and Mylar bags with oxygen absorbers for long-term storage.

2 Add Oxygen Absorbers and Desiccants (Moisture Absorbers)

Oxygen absorbers help maintain freshness by removing oxygen, which can lead to spoilage. Desiccant packs are also effective for absorbing any residual moisture inside the container. These are especially useful for foods intended for extended storage.

3 Store in a Cool, Dry Place

A consistent storage environment is critical. Choose a location that is cool (ideally below 75°F/24°C), dry, and free from direct sunlight. Avoid areas like attics or garages where temperature and humidity levels fluctuate.

4 Avoid Freezing Stored Foods

While it may seem beneficial to freeze stored foods, the freezing and thawing process can introduce condensation into the containers, compromising the dryness needed for both dehydrated and freeze-dried foods.

5 Label and Date Containers

Clearly label each container with the contents and the date it was preserved. While freeze-dried foods can last 10 to 25 years, and dehydrated foods last 6 months to a year, this ensures proper rotation of your stock.

6 Regularly Check for Integrity

Periodically inspect containers for signs of moisture, pests, or compromised seals. Any exposure to moisture can rehydrate the food and lead to spoilage.

7 Portion Appropriately

For ease of use, store foods in portions that match your needs. This minimizes repeated exposure to air when opening larger containers.

By following these tips, you can maximize the shelf life of both dehydrated and freeze-dried foods and ensure they remain safe and high quality for as long as possible.

The best storage environment for both dehydrated and freeze-dried foods is cool, dark, and dry. Ideally, the temperature should be consistent, between 50°F (10°C) and 70°F (21°C), as higher temperatures can accelerate the degradation of nutrients and flavors. Avoid direct sunlight or even indirect light, as exposure to UV rays can break down vitamins and cause discoloration. Humidity should be kept low, as moisture can rehydrate foods prematurely, leading to spoilage.

Airtight containers, such as vacuum-sealed bags, Mylar bags with oxygen absorbers, or jars with tightly sealed lids, are essential to protect against air and moisture. Additionally, storing foods in a location with minimal temperature fluctuations, like a pantry, basement, or dedicated food storage room, will help ensure the longest possible shelf life and maintain the quality of your preserved foods.

Shelf Life of Dehydrated and Freeze-Dried Foods in Long-Term Storage

Dehydrated Foods (Properly Stored):

- High-Protein Foods (e.g., Jerky, Meat Strips): 6 months to 1 year
- Carbohydrate-Rich Foods (e.g., Grains, Pasta): 1 to 2 years
- Fruits and Vegetables: 1 to 2 years
- Herbs: 1 to 3 years
- High-Fat Foods (e.g., Nuts, Seeds): 6 months to 1 year

Freeze-Dried Foods (Properly Stored):

- High-Protein Foods (e.g., Chicken, Beef): 10 to 25 years
- Carbohydrate-Rich Foods (e.g., Potatoes, Pasta): 10 to 25 years
- Fruits and Vegetables: 10 to 25 years
- Herbs: 10 to 25 years
- High-Fat Foods (e.g., Avocados, Nuts): 2 to 5 years

Shelf Life of Dried Foods Once Their Container Is Opened

Once a container of dried food is opened, the food's shelf life—the length of its viability—depends on the preservation method and its chemical makeup. In general terms:

- **Freeze-dried foods**, when properly resealed and stored in a cool, dark, and dry environment, typically remain safe and flavorful for up to 6 months to 1 year after opening. This assumes that moisture or contaminants have not entered the container.
- **Dehydrated foods** generally have a shorter shelf life after opening, typically 2 to 6 months depending on the food type, storage conditions, and exposure to air and moisture. For instance, dried fruits and vegetables may last closer to 6 months, while meats like jerky are best consumed within 2 months due to the risk of spoilage.

The stability of dried foods opened after storage depends on the food's composition, the effectiveness of storage after opening, and environmental factors like temperature and humidity. The chemical makeup of dried foods significantly influences their shelf life after opening. Here's how their composition affects longevity:

High-Protein Foods

- **Shorter Shelf Life.** High-protein foods, such as dried meats (jerky) and freeze-dried chicken, are more prone to spoilage once exposed to air and moisture. Proteins can break down faster due to oxidation, and any residual fat in the food can turn rancid, particularly if not stored in a cool, airtight environment.

- **Safety Considerations.** Protein-rich foods are also more susceptible to bacterial growth if moisture is introduced, making it critical to consume them sooner—typically within 1 to 2 months after opening for dehydrated items and 6 to 12 months for freeze-dried proteins.

Carbohydrate-Rich Foods (Starches)

- **Longer Shelf Life.** Starch-based dried foods, such as freeze-dried potatoes, pasta, and grains, tend to be more stable because they lack the fats and proteins more prone to spoilage. These items can often remain safe for 6 months to 1 year after opening, provided they're stored in a cool, dry place.

- **Resistance to Rancidity.** Starches are less likely to degrade or oxidize quickly, making them more forgiving even if storage conditions are less than ideal.

Fruits and Vegetables

- **Moderate Shelf Life.** Dried fruits and vegetables fall in between. While they generally lack the fat content that leads to rancidity, their natural sugars can attract moisture and lead to spoilage if not resealed properly. They usually last 2 to 6 months for dehydrated items and up to 12 months for freeze-dried versions.

Fats and Oils

- **Very Short Shelf Life.** Foods high in fat, even when dried, degrade quickly due to oxidation, with exposure to oxygen leading to rancidity. For example, dried or freeze-dried avocado and nuts have a much shorter shelf life once exposed to air and should be consumed within 1 to 2 months of opening.

Understanding these differences helps ensure the optimal use and safety of your stored foods. To maximize the shelf life of both freeze-dried and dehydrated foods after opening, reseal containers tightly, use airtight bags or jars with oxygen absorbers, and return them to a cool, dark storage area. Monitoring changes in smell, texture, or visible signs of spoilage is also essential to ensure food safety.

Common Mistakes to Avoid

Dehydrating and freeze-drying are effective methods for preserving food, but certain common mistakes can compromise the quality and safety of the preserved items. In dehydrating, one frequent error is overcrowding the dehydrator trays. Placing too many items on a tray or allowing the food pieces to overlap can obstruct airflow. This leads to uneven drying, where some pieces become over-dried while others remain moist, potentially causing spoilage.

Another mistake is skipping necessary pretreatments, such as blanching vegetables or soaking fruits in lemon juice or an ascorbic acid solution, which can result in nutrient loss and diminished flavor. Additionally, improper storage

COMMON MISTAKES TO AVOID

Method	Common Mistake	Potential Consequence	Preventive Measure
Dehydrating	Overcrowding trays	Uneven drying; risk of spoilage	Arrange food in a single layer with space between pieces to allow proper airflow.
Dehydrating	Skipping pre-treatments	Nutrient loss; diminished flavor and color	Blanch vegetables and soak fruits in lemon juice or ascorbic acid solution before dehydrating.
Dehydrating	Improper storage	Accelerated spoilage; reduced shelf life	Store dehydrated foods in airtight containers, away from light and oxygen.
Dehydrating	Drying at the wrong temperature	Temperatures too high can scorch food or result in uneven drying; temperatures too low can fail to remove sufficient moisture, leading to spoilage.	Follow recommended temperature guidelines for each type of food (e.g., 125°F/52°C for herbs, 135°F/57°C for fruits, 160°F/71°C for meats).
Dehydrating	Too thick or inconsistent sized pieces	Thicker or uneven pieces take longer to dry, leaving moisture in some areas and increasing the risk of mold or bacteria growth.	Slice all pieces to uniform thickness for consistent drying times.
Freeze-Drying	Overloading trays	Extended drying times; incomplete moisture removal	Adhere to recommended load sizes for your freeze-dryer model to ensure efficient drying.
Freeze-Drying	Freeze-drying high-fat or high-sugar foods	Rancidity in fats; stickiness in sugary items	Limit freeze-drying of high-fat foods; pre-treat sugary items or be prepared for longer drying times.
Freeze-Drying	Mixing foods with strong odors	Cross-contamination of flavors	Freeze-dry foods with strong odors separately to prevent flavor transfer.
Freeze-Drying	Failing to pre-freeze foods	Skipping this step can lengthen the freeze-drying process and lead to inconsistent results, especially for liquid-based or dense foods.	Always pre-freeze foods for 12 to 24 hours in a standard freezer before placing them in the freeze-dryer.
Freeze-Drying	Removing food too soon from the chamber	Prematurely ending the freeze-drying process can leave residual moisture in the food, which can spoil over time or fail to store properly.	Allow the freeze-dryer to complete its full cycle and test food for brittleness or dryness before storing.

DEHYDRATING AND FREEZE-DRYING COMPARED

Aspect	Dehydrating	Freeze-Drying
Moisture Removal Process	Removes moisture through heat and airflow.	Removes moisture through freezing and sublimation under vacuum.
Nutritional Retention	Retains nutrients but loses some during the heating process.	Retains up to 97% of nutrients due to low-temperature process.
Shelf Life	Shelf life of 6 months to 1 year (proper storage needed).	Shelf life of 10 to 25+ years (in ideal conditions).
Texture of Final Product	Chewy or leathery texture for most foods.	Crisp and airy texture, closely resembling the original product.
Flavor Intensity	Concentrated flavor due to moisture removal.	Retains original flavor more accurately than dehydrating.
Initial Investment	Low cost; equipment ranges from $40 to $200.	High cost; freeze-dryers range from $2,500 to $6,000+.
Energy Requirement	Moderate energy requirement for electric dehydrators.	High energy requirement for freeze-dryers.
Storage Requirements	Requires airtight containers to prevent rehydration.	Requires vacuum-sealed bags or containers with desiccants.
Usability After Preservation	Often requires soaking or cooking before use for certain foods.	Can often be rehydrated to closely resemble fresh food.

of dehydrated foods, like using non-airtight containers or exposing them to light and oxygen, can accelerate spoilage.

In freeze-drying, a common issue is mixing foods with strong odors, as freeze-drying preserves all aspects of the food, including any bacteria present. This can lead to cross-contamination of flavors.

By being aware of these common mistakes and implementing the suggested preventive measures, preservers can enhance the quality and safety of their dehydrated and freeze-dried foods. The chart on page 123 outlines common mistakes in both dehydrating and freeze-drying, along with their potential consequences and preventive measures.

The Importance of Proper Reconstituting

Reconstituting dried foods involves restoring their original moisture content by adding water, allowing them to regain their natural texture, flavor, and nutritional profile. This process is essential for making dried foods easier to digest and enjoyable to eat, as our bodies require moisture to break down and process food. When foods aren't properly rehydrated, our digestive system must work harder to extract moisture from internal reserves, which can lead to dehydration and strain on the body—especially if large amounts of dry food are consumed.

Proper reconstitution not only prevents digestive discomfort but also enhances the eating experience by improving the texture and flavor of preserved foods. Additionally, rehydrating foods ensures they retain their intended nutritional benefits, making them more comparable to fresh options. This step is crucial for maintaining a balanced diet and ensuring that dried foods are both safe and satisfying to consume.

Reconstituting Dehydrated Foods

Reconstituting dehydrated foods is a straightforward process that typically involves soaking or simmering the food in water until it regains its original texture and flavor. The ideal water temperature for rehydration is warm to hot, as heat helps soften the food and speeds up the absorption of moisture. For most fruits and vegetables, soaking in warm water for 20 to 30 minutes is sufficient, while tougher items like dehydrated meats may require simmering for up to an hour to fully rehydrate. Herbs, on the other hand, rehydrate almost instantly in hot water or directly in the cooking process. It's essential to use just enough water to cover the food, as excessive water can dilute flavors.

Consuming improperly rehydrated dehydrated foods can cause digestive discomfort, as the body must work harder to absorb the necessary moisture during digestion. To avoid this, ensure foods are thoroughly softened before consumption. And to support hydration, consider drinking water alongside meals made from dehydrated products.

Reconstituting Freeze-Dried Foods

Rehydrating freeze-dried foods is an efficient process, as the unique structure of freeze-dried products allows them to absorb water quickly and return to near-fresh quality. For best results, use warm water, as it mimics natural moisture absorption and helps restore texture without over-softening the food. Most freeze-dried fruits, vegetables, and cooked meals will rehydrate within 5 to 10 minutes.

To rehydrate, cover the food with enough water to match its original weight or volume, then let it sit until fully absorbed. Stirring occasionally can help distribute moisture evenly. Meats and dense meals like stews may benefit from hot water and a slightly longer rehydration time.

While some freeze-dried foods, such as fruits, make excellent snacks in their dry state, it's important to consume them mindfully. Eating large amounts of freeze-dried products without rehydration can strain the digestive system, as the body pulls moisture from internal reserves to process the food. This can lead to dehydration,

Turning Up the Heat!—Perfect Rehydration Temps

Hotter isn't always better when it comes to reconstituting food. To help you gain a better outcome when reconstituting your dehydrated or freeze-dried foods, here's more detail. These temperature ranges ensure effective rehydration without compromising the texture or quality of the food.

- **Warm Water.** Approximately 110°F (43°C) to 130°F (54°C). This is comfortable to touch, similar to a warm bath, and suitable for gently rehydrating delicate foods like fruits or herbs without causing them to get overly mushy or overcooked.
- **Hot Water.** Approximately 140°F (60°C) to 160°F (71°C). This is hot enough to speed up the rehydration process for sturdier foods like vegetables, beans, and grains, but not boiling, which could cook the outer layer too quickly.
- **Boiling Water.** Approximately 212°F (100°C). Boiling water is ideal for rehydrating foods that need rapid and complete moisture absorption, such as potato hash browns, couscous, and some freeze-dried meals. The high temperature quickly softens these items and prepares them for immediate use.

especially if water intake isn't sufficient. To maintain proper hydration, drink plenty of water alongside freeze-dried snacks or meals that are consumed without rehydration. Proper rehydration ensures both enjoyable and safe consumption of freeze-dried foods.

How to Enhance Flavor and Texture After Rehydrating

Enhancing the flavor and texture of foods after rehydrating can turn simple dried ingredients into exciting culinary creations. One way to elevate flavor is to sauté rehydrated vegetables, such as bell peppers and mushrooms, in olive oil or butter with garlic, herbs, or a dash of soy sauce. This adds a rich, caramelized depth that transforms their taste and texture.

Another approach is to coat rehydrated fruits, like apple slices or cherries, in cinnamon sugar and bake them until they're lightly caramelized. This creates a sweet, slightly crisp exterior that's perfect for snacking or dessert toppings. For proteins, like rehydrated beef or chicken, searing them in a hot skillet with a flavorful marinade or dry rub can bring out bold flavors and add a satisfying crust.

Experimenting with these techniques not only makes rehydrated foods more enjoyable but inspires creativity in the kitchen, encouraging you to explore new ways to bring dried ingredients to life.

Here are additional ideas to enhance texture after rehydrating your dehydrated or freeze-dried foods:

1 Roasting or Air-Frying

After rehydrating foods like chickpeas, potatoes, or zucchini, toss them in oil and seasoning, then roast or air-fry for a crisp, golden exterior and tender interior.

2 Grilling

For rehydrated vegetables like eggplant and asparagus, brushing them with oil and grilling over high heat creates smoky, charred edges that add depth and texture.

3 Coating with Breadcrumbs

After rehydrating mushrooms, zucchini slices, or even meats, coat them in breadcrumbs and bake or fry. This adds a crunchy exterior while keeping the inside moist and tender.

4 Pan-Frying

Rehydrated items like tofu or tempeh can be pan-fried in a small amount of oil to develop a crisp crust while maintaining a soft center.

5 Adding a Crunchy Topping

For softer rehydrated dishes like casseroles or baked pasta, sprinkle breadcrumbs, nuts, or grated cheese on top and broil for a golden, crunchy layer.

6 Mixing with Fresh Ingredients

Combine rehydrated foods with fresh ones for a textural contrast. For instance, add rehydrated cranberries to a fresh green salad or blend rehydrated lentils with raw vegetables in a hearty grain bowl.

7 Freezing and Shredding

For unique applications, rehydrate dense foods like cooked meats, then freeze and shred them to use as a topping or filler for an interesting flaky texture.

COMPREHENSIVE DEHYDRATING GUIDE

Category	Food Examples	Drying Temperature (°F)
Herbs	Basil, Parsley, Mint, Cilantro, Oregano, Thyme, Rosemary, Sage, Dill, Chives	95°
Herbs	Tarragon, Marjoram, Lemon Balm, Bay Leaves, Lavender, Mint	95°
Fruits	Apples, Bananas, Strawberries, Pineapple, Mango, Peaches, Pears, Plums, Cherries, Kiwi	135°
Fruits	Blueberries, Cranberries, Grapes, Papaya, Figs, Oranges, Watermelon, Cantaloupe, Blackberries	135°
Vegetables	Carrots, Tomatoes, Zucchini, Bell Peppers, Onions, Spinach, Kale, Broccoli, Green Beans, Mushrooms	125°
Vegetables	Cabbage, Cauliflower, Sweet Potatoes, Asparagus, Corn, Celery, Beets, Okra, Eggplant, Pumpkin	125°
Meats	Beef Jerky, Chicken Strips, Turkey Jerky, Fish Fillets, Venison, Pork Slices, Duck, Game Meat	160°
Leathers	Fruit Leathers (Mixed Berries, Applesauce, Pears), Vegetable Leathers (Carrot, Pumpkin, Sweet Potato)	135°
Other	Nuts (Almonds, Walnuts, Pecans), Seeds (Sunflower, Pumpkin), Tofu, Cooked Beans, Lentils, Pasta	105° to 135°

Use any of these techniques to make your rehydrated foods more vibrant and flavorful, adding variety and interest to your meals. No one says using dried foods must be bland! Also feel free to get creative with sauces, oils, and dried seasonings so every bite packs a delicious punch of flavor.

Comprehensive Dehydrating Guide for Common Food Items

The comprehensive chart above has expanded food groups, including several examples for each, all grouped by drying times and temperatures. This user-friendly guide is perfect for quick reference. Feel free to make a copy and store it in your kitchen for easy access.

In addition to standard food categories, I've shared some unique food items in the chart. Here are more detailed instructions to help you dehydrate and preserve them for the long-term.

- **Tofu.** Begin by pressing extra-firm tofu to remove excess moisture. Slice it into thin pieces, approximately ¼ inch thick. Marinate if desired to enhance flavor.

Drying Temperature (°C)	Drying Time Range	Notes
35°	2 to 4 hours	Dry until crumbly; store in airtight containers to preserve flavor.
35°	2 to 4 hours	Dry until leaves crumble easily; avoid overdrying.
57°	6 to 12 hours	Dry until leathery and pliable; avoid sticky or wet spots.
57°	8 to 16 hours	Dry until leathery and pliable; larger fruits may need additional time.
52°	8 to 12 hours	Dry until crisp or brittle; store in airtight containers to prevent moisture absorption.
52°	10 to 16 hours	Dry until leathery or flexible with no wet spots; suitable for soups and stews.
71°	4 to 8 hours	Dry until firm and chewy; ensure meats are fully cooked before dehydrating.
57°	4 to 8 hours	Dry until pliable and slightly tacky; store in wax paper for best results.
41° to 57°	6 to 24 hours	Dry until firm and crisp; suitable for long-term storage.

Arrange the slices on dehydrator trays without overlapping. Dehydrate at 140°F (60°C) for 4 to 8 hours until the tofu is firm and dry to the touch. Properly dehydrated tofu should break easily rather than bend.

- **Cooked Beans.** After cooking the beans until tender, drain and rinse them. Then spread them in a single layer on dehydrator trays. Dehydrate at 130°F (55°C) for 6 to 8 hours until they're hard and dry. Properly dehydrated beans should be brittle and break easily.
- **Lentils.** Cook lentils until just tender, then drain well before distributing them evenly on dehydrator trays. Dehydrate at 125°F (52°C) for 6 to 8 hours until they're hard and dry. Dehydrated lentils should be brittle and break easily.
- **Pasta.** Cook pasta slightly al dente, drain it thoroughly, and then spread it in a single layer on dehydrator trays. Dehydrate at 135°F (57°C) for 6 to 8 hours until the pasta is completely dry and brittle. Ensure pasta is fully dry before storage to prevent mold growth.

6

Storing Dry Goods and Cold-Storage Techniques

The wise store up choice food and olive oil, but fools gulp theirs down.

PROVERBS 21:20 (NIV)

Proverbs 21:20 says, "The wise store up choice food and olive oil, but fools gulp theirs down" (NIV). At its heart, this verse speaks to the value of foresight, stewardship, and the intentional care of one's resources. On a personal level, it encourages us to not only gather provisions, but to cherish and protect them, ensuring they sustain us in times of need. It's a call to thoughtful living.

This wisdom extends to how we view our pantry and our lives. Are we devouring everything at once, leaving nothing for tomorrow? Or are we approaching our resources with care, planning for both today and the future? A well-organized pantry and cold stores become more than just conveniences; they're a reflection of our ability to adapt, prepare, and appreciate what we have. It's my goal that we all strive to cultivate a mindset of self-sufficient living, one that balances the joy of the present with the wisdom of preparation.

Storing and Organizing Dry Goods for a Well-Stocked Pantry

The timeless wisdom in Proverbs reminds us of the importance of planning and stewardship. These values resonate deeply when building a well-stocked pantry. A wise approach to dried-goods storage and their organization ensures the resources you've worked hard to gather are preserved and used efficiently, reducing waste and preparing for the future.

Learning practical techniques for storing pantry staples like flour, sugar, rice, and grains to maintain their freshness and usability involves employing airtight containers to protect against pests and moisture. Proper storage means keeping items in cool, dark, and dry locations, as well as rotating stock regularly to ensure older items are used first.

Seasonal stocking habits, such as purchasing baking ingredients before the holidays or grains during harvest seasons, can help maximize savings and ensure a steady supply of essentials. The goal with learning these strategies is that your pantry will remain well-organized and ready to meet everyday needs and future demands, with an emphasis on resourcefulness and careful planning.

Proper Dried-Goods Storage Techniques

Proper storage of dried goods is essential for maintaining their quality, nutritional value, and usability in a seasonal pantry. Bulk quantities of flour, rice, grains, and sugars should be stored in airtight containers made of food-grade plastic, glass, or stainless steel to protect them from pests, moisture, and light. Containers with secure lids and gasket seals are ideal for long-term storage, and oxygen absorbers or silica gel packs can be added to further preserve freshness.

For smaller quantities intended for everyday use, consider using labeled mason jars or smaller containers that are easy to access and refill from the bulk supply. Keeping items like flour and grains in a cool, dry, and dark environment—such as a pantry, basement, or root cellar—extends their shelf life and reduces the risk of spoilage. It's also helpful to store high-turnover items, like sugar or rice, in stackable containers for better organization and accessibility.

Seasonal buying habits often influence how a pantry is stocked. For instance, during the fall and early winter, many people purchase baking essentials such as flours, sugars, and spices in larger quantities to prepare for holiday baking. Similarly, grains like wheat berries, oats, and quinoa may be bought in bulk during harvest seasons when they're fresher and often more affordable. For these seasonal purchases, it's wise to rotate older stock forward to ensure nothing is wasted.

Labeling containers with purchase and expiration dates provides an easy way to manage inventory and prioritize use. Smaller seasonal buys, like specialty baking flours or alternative sweeteners, can be stored in resealable bags within larger airtight bins to maintain their freshness. Overall, keeping your dry goods well organized by category, using stackable storage solutions, and aligning your stocking practices with the seasons ensures a functional and resourceful pantry that reflects the rhythm of your kitchen year-round.

The Importance of Pantry Pest Control

Pest control is essential for maintaining a clean, functional pantry and protecting your dried food items from contamination and waste. Infestations of weevils, moths, ants, or rodents can compromise the safety and quality of pantry staples like flour, beans, rice, and grains, leading to financial loss and unnecessary stress.

Beyond the visible damage pests cause, they can leave behind eggs, larvae, or waste that may go unnoticed until it's too late. A proactive approach to pest control ensures your pantry remains a safe and sanitary space for food storage, supporting your efforts to create a reliable and well-stocked supply of essentials. Natural pest control methods, such as adding bay leaves to containers or using

Proper Storage and Organizational Techniques for Dried Goods

1. **Use Airtight Containers**
   Store bulk items like flour, rice, grains, and sugar in food-grade plastic, glass, or stainless steel containers with secure lids to protect against pests and moisture.
2. **Add Oxygen and Moisture Absorbers**
   For long-term storage, include these items in airtight containers to preserve freshness and prevent spoilage. Clay desiccants are generally the better choice, because they're non-toxic and safe for use with food, and they provide effective moisture absorption. Food-grade silica gel packs may also be used.
3. **Control Pests and Moisture Naturally**
   Add dried bay leaves, rosemary, or mint to containers to repel pests naturally. Place a few soda crackers or rice grains in containers to absorb excess moisture.
4. **Store in Cool, Dry, and Dark Locations**
   Keep dried goods in a pantry, basement, or root cellar to maintain quality and extend shelf life. No direct or indirect sunlight is also required to lengthen the shelf life of your pantry items.
5. **Divide Bulk and Daily-Use Quantities**
   Keep bulk supplies in large containers and transfer smaller amounts into easily accessible jars or containers for daily use. The bulk supplies should be stored in optimal conditions, like your designated pantry or root cellar, while the smaller quantities for daily use can be stored in your kitchen for easy access.
6. **Label Containers Clearly**
   Include purchase or expiration dates to track inventory and ensure older items are used first. This holds true for both long-term storage items as well as daily use ingredients. Once a long-term storage food item is opened, it's also prudent to label the smaller-use container with the "open date" to know how much time you have to use it before it loses its nutritional value and potency.
7. **Rotate Stock Regularly**
   Place older items at the front of shelves and newly purchased items behind them to ensure nothing goes to waste. If you choose to stack your bulk supplies, make sure the oldest is on top and the newest is on the bottom.
8. **Group Items by Category**
   Organize dried goods by type—flours, grains, sugars, spices—so everything is easy to locate. These are the same principles used to organize your home-canned, dehydrated, and freeze-dried items.
9. **Plan Seasonal Purchases**
   Stock up on baking essentials before the holidays or grains during harvest seasons and store them with long-term freshness in mind. Take advantage of discounts, specials, and local coupons to stretch your budget, giving you access to low-cost ingredients from your pantry when commercial prices are high.
10. **Inspect Storage Regularly**
    Check containers for signs of pests, moisture, or spoilage and address issues promptly. Annually create a quarterly schedule to sort and arrange items on your shelves and in your stacks to ensure no container is forgotten in the back of the supplies.

garlic cloves as repellents, offer effective, non-toxic solutions that align with sustainable practices.

By combining thoughtful storage techniques with regular inspections and preventative measures, you can safeguard your pantry, reduce food waste, and ensure your dried goods are always fresh and ready to use.

Common pantry pests can invade households regardless of location, climate, or season. These pests are particularly attracted to stored food items like grains, flours, beans, and sugary foods. Here is a list of the most common pests we all fight no matter what part of the world we live in.

- **Weevils:** These tiny beetles often infest grains, rice, and dried beans. They can chew through packaging like paper, cardboard, and even thin plastic bags to lay eggs inside stored food.
- **Pantry Moths (Indian Meal Moths):** These moths lay eggs in grains, flours, nuts, and dried fruits. The larvae spin silk webs inside the food, making infestations easy to spot. Additionally, larvae can penetrate thin packaging materials, especially cardboard and lightweight plastic, to access stored food.
- **Ants:** Drawn to sugary or greasy foods, ants can quickly infiltrate pantries through even the smallest cracks.
- **Flour Beetles:** Found in flours, cereals, and baking mixes, these beetles thrive in poorly sealed containers or infested store-bought goods. Worse, some species of flour beetles can chew through thin, poorly sealed packaging, like paper or cardboard.
- **Rodents (Mice and Rats):** These are among the most destructive pests, capable of gnawing through thick plastic, cardboard, and even wood to access food. Attracted to a variety of dried goods, rodents leave behind contamination from their droppings and urine.
- **Cockroaches:** These resilient pests are drawn to crumbs, spilled food, and improperly sealed pantry items. They can also contaminate food with bacteria.
- **Fruit Flies:** While primarily drawn to fresh produce, fruit flies can also infest dried fruits or sugary residues on pantry shelves.
- **Silverfish:** These insects are attracted to starchy materials like flour, pasta, and paper packaging, as well as the glue in some cardboard containers.

By recognizing these common pests, you can take steps to prevent infestations, such as using airtight containers, regularly inspecting food storage, and employing natural pest deterrents to keep your pantry safe and pest-free.

Preventative Pest Control Options

In addition to keeping an eye out for pantry pests, you can avoid bringing any home from stores or commercial manufacturing facilities. A quick way to ensure your bulk purchase of, for instance, dried

WARNING
Garlic DILLS

beans doesn't go to waste is to spread them on a tray or tabletop for a few hours in direct sunlight. Or place them in the oven on a low temperature—at around 120°F (49°C) to 140°F (60°C)—for 30 minutes. This will kill any pests before storage.

Another option is to freeze-dry beans, grains, and flour for 48 to 72 hours before storing them. Freezing kills any potential pests, their eggs, and their larvae if present. This helps prevent any infestations later during storage.

If you choose to freeze your dried pantry items as an added step toward preventative pest control, be sure to use proper handling afterward. Failure to do so can lead to moisture issues that may compromise the quality of the food. When dried goods are removed from the freezer, condensation can form on the surface as the items thaw, potentially introducing moisture that encourages mold growth or clumping.

Top 5 Tips to Prevent Moisture Issues After Freezing Dried Goods

1. Before freezing, store dried goods in airtight, moisture-proof containers such as vacuum-sealed bags, heavy-duty freezer bags, or glass jars with tight-fitting lids. This minimizes the risk of freezer burn and condensation.
2. After removing dried goods from the freezer, let them come to room temperature while still sealed in their container. This prevents condensation from forming inside the container as the temperature equalizes.
3. Ensure the containers are completely dry before placing dried goods in them for freezing. Any pre-existing moisture inside the container can freeze and then melt during thawing, introducing unwanted dampness.
4. After freezing and thawing, place a food-safe desiccant, like a clay packet or food-grade silica gel, inside the storage container to absorb any residual moisture and maintain dryness.
5. Before transferring them to your pantry or long-term storage, check dried goods for any signs of moisture or clumping. If any dampness is detected, spread the items on a baking sheet and dry them in a low-temperature oven—120°F (49°C) to 140°F (60°C)—to remove moisture completely.

By carefully managing the freezing and thawing process, you can safely use freezing as a pest control method without compromising the integrity of your dried goods.

Stocking Up on Seasonal Staples

Stocking up on seasonal staples is a practical and cost-effective way to ensure your pantry and cold storage are prepared for the year ahead. Seasonal sales and harvests provide ideal opportunities to purchase essentials like flours, sugars, vinegars, oils, spices, and fresh produce when prices are lower and availability is at its peak.

Whether it's the abundance of stone fruits in summer, hardy root vegetables in fall, or baking

Natural Pest Control Methods for Dried-Goods Storage

These methods are non-toxic, are easy to implement, and align well with a natural, sustainable approach to food storage. Regularly replacing the herbs and spices ensures continued effectiveness.

1. **Bay Leaves:** Bay leaves are a natural deterrent for pantry pests like weevils and moths. Place a few dried bay leaves inside flour, rice, or grain containers. Replace the leaves every few months to maintain their potency.
2. **Whole Cloves:** Whole cloves emit a strong aroma that pests dislike. Scatter a few in sugar, rice, or other dry goods to keep insects away without altering the flavor of the food.
3. **Dried Mint or Rosemary:** Place sachets of dried mint or rosemary in pantry corners or on shelves to repel ants and moths. These herbs create a barrier that discourages pests from entering the pantry.
4. **Cinnamon Sticks:** Cinnamon sticks can be placed in jars or directly on pantry shelves to repel pests. Their strong scent works particularly well against ants and pantry moths.
5. **Black Peppercorns:** Bundle black peppercorns in cheesecloth and tuck the sachets into containers or on shelves. Peppercorns naturally deter pests like ants and rodents.
6. **Diatomaceous Earth (Food Grade):** Sprinkle a small amount of food-grade diatomaceous earth in the bottom of storage containers for dried beans, grains, or seeds. It's safe for consumption and acts as a physical pest deterrent by dehydrating insects.
7. **Garlic Cloves:** Place whole, unpeeled garlic cloves near dried food storage containers or on pantry shelves. The smell of garlic deters pantry pests without affecting the flavor of the food inside sealed containers.
8. **Lavender or Thyme:** Create small sachets using dried lavender or thyme and place them in your pantry or near food containers. Both herbs have strong scents that naturally repel moths and ants.

staples during holiday promotions, buying strategically during these times can save money and reduce reliance on last-minute shopping.

This approach not only supports your baking and cooking endeavors but ensures you're ready for preserving seasonal foods, creating holiday favorites, or preparing everyday meals. By stocking up when items are plentiful, you can avoid shortages of high-demand ingredients and stretch your budget further.

Key Ingredients to Stock Up for Different Seasons

Staple ingredients and food items should align with the seasonal rhythms of the year, allowing you to plan meals, preserve foods, and enjoy the unique flavors of each season with ease. The following list highlights key ingredients to stock up during every season, helping you build a well-rounded pantry and cold-storage system that fosters preparedness and resourcefulness year-round.

Winter (Comfort Foods, Holiday Baking, and Preserving Leftovers)

ALL-PURPOSE AND BREAD FLOUR

Essential for holiday baking (cookies, breads, pastries) and for baking bread and pastries and making pasta year-round. Stock up during holiday sales when prices drop.

SUGARS (GRANULATED, BROWN, POWDERED)

Used in cookies, candies, and frostings. Even if you aren't a baker, having sugar on hand for home canning and jam making is ideal. Brown sugar adds depth to recipes and is used in many canning recipes. Think of your canning calendar when stocking up in the winter season.

BUTTER (FREEZER-FRIENDLY)

A staple for baking and cooking. Stock up when sales align with the holidays and freeze for later use. I try to purchase a four-pack of stick butter every time I go grocery shopping to keep a continual supply in the freezer.

SPICES (CINNAMON, NUTMEG, GINGER, CLOVES)

Key for festive desserts like gingerbread and spiced cakes as well as holiday chutney and jam for gift-giving. Purchase fresh each year for optimal flavor.

VANILLA EXTRACT AND FRESH WHOLE VANILLA BEANS

A must-have flavor enhancer for nearly all baked goods. Prices for extract can be lower during holiday sales. This is also the perfect time of year to purchase whole vanilla beans and vodka so you can make your own vanilla extract to enjoy the following year. (See more on pages 186–189.)

NUTS (PECANS, WALNUTS, ALMONDS)

Used in pies, breads, and cookies. These can be stored in your pantry or in the freezer to maintain freshness. Nuts have a shorter shelf life than most ingredients, so be sure to rotate your inventory regularly to ensure you have fresh ingredients year-round.

ROOT VEGETABLES

Ideal for long-term storage. Be sure to cold-store potatoes, onions, and garlic for hearty winter meals, soups, and stews in cool, dark, and dry conditions.

Spring (Lighter Meals and Early Preserving)

CAKE FLOUR

Ideal for delicate cakes and desserts. Stock up before Easter for pastel-themed and lighter recipes.

YEAST AND BAKING POWDER

Used for homemade breads and rolls. Fresh yeast ensures successful rising for spring gatherings as well as annual baking. Once opened, it's important to transfer yeast from long-term storage to cold storage (refrigerator) for optimal effectiveness.

WHITE WINE AND RICE VINEGARS

Used in pickling spring vegetables like radishes and asparagus and making chutney. Employing these is also a great way to flavor a variety of dishes when canning and preserving.

GELATIN, PECTIN, AND CLEARJEL

A key ingredient for creating jams, jellies, molded desserts, and more. Ensuring these items are restocked annually for ultimate freshness is key to getting a good "gel" when making and canning preserves. Cook-Type ClearJel is also ideal for making and canning fruit pie fillings and low-sugar berry jam, as well as for everyday cooking.

BOTTLED LEMON JUICE

Essential when home canning to increase a recipe's acidity without destroying the flavor. A necessity when making jams and pie fillings as well as other canning recipes in the upcoming summer months.

RADISHES AND SPRING TURNIPS

Ideal for cold storage in a refrigerator or root cellar. These crisp, versatile vegetables are perfect for early pickling, roasting, or adding to fresh, spring-inspired meals.

Summer (Fresh Produce, Grilling, and Bulk Preserving)

SALT (REGULAR AND CANNING)

An essential element to our everyday diets and a necessity for baking, seasoning, curing, and preserving. Be sure to have a variety of salt on hand to enhance your nutrition, such as Celtic salt, Himalayan sea salt for seasoning, iodized salt for baking and canning, and pickling salt for preserving.

OILS (AVOCADO, OLIVE, COCONUT)

Versatile for grilling, cooking, and preserving. Having high-quality olive oil on hand is key when making herb-infused oils. Keeping coconut or avocado oil handy year-round is vital to protecting and seasoning your cast iron cookware as well as using in everyday cooking and canning.

SWEETENED CONDENSED MILK AND EVAPORATED MILK

Perfect for no-bake pies and creamy desserts. Their long shelf life makes them pantry staples for summer. They're also a great preparedness item in the event you lose power and don't have access to refrigerated milk.

RICE, QUINOA, AND PASTA

Easy staples that are incredibly versatile and pair well with fresh, seasonal produce like tomatoes, zucchini, peppers, and herbs, all abundant in summer. Bulk purchasing these items during summer allows you to prepare for a busier fall and winter season when hearty meals become the focus.

VINEGARS (WHITE, APPLE CIDER, BALSAMIC)

Essential for pickling, dressings, and marinades often made as accompaniments to meals. Having a variety of vinegars on hand for home canning or creating chutney, pickling, glazes, and marinades is key.

Fall (Harvest Baking, Comfort Meals, and Preserving Abundance)

MOLASSES, MAPLE SYRUP, AND HONEY

Used in gingerbreads, spiced cookies, and marinades. These keep well and add depth to seasonal baking. They can also be used as a substitution for granulated sugar when home canning and preserving. And they're often found in greater abundance in stores during the fall months.

DRIED CRANBERRIES AND RAISINS

Great for stuffing, breads, and oatmeal cookies as well as chutneys, meals in a jar, and everyday cooking. Bulk-buy during harvest seasons for cost savings and use throughout the next year.

CINNAMON, GINGER, ALLSPICE, AND CLOVES

Enhance your fall cooking, canning, and dehydrating recipes. These whole and powdered spices are also staples for seasonal baking. And whole cinnamon and cloves are important natural means of rodent and pest control in your pantry.

DRY BEANS AND LENTILS

Protein-rich staples that help round out your pantry, providing an alternative source of protein if meat isn't available or you have a meatless diet. They make excellent soups and stews commonly consumed in the fall and winter months. In addition, they're perfect for home canning so you can have ready-to-eat essentials in a jar without the need for soaking and pre-cooking.

OATS AND CORNMEAL

Versatile for making breakfast, baking, thickening recipes, and creating tasty side dishes to accompany meals.

WINTER SQUASH

Make versatile soups and casseroles. They're also perfect for roasting and fall staples in meal creation. Be sure to cold-store a variety of winter squash, like acorn, butternut, and spaghetti, which are ideal for pressure canning.

STOCKS AND BROTHS (HOME CANNED OR STORE-BOUGHT)

Essential for soups, stews, and casseroles, providing a rich, flavorful base for hearty comfort foods. Stocking up on or preparing these in the fall ensures you have quick, ready-to-use options for meals, saving time while enhancing the depth of your dishes all year long.

This list is designed as a guide to help you stock your pantry and cold storage with key seasonal staples, but it's only the beginning. Your cooking habits, dietary preferences, and preserving goals will ultimately shape the items most important to have on hand. Think about the meals and treats you prepare most often, the ingredients you reach for regularly, and the unique flavors and staples you and your family enjoy.

Consider what you preserve seasonally, from jams to pickles, or any cultural or regional specialties that are part of your routine. By reflecting on how you cook and what you use most, you can customize and expand this list to suit your needs, ensuring your pantry and cold-stored reserves are not only well-stocked but truly personalized. Planning ahead with these considerations will help you create a kitchen that works efficiently and supports your seasonal cooking all year long.

Inventory Rotation and Management

To maintain a well-stocked home year-round, it's essential to develop a system for regular inventory management and restocking. Start by designating a specific space for baking ingredients and organizing them in clear, labeled containers for easy visibility.

Keep a running list of food items, whether cold-stored or dried staples, and update it as you use or replenish ingredients. This running list can be either written on paper or saved in digital form. Plan to review your inventory at least every 3 months, checking for low supplies or items nearing their expiration dates. When possible, take advantage of seasonal sales to restock staples like flours, sugars, spices, and vinegars, buying enough to last until the next sale cycle.

Rotate older ingredients to the front and store newer ones behind them to ensure nothing goes to waste. Regularly cleaning your pantry and inspecting for pests or damage will also help maintain the quality of your supplies. Regularly cleaning your freezer, deep freezer, and refrigerator will help you find and use forgotten items at the bottom or shoved way in the back, reducing food waste. By staying organized and proactive, you can keep your pantry ready for any baking or cooking need while saving time and money throughout the year.

Cold Storage Beyond Refrigeration

Cold storage doesn't necessarily require refrigeration. Long before modern technology, people relied on nature's principles to preserve their food, a practice that remains accessible and practical even today. By understanding and applying these traditional methods, we can create simple, effective cold-storage solutions that work in a variety of settings, including homes without basements or root cellars and even small apartments.

One of the most enduring methods is storing root vegetables like potatoes, carrots, and beets in sand. This technique mimics the natural insulation and moisture regulation of soil. A sturdy wooden box or deep plastic bin filled with slightly damp sand can be placed in a cool, dark space like a pantry, basement, or garage. Vegetables are nestled into the sand so they remain cool and retain their firmness without drying out. For apartment dwellers, this setup can be tucked away in a cabinet or closet, or under a countertop, offering an easy way to keep produce fresh for weeks or even months.

Those without access to outdoor storage or a basement can adopt other natural cold-storage techniques. Certain fruits and vegetables, like apples and winter squash, require cool, dry conditions and can be stored on racks or shelves in a well-ventilated area away from direct sunlight. Wrapping each item in newspaper or storing them in breathable bags helps prevent bruising and rot. Similarly, onions and garlic can be braided and hung or placed in mesh bags while maintaining airflow to extend their shelf life.

Even in small spaces, refrigerators can be optimized to mimic traditional cold storage. Adjustable crisper drawers allow you to control humidity, making them ideal for leafy greens or root vegetables. Stacking produce in containers with small vents can mimic the air circulation of larger storage setups. Freezer space can be used for longer-term storage, with blanched vegetables, fruits, and herbs sealed in vacuum-packed bags to preserve their nutrients and texture.

The key to maximizing cold storage, whether with natural methods or refrigeration, is organization and understanding the needs of each food item. Combining traditional techniques like sand storage with modern refrigeration allows anyone, from homesteaders to apartment dwellers, to preserve fresh produce and reduce food waste, making the most of their available space and resources.

Using Nature's Own Preservation Method

Cold storage allows you to keep fresh produce through the winter months. By mimicking the cool, dark conditions of traditional root cellars, you can create a cold-storage area in your home to extend the life of your harvest well beyond the growing season.

Cold storage works by slowing down the natural processes that cause food to spoil. Different types of produce thrive under slightly different conditions, so grouping compatible vegetables and fruits together is key.

Here are a few time-honored methods for storing various crops in your home:

Potatoes and Carrots in Sand

Potatoes and carrots are some of the easiest vegetables to store through the winter. Both require a cool, dark environment with some humidity to prevent them from drying out. A simple storage solution involves using damp sand to provide insulation and regulate moisture. Start by filling a wooden crate or a plastic storage bin with a layer of slightly damp sand. Place a single layer of potatoes or carrots on top, then cover them with more sand. Repeat the process, alternating layers, until the bin is full.

This method keeps the vegetables from touching, which helps reduce the spread of spoilage. The sand also maintains a consistent moisture level, preventing the vegetables from shriveling. Potatoes and carrots stored this way can last for several months, making them available for soups, stews, and other hearty dishes all winter long.

Storing Apples on Racks

Apples store best in a cool, slightly humid environment, but it's important to keep air circulating around them to prevent mold. One of the simplest and most effective ways to store apples is by placing them on wooden racks. Lay the apples out in a single layer, ensuring they don't touch one another. If space is limited, you can stack the racks, leaving a few inches between each level to allow for proper airflow.

Before placing the apples on the racks, inspect each one for bruises or blemishes, as damaged apples will spoil faster and can affect the others. As the saying goes, one bad apple spoils the bunch. Once a week, check your stored apples and remove any that show signs of spoilage. With proper care, some apple varieties can last 3 to 6 months in cold storage, providing you with fresh, crisp fruit through the winter.

Root Vegetables in Bins of Sawdust or Wood Shavings

Many root vegetables, such as beets, turnips, and parsnips, benefit from being stored in sawdust or wood shavings, because this helps regulate moisture and temperature. Fill a bin with a few inches of sawdust, then place the vegetables in a single layer. Cover them with more sawdust, repeating until the bin is full. This method is similar to storing in sand but has the added benefit of keeping the vegetables dry, reducing the risk of mold. Root vegetables stored in sawdust can last through the winter and remain firm and flavorful.

Cabbage and Winter Squash on Shelves

Cabbage and winter squash varieties, like butternut and acorn, are ideal candidates for cool storage and can last for several months when stored correctly. For cabbage, it's best to harvest the heads with a few outer leaves intact. Place them on a shelf in a cool, humid area, like a basement, but avoid stacking them as they need airflow to stay fresh.

Winter squash, on the other hand, prefer a dry environment. Store them on a shelf, spacing them out so air can circulate around each one. Avoid placing them on a cold concrete floor, which holds moisture and fluctuates in temperature, causing chilling injuries and reducing shelf life. A wooden or metal shelf works best, as it provides insulation from the cold ground.

Maintaining Your Cold Storage Area in a Basement

The success of a cold-storage area relies on maintaining the right conditions. Basements are typically cool and dark, but they can vary in temperature and humidity. If you're serious about long-term storage, invest in a thermometer and hygrometer to monitor these conditions. Ideally, a cold-storage area should stay between 32°F (0°C) and 50°F (10°C), with humidity levels of 85 to 95 percent for most root vegetables and slightly lower for squash.

To maintain these conditions, try to keep the storage area as undisturbed as possible. The less frequently you open the door, the more stable the temperature and humidity will remain. You can also increase humidity by periodically misting the area or placing a bucket of water nearby to evaporate slowly. If the basement is too dry, cover stored vegetables with damp burlap sacks to help retain moisture.

Cold storage allows you to enjoy the fruits of your labor long after the garden has gone dormant. By carefully setting up your basement as a cold-storage area, you're essentially extending the season, creating a natural pantry that can feed you well into the next growing cycle.

Refrigeration: A Convenient Form of Cold Storage

Refrigeration is a modern and accessible form of cold storage that provides an ideal environment for preserving fresh foods. The optimal refrigerator temperature is 35°F (2°C) to 38°F (3°C). This range is cold enough to slow the growth of bacteria and mold, keeping your food safe and fresh, yet warm enough to prevent freezing, which can damage delicate foods like leafy greens or milk. Many homeowners have a second refrigerator in their garage or outbuilding, or in a separate room of the home, for this purpose.

For effective refrigeration you must:

- **Monitor the Temperature.** Use a refrigerator thermometer to ensure the temperature stays within the ideal range.
- **Organize for Airflow.** Avoid overcrowding your fridge, as proper airflow is essential for even cooling.
- **Reduce Door Opening.** Minimize the number of times the door is open—and for how long—to help maintain consistent temperatures.

Refrigeration offers a practical solution for those without a root cellar, providing a reliable way to extend the life of perishables like fruits, vegetables, dairy, and meats. By properly managing your refrigerator, you can enjoy fresh ingredients and reduce food waste, even in urban or small-space living situations.

Best Practices for Refrigeration: Preparing and Storing Fresh Foods

Refrigeration is another form of cold storage and an essential method for preserving the quality and freshness of raw ingredients and fresh foods. By maintaining a stable, cool environment, you can extend the shelf life of fruits, vegetables, dairy, and even raw meats. Following these best practices ensures your stored items will retain their nutritional value, flavor, and texture.

How to Prepare Foods for Refrigeration

1. **SORT AND INSPECT:**
   - Only store high-quality produce or ingredients.
   - Check for bruises, rot, or other signs of decay, and avoid placing damaged items in storage, as they can spoil surrounding foods.
2. **WASH OR NOT WASH:**
   - **Do Wash:** Hardy vegetables like carrots, potatoes, and turnips benefit from a light rinse to remove dirt if they're stored in a humid environment. Dry thoroughly before storing to prevent mold.
   - **Do Not Wash:** Produce like berries, apples, and cucumbers should remain unwashed to avoid introducing excess moisture that accelerates spoilage. Wash them just before use.
3. **TRIM:**
   - Remove tops from root vegetables like carrots or beets to reduce moisture loss during storage.
   - Leave the skins intact as they provide a natural barrier to dehydration.
4. **USE PROPER WRAPPING TECHNIQUES:**
   - Use breathable materials for high-moisture items. For example, wrap leafy greens in damp paper towels and place them in perforated plastic bags.
   - For items prone to drying out, such as cheeses or meats, use wax paper or butcher paper followed by a loose plastic wrap to maintain a balance between moisture retention and air circulation.
   - Vacuum sealing is excellent for raw meats and some cheeses to prevent spoilage.
5. **CONSIDER TEMPERATURE:**
   - Store fruits and vegetables separately. Some fruits like apples and bananas release ethylene gas, which can cause nearby vegetables to ripen and spoil faster.
   - Keep dairy products in the coldest part of the refrigerator, typically the back of the lower shelves, where temperatures are most stable.
   - Maintain a steady temperature, ideally between 35°F (2°C) and 38°F (3°C) for fresh produce and perishable items.

Best Refrigeration Practices for Specific Foods

Refrigeration is an excellent way to extend the life of fresh foods and maintain their quality, but each type of food has unique needs. Here are best practices to keep your produce, dairy, and proteins fresh and safe for longer:

Fruits

- **Apples, Pears, and Citrus:** Store these fruits in the crisper drawers without sealed bags to allow air circulation and prevent moisture buildup. Dry thoroughly to remove excess moisture, which can lead to mold and bacteria growth. Always pat fresh produce dry before storing to prolong freshness.

- **Bananas:** Bananas are best kept at room temperature unless they're overripe, in which case refrigeration can slow further ripening. The peel may darken, but the fruit inside remains edible.

Vegetables

- **Root Vegetables (Potatoes, Onions, Garlic):** Do *not* store root vegetables in a refrigerator. Instead, store them in a cool, dark place to prevent sprouting or softening. Also keep them separate—potatoes emit ethylene gas that can speed up spoilage in onions and garlic.

- **Leafy Greens and Fresh Herbs:** Before refrigeration, place leafy greens and fresh herbs in a jar of water with a loose plastic cover (like a bouquet), or wrap them in a slightly damp cloth or sheet of paper towel to retain freshness and crispness.

Dairy

- **Butter:** Butter can be refrigerated for immediate use or frozen for long-term storage. It can also be stored at room temperature in a butter dish, keeping it softer and easier to spread.

- **Milk and Yogurt:** Milk and yogurt should be kept in the coldest part of the refrigerator, which is generally toward the back. Store them sealed in their original containers to prevent contamination and retain freshness.

- **Hard Cheeses (e.g., Parmesan):** Hard cheeses should be kept in crisper drawers where the environment is slightly drier.

- **Soft Cheeses (e.g., Brie, Cream Cheese):** Soft cheeses should be wrapped in airtight packaging to maintain their moisture and prevent odors from transferring.

Raw Meats and Fish

Raw meats and fish can be refrigerated in their packaging on a tray or in a sealed container to catch drips and prevent cross-contamination. Keep them on the lowest shelf to avoid accidental leakage onto other foods. Freeze the meats you don't plan to use within 1 to 2 days, and always thaw them in the refrigerator rather than on a countertop to keep them at a safe temperature.

By following these best practices, you can maximize the lifespan and quality of your fresh foods. Thoughtful refrigeration not only reduces waste but ensures that every meal you prepare is safe, flavorful, and satisfying.

500
400
300
200
100

7

Freezing Techniques and Recipes

Gather up the fragments that remain, that nothing be lost.

JOHN 6:12 (KJV)

Freezing food is one of the most effective and accessible methods for preserving its freshness, flavor, and nutritional value. This technique dates back centuries, with evidence suggesting that ancient cultures in cold climates naturally froze food during winter months to extend its shelf life.

Freezing Foods: A Timeless Food Preservation Method

A huge benefit to freezing food is that it halts bacterial growth and slows the enzymatic processes that cause spoilage, making it an invaluable tool for preserving everything from fresh produce and meats to prepared meals. For home gardeners, cooks, and families, freezing provides a convenient way to store seasonal harvests, bulk purchases, or leftovers while reducing waste.

To ensure the longevity of frozen foods, proper preparation and packaging are essential. Foods that are poorly prepared or improperly stored may suffer from freezer burn, loss of quality, and even contamination. By following a few key guidelines, you maximize the shelf life of your frozen foods while retaining their taste and nutritional benefits.

The Importance of Proper Food Handling Before Freezing

While freezing food halts bacterial growth by reducing the temperature to levels where microorganisms can't multiply, it does *not* kill foodborne pathogens already present. Harmful bacteria such as salmonella, listeria, and E. coli can survive freezing temperatures and become active again once the food is thawed. This means improper handling or contamination of food before freezing can pose a significant risk to health, even after the food is frozen and later consumed.

To minimize this risk, following these two proper food handling practices is essential before freezing.

- Always wash fresh produce thoroughly to remove dirt, bacteria, and pesticide residues. For meats, ensure they're fresh and handle them in a clean environment to avoid cross-contamination.
- Cooked foods should be cooled quickly and stored in clean, airtight containers to prevent bacterial growth before freezing.

By taking these precautions, you can help ensure that the food you freeze remains safe and nutritious when thawed and consumed. Proper handling not only preserves food quality but protects your family from the potential dangers of foodborne illness, making freezing a reliable method for long-term storage.

Proper Preparation for Freezing Foods

Attention to preparation, packaging, and storage ensures optimal quality and longevity. By following the correct techniques for different food types, you can preserve freshness, flavor, and nutrition while also minimizing waste.

Freezing Fish and Meats

Fish and meats are particularly susceptible to freezer burn, which occurs when air reaches the food, causing dehydration and oxidation. Proper wrapping and packaging are essential to maintaining their quality over time.

Wrapping for Optimal Storage

- Wrap fish or meat tightly in plastic wrap or aluminum foil to prevent exposure to air. Use multiple layers if not vacuum sealing.
- Place the wrapped portions in a freezer-safe zip-top bag, squeezing out as much air as possible before sealing.
- Label the bag with the type of meat or fish and the date of freezing for easy identification.

Vacuum Sealing

- Vacuum sealing removes air completely, significantly extending the freezer life of fish and meats. This method is especially useful for large quantities or expensive cuts.
- For best results, freeze the meat or fish flat to optimize space and ensure even freezing.
- Label the bag with the type of meat or fish and the date of freezing for easy identification.

Portioning

- Freeze meats and fish in portion sizes that suit your cooking needs. This avoids repeated thawing and refreezing, which can compromise their texture and safety.

Freezing Berries

Berries such as strawberries, blueberries, and raspberries tend to clump together when frozen, but proper preparation prevents them from forming a solid mass. Spreading berries in a single layer on a cookie sheet allows each berry to freeze individually. Once frozen, they can be transferred to a freezer-safe bag or container without sticking

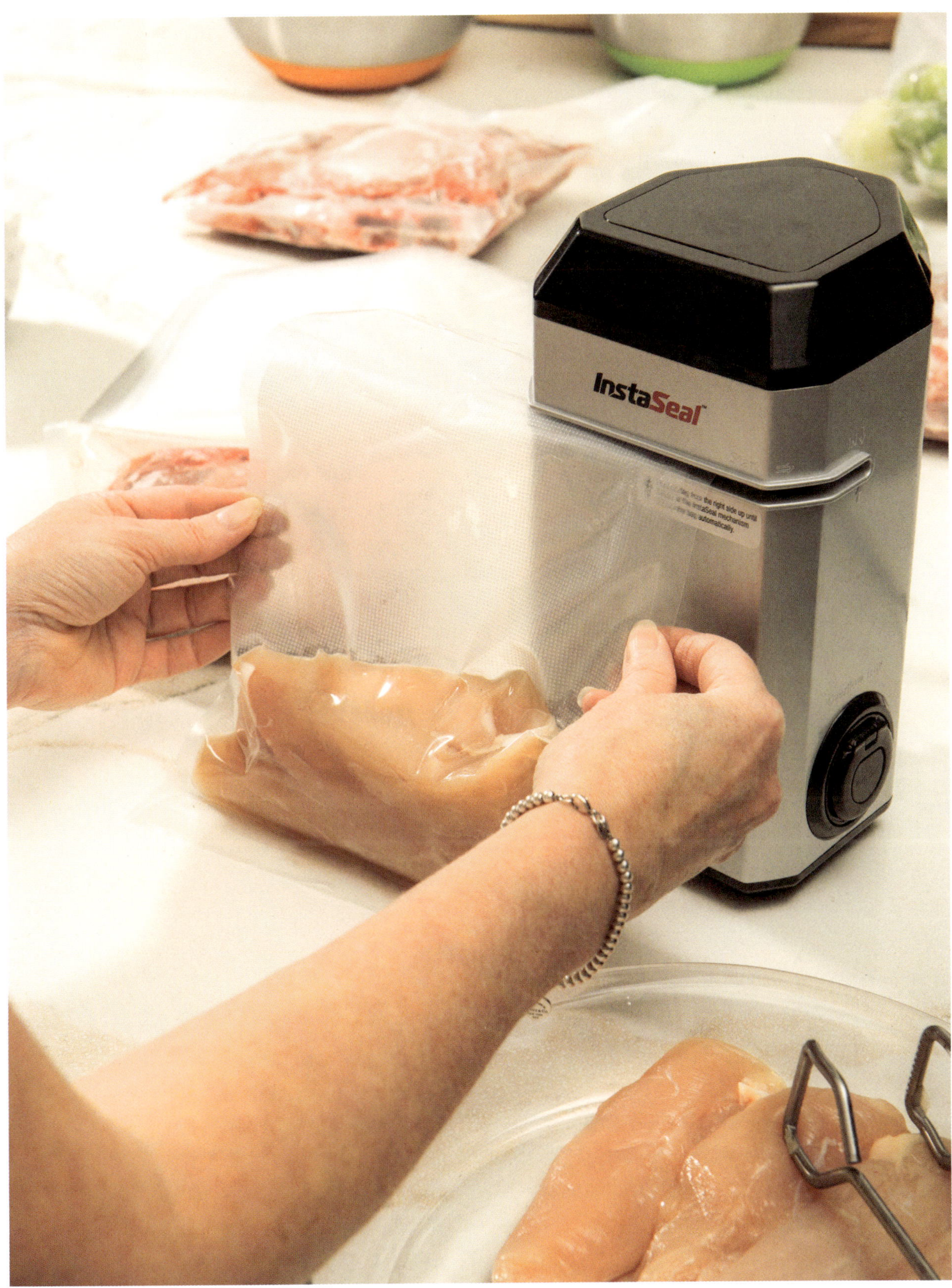
InstaSeal

together. This method makes it easier to remove only the amount needed for recipes.

Steps for Freezing Berries:

1. Wash berries gently under cool water and pat dry with a clean towel.
2. Remove stems and hulls (for strawberries) or any damaged parts.
3. Spread the berries in a single layer on a parchment-lined cookie sheet.
4. Freeze for 2 to 4 hours until firm, then transfer to a freezer bag or container. Remove as much air from the bag as possible before sealing.

Freezing Vegetables

Vegetables require special preparation to preserve their color, texture, and nutrients during freezing. Blanching, a process of briefly boiling and then cooling vegetables, is essential for most types. Blanching inactivates enzymes that cause vegetables to lose quality over time, even in the freezer, and helps maintain their vibrant colors and crisp textures.

Steps for Freezing Vegetables:

1. Wash vegetables thoroughly and trim any inedible parts.
2. Chop or slice into the desired size for cooking or later use.
3. Boil a pot of water and blanch vegetables according to the time specified in the chart.
4. Immediately transfer blanched vegetables to an ice water bath to stop the cooking process and follow the cooling times listed in the chart.
5. Drain and pat dry completely to prevent ice crystals from forming.
6. Pack the vegetables in freezer-safe bags or containers, removing as much air as possible. Vacuum sealing is also ideal for freezing vegetables.

Vegetables That Require Blanching Before Freezing

- Asparagus
- Beans (Green, Wax)
- Broccoli
- Brussels Sprouts
- Carrots
- Cauliflower
- Corn (on the cob or kernels)
- Kale, Collards, Spinach, and other leafy greens
- Peas (Shell, Sugar Snap, Snow)
- Zucchini and Summer Squash

General Freezing Tips

- To prevent freezer burn, always use high-quality freezer bags, containers, or vacuum-sealing systems designed for freezing.
- Maintain your freezer at 0°F (-18°C) or lower to ensure food remains safely frozen.
- Organize your freezer to rotate older items forward and use them first, reducing waste.
- Avoid overloading your freezer, as this can reduce airflow and slow freezing, compromising food quality.

By taking these steps for meats, fish, berries, and vegetables, you can ensure your frozen foods remain

VEGETABLES BLANCHING AND COOLING TIME CHART

Vegetable	Boiling Time	Cooling Time (in Ice Water)
Asparagus (thin spears)	2 minutes	2 minutes
Asparagus (thick spears)	3 minutes	3 minutes
Beans (Green/Wax)	3 minutes	3 minutes
Broccoli (florets)	3 minutes	3 minutes
Brussels Sprouts (small)	3 minutes	3 minutes
Brussels Sprouts (large)	5 minutes	5 minutes
Carrots (sliced)	2 minutes	2 minutes
Carrots (whole, small)	5 minutes	5 minutes
Cauliflower (florets)	3 minutes	3 minutes
Corn (kernels)	4 minutes	4 minutes
Corn (whole cob)	7 to 9 minutes	7 to 9 minutes
Kale/Collards (leaves)	2 minutes	2 minutes
Spinach/Other Greens	1½ minutes	1½ minutes
Peas (Shell)	1½ minutes	1½ minutes
Peas (Sugar Snap/Snow)	2 minutes	2 minutes
Zucchini/Summer Squash	3 minutes	3 minutes

FREEZER STORAGE LONGEVITY BY FOOD GROUP

Food Category	Freezer Shelf Life
Baked Goods (e.g., Bread, Muffins)	Up to 3 months
Bacon and Sausage	6 to 8 months
Bananas (Peeled)	2 to 3 months
Berries	Up to 12 months
Blanched Vegetables	Up to 12 months
Citrus Slices/Zest	3 to 4 months
Cooked Casseroles/Pasta Dishes	Up to 3 months
Cooked Poultry	Up to 4 months
Fish (Fatty)	Up to 3 months
Fish (Lean)	Up to 6 months
Ground Meats	Up to 3 to 4 months
Herbs (in Water/Oil)	6 to 8 months
Poultry Parts	Up to 9 months
Processed Meats (e.g., deli meats)	1 to 2 months
Root Vegetables (e.g., Carrots, Parsnips)	10 to 12 months
Soups, Stews, Broths	4 to 6 months
Steaks, Chops, Roasts	Up to 6 to 12 months
Stone Fruits (e.g., Peaches, Cherries)	10 to12 months
Whole Poultry	Up to 12 months

From Scraps to Stock: A Freezer Treasure Trove

Don't toss those veggie scraps! Instead, turn them into liquid gold. Freezing vegetable trimmings like onion skins, carrot tops, celery ends, and herb stems is an easy way to stockpile ingredients for homemade broths and stocks (see recipe page 83).

Keep a designated freezer bag or container and add scraps as you cook throughout the week. Once it's full, toss them into a pot with water, a pinch of salt, and your favorite spices, then simmer away to create a rich, flavorful stock. It's a budget-friendly, waste-reducing way to make the most of every veggie, and your future soups and stews will thank you!

safe, flavorful, and nutritious for months to come. Not only is freezing a convenient preservation method, but it's an excellent way to enjoy seasonal produce and high-quality proteins year-round.

From the Freezer to the Jar: Combining Freezing and Canning for Food Preservation

Freezing and canning go hand in hand as complementary methods of food preservation, particularly for gardeners and home cooks. Freezing allows you to capture ingredients at their peak freshness, even when the timing isn't right to start a canning project. For example, gardeners often find themselves with tomatoes ripening gradually over the season. Instead of letting small quantities go to waste, freeze them until you've gathered enough to make a full canning batch. This approach ensures nothing from your garden goes unused, and it lets you home can your bounty when your schedule permits.

Canning also provides a safety net for foods approaching the end of their freezer life. As frozen produce, meats, or prepared foods are near their storage limits, canning offers a way to extend their usability and avoid waste. For instance, blanched green beans frozen in summer can be transformed into a flavorful canned vegetable medley when winter arrives. Similarly, berries stored in the freezer can be turned into jams and jellies now lasting far longer than their frozen counterparts.

By combining these preservation techniques, you can take full advantage of seasonal abundance, prevent freezer burn, and enjoy homemade, shelf-stable foods year-round. This dual approach maximizes your resources, reduces waste, and keeps your pantry stocked with nutritious, flavorful meals and ingredients. Whether you're freezing in preparation for canning or canning to extend the life of frozen foods, these methods emphasize sustainability and efficiency in your kitchen.

SLOW-COOKER FREEZER BAG MEAL RECIPES

Freezer bag meals are a game changer for busy families, meal preppers, or anyone looking to save time in the kitchen. They're wonderful to have on hand in the event a neighbor is sick or you just don't feel like cooking from scratch. By combining wholesome ingredients into 1-gallon freezer bags and storing them in the freezer, you can have nutritious, ready-to-cook meals on hand anytime.

To make the preparation process even easier, consider using suction-cupped bag stands to hold your freezer bags upright while you fill them. These stands keep the bags steady and open, leaving your hands free to add ingredients without tipping them or spilling. For a mess-free seal, press out as much air as possible before zipping the bag shut. Lay flat in your freezer to maximize space and freeze quickly.

Freezer Bag Filling Instructions

1. Wash, cut, and prepare each ingredient and measure to ensure you have the required amount to make six 1-gallon freezer-safe bags' worth, indicated in each recipe.
2. Working in an assembly-line fashion, start with the first ingredient and place its "per bag" amount into each bag. Then move on to the next ingredient. Repeat until each ingredient has been placed into each bag.
3. Remove as much air as possible from the bag, seal it tightly, and label the bag with the recipe name and the date.
4. Lay flat in the freezer for efficient storage.

When you're ready to eat, simply transfer the frozen contents of a bag to your slow cooker. Add 2 cups of broth or water to the slow cooker, then cook on low for 6 to 8 hours or on high for 3 to 4 hours, creating delicious, fuss-free meals. Do not thaw the contents prior to slow cooking. Each recipe in this section is designed to yield six freezer bags, with each bag serving approximately 4 to 6 people, depending on their individual portion sizes.

Hearty Vegetable and Lentil Stew

This hearty stew is true *comfort in a bowl.* It's packed with earthy lentils, vibrant vegetables, and warm spices like cumin, paprika, and turmeric. The lentils provide a hearty texture, and as they cook, they release a richness that thickens the stew beautifully. Serve with crusty bread or a side of rice.

YIELD: Serves 4 to 6 people

INGREDIENTS

6 cups dried lentils (green or brown) (1 cup per bag)
6 medium carrots, peeled and chopped (1 cup per bag)
6 celery ribs, chopped (1 cup per bag)
6 medium zucchinis, chopped (1 cup per bag)
6 medium yellow onions, chopped (1 cup per bag)
12 garlic cloves, minced (2 tsp. per bag)
3 medium tomatoes, cored and diced (½ cup per bag)
1 bunch kale, destemmed and coarsely chopped (½ cup per bag)
6 tsp. ground cumin (1 tsp. per bag)
6 tsp. smoked paprika (1 tsp. per bag)
3 tsp. turmeric (½ tsp. per bag)
3 tsp. black pepper (½ tsp. per bag)
6 tsp. salt (1 tsp. per bag, adjust to taste)
12 cups vegetable broth or water (2 cups per bag)
12 T. olive oil (2 T. per bag)

DIRECTIONS

Follow the instructions on page 156 to fill six freezer bags with equal amounts of the ingredients for this recipe, then freeze for long-term storage. When you're ready to eat, remove one bag from the freezer and simply transfer its contents to your slow cooker. Cook on low for 6 to 8 hours or on high for 3 to 4 hours.

Savory Chicken and Sweet Potato Curry

This flavorful curry combines tender chicken, sweet potatoes, and aromatic spices in a creamy coconut-based sauce. It's a perfectly balanced, wholesome meal that brings warmth and comfort to your table. This dish is rich in nutrients and naturally gluten-free.

YIELD: Serves 4 to 6 people

INGREDIENTS

6 lbs. boneless, skinless chicken thighs, cut into bite-size pieces (1 lb. or 2 cups per bag)
6 medium sweet potatoes, peeled and cubed (1 cup per bag)
6 medium yellow onions, chopped (1 cup per bag)
18 garlic cloves, minced (1 T. per bag)
6 cups diced tomatoes (1 cup per bag)
6 T. curry powder (1 T. per bag)
6 tsp. ground cumin (1 tsp. per bag)
3 tsp. ground coriander (½ tsp. per bag)
6 tsp. smoked paprika (1 tsp. per bag)
3 tsp. black pepper (½ tsp. per bag)
6 tsp. salt (1 tsp. per bag, adjust to taste)
3 tsp. crushed red pepper flakes (optional; ½ tsp. per bag, for extra heat)
3 (13.5 oz.) cans coconut milk, unsweetened (½ can per bag)
6 T. lime juice (1 T. per bag)
12 T. avocado or olive oil (2 T. per bag)

DIRECTIONS

Follow the instructions on page 156 to fill six freezer bags with equal amounts of the ingredients for this recipe, then freeze for long-term storage. When you're ready to eat, remove one bag from the freezer and simply transfer its frozen contents to your slow cooker. Cook on low for 6 to 8 hours or on high for 3 to 4 hours. For best results and to prevent sticking when transferring frozen contents to slow cooker, add ½ to 1 cup of water or chicken broth.

Beef and Barley Mushroom Soup

This hearty soup is a cozy, comforting meal perfect for any time of year. Tender beef, earthy mushrooms, and nutty barley simmer together in a flavorful broth, creating a satisfying dish that's both nourishing and delicious.

YIELD: Serves 4 to 6 people

INGREDIENTS

6 lbs. beef stew meat, cut into bite-size pieces (1 lb. or 2 cups per bag)
6 cups barley, rinsed (1 cup per bag)
6 cups sliced mushrooms (1 cup per bag)
6 medium carrots, peeled and chopped (1 cup per bag)
6 celery ribs, chopped (1 cup per bag)
6 medium yellow onions, chopped (1 cup per bag)
18 garlic cloves, minced (1 T. per bag)
6 tsp. dried thyme (1 tsp. per bag)
6 tsp. dried parsley (1 tsp. per bag)
3 tsp. black pepper (½ tsp. per bag)
6 tsp. salt (1 tsp. per bag, adjust to taste)
6 bay leaves (1 per bag)
12 cups beef broth (2 cups per bag)
6 T. Worcestershire sauce (1 T. per bag)
6 T. olive oil (1 T. per bag)

DIRECTIONS

Follow the instructions on page 156 to fill six freezer bags with equal amounts of the ingredients for this recipe, then freeze for long-term storage. When you're ready to eat, remove one bag from the freezer and simply transfer its frozen contents to your slow cooker. Add 6 cups additional beef broth or water to the slow cooker. Cook on low for 6 to 8 hours or on high for 3 to 4 hours.

Tuscan White Bean and Sausage Ragu

This rich and flavorful ragu combines hearty white beans, savory Italian sausage, and aromatic herbs in a tomato-based sauce. It's a comforting, rustic dish that brings the flavors of Tuscany to your table with ease. Toss with pasta or serve over garlic mashed potatoes.

YIELD: Serves 4 to 6 people

INGREDIENTS

6 lbs. cooked Italian sausage (mild or spicy), browned (2 cups per bag)

4 pint jars or 4 (15 oz.) cans white beans, drained and rinsed (1 cup per bag)

6 medium carrots, peeled and diced (1 cup per bag)

6 celery ribs, chopped (1 cup per bag)

6 medium yellow onions, chopped (1 cup per bag)

18 garlic cloves, minced (1 T. per bag)

6 tsp. dried rosemary (1 tsp. per bag)

6 tsp. dried oregano (1 tsp. per bag)

6 tsp. smoked paprika (1 tsp. per bag)

3 tsp. crushed red pepper flakes (optional; ½ tsp. per bag)

6 tsp. salt (1 tsp. per bag, adjust to taste)

3 tsp. black pepper (½ tsp. per bag)

6 cups crushed tomatoes (1 cup per bag)

6 cups chicken or vegetable broth (1 cup per bag)

12 T. olive oil (2 T. per bag)

DIRECTIONS

Follow the instructions on page 156 to fill six freezer bags with equal amounts of the ingredients for this recipe, then freeze for long-term storage. When you're ready to eat, remove one bag from the freezer and simply transfer its frozen contents to your slow cooker. Cook on low for 6 to 8 hours or on high for 3 to 4 hours.

Zesty Lemon Garlic Herb Chicken with Vegetables

Bright, tangy lemon, aromatic garlic, and a medley of fresh herbs bring this slow-cooker chicken dish to life. Paired with hearty root vegetables, it's a flavorful and wholesome meal perfect for any night of the week. Feel free to use a mixture of chicken breasts and thighs to create this recipe.

YIELD: Serves 4 to 6 people

INGREDIENTS

6 lbs. boneless, skinless chicken thighs or breasts, left whole (1 lb. or 2 cups per bag)
6 medium carrots, peeled and chopped (1 cup per bag)
6 medium parsnips, peeled and chopped (1 cup per bag)
6 small red onions, quartered (4 quarters per bag)
12 garlic cloves, minced (2 tsp. per bag)
6 tsp. dried oregano (1 tsp. per bag)
6 tsp. dried thyme (1 tsp. per bag)
6 tsp. smoked paprika (1 tsp. per bag)
3 tsp. black pepper (½ tsp. per bag)
6 tsp. salt (1 tsp. per bag, adjust to taste)
Zest of 6 lemons (1 lemon per bag)
Juice of 6 lemons (2 T. per bag)
12 T. olive oil (2 T. per bag)
6 cups chicken broth (1 cup per bag)

DIRECTIONS

Follow the instructions on page 156 to fill six freezer bags with equal amounts of the ingredients for this recipe, then freeze for long-term storage. When you're ready to eat, remove one bag from the freezer and simply transfer its frozen contents to your slow cooker. Cook on low for 6 to 8 hours or on high for 3 to 4 hours.

Southwest Black Bean and Sweet Corn Chili

This vibrant chili is bursting with bold southwestern flavors, hearty black beans, and sweet corn. It's a satisfying, wholesome meal perfect for busy nights, offering a delicious blend of spices and natural ingredients. When serving, top each steamy bowl with a dollop of sour cream and shredded cheddar cheese.

YIELD: Serves 4 to 6 people

INGREDIENTS

6 cups cooked or 4 (15 oz.) cans black beans, drained and rinsed (1 cup per bag)
6 cups frozen sweet corn kernels (1 cup per bag)
6 medium red bell peppers, diced (1 cup per bag)
6 medium yellow onions, chopped (1 cup per bag)
18 garlic cloves, minced (1 T. per bag)
6 T. chili powder (1 T. per bag)
6 tsp. ground cumin (1 tsp. per bag)
3 tsp. smoked paprika (½ tsp. per bag)
6 tsp. dried oregano (1 tsp. per bag)
6 tsp. salt (1 tsp. per bag, adjust to taste)
3 tsp. black pepper (½ tsp. per bag)
3 tsp. crushed red pepper flakes (optional; ½ tsp. per bag)
6 cups crushed tomatoes (1 cup per bag)
12 cups vegetable or chicken broth (2 cups per bag)
6 T. olive oil (1 T. per bag)

DIRECTIONS

Follow the instructions on page 156 to fill six freezer bags with equal amounts of the ingredients for this recipe, then freeze for long-term storage. When you're ready to eat, remove one bag from the freezer and simply transfer its frozen contents to your slow cooker. Cook on low for 6 to 8 hours or on high for 3 to 4 hours. If you prefer a thicker chili, remove the slow cooker lid for the final 15–20 minutes of cooking to allow excess moisture to evaporate.

Mediterranean Lemon Herb Salmon with Vegetables

This light and flavorful dish combines tender salmon, vibrant vegetables, and a medley of Mediterranean-inspired herbs. Finished with a zesty lemon kick, it's a healthy, no-fuss meal perfect for any night of the week. Serve over a bed of herbed couscous or with a side of creamy mashed potatoes.

YIELD: **Serves 4 to 6 people**

INGREDIENTS

6 lbs. salmon fillets, skinless (cut into portions; 1 lb. per bag)
6 cups cherry tomatoes, halved (1 cup per bag)
6 medium zucchini, sliced (1 cup per bag)
6 medium yellow bell peppers, chopped (1 cup per bag)
6 medium red onions, sliced (1 cup per bag)
33 oz. artichokes in oil, excess oil shaken off (⅔ cup per bag)
4 (6 oz.) cans whole black olives (¾ cup per bag)
6 tsp. dried oregano (1 tsp. per bag)
6 tsp. dried parsley (1 tsp. per bag)
6 tsp. garlic powder (1 tsp. per bag)
6 tsp. salt (1 tsp. per bag, adjust to taste)
3 tsp. black pepper (½ tsp. per bag)
Zest of 6 lemons (1 lemon per bag)
Juice of 6 lemons (2 T. per bag)
12 T. olive oil (2 T. per bag)
6 cups vegetable or chicken broth (1 cup per bag)

DIRECTIONS

Follow the instructions on page 156 to fill six freezer bags with equal amounts of the ingredients for this recipe, then freeze for long-term storage. When you're ready to eat, remove one bag from the freezer and simply transfer its frozen contents to your slow cooker. Cook on low for 2 to 3 hours or high for 1½ to 2 hours, until salmon is tender and vegetables are fork-soft. For more a more concentrated flavor, remove the slow cooker lid during the last 15 minutes of cooking to reduce excess liquid.

Coconut Curry Chickpea Stew

This creamy and flavorful stew combines hearty chickpeas, tender vegetables, and a rich coconut curry base. It's a plant-based delight that's perfect for warming up any day with its vibrant spices and nourishing ingredients.

YIELD: Serves 4 to 6 people

INGREDIENTS

6 cups cooked or 4 (15 oz.) cans chickpeas, drained and rinsed (1 cup per bag)
6 medium sweet potatoes, peeled and cubed (1 cup per bag)
6 cups diced butternut squash (1 cup per bag)
6 medium carrots, peeled and sliced (1 cup per bag)
6 medium yellow onions, chopped (1 cup per bag)
18 garlic cloves, minced (1 T. per bag)
6 T. grated fresh ginger (1 T. per bag)
6 T. yellow curry powder (1 T. per bag)
6 tsp. ground cumin (1 tsp. per bag)
6 tsp. smoked paprika (1 tsp. per bag)
3 tsp. turmeric (½ tsp. per bag)
6 tsp. salt (1 tsp. per bag, adjust to taste)
3 tsp. black pepper (½ tsp. per bag)
3 tsp. crushed red pepper flakes (optional; ½ tsp. per bag)
3 (13.5 oz.) cans coconut milk, unsweetened (½ can per bag)
12 cups vegetable broth (2 cups per bag)
6 T. lime juice (1 T. per bag)
12 T. olive oil (2 T. per bag)

DIRECTIONS

Follow the instructions on page 156 to fill six freezer bags with equal amounts of the ingredients for this recipe, then freeze for long-term storage. When you're ready to eat, remove one bag from the freezer and simply transfer its frozen contents to your slow cooker. Cook on low for 6 to 7 hours only. Avoid high heat, as it may cause the coconut milk to separate. If a thicker texture is desired, remove the lid for the final 30 minutes of cooking to reduce excess liquid.

Honey Mustard Glazed Pork with Apples and Root Vegetables

This sweet and savory dish features tender pork, crisp apples, and hearty root vegetables, all coated in a rich honey mustard glaze. It's a comforting, wholesome meal perfect for any time of year. Serve it alongside a wild rice pilaf and roasted Brussels sprouts for a complete meal.

YIELD: Serves 4 to 6 people

INGREDIENTS

6 lbs. pork tenderloin, cut into 1-inch medallions (1 lb. or 2 cups per bag)

6 medium apples (Granny Smith or Honeycrisp), cored and sliced (1 cup per bag)

6 medium carrots, peeled and sliced (1 cup per bag)

6 medium parsnips, peeled and chopped (1 cup per bag)

6 medium yellow onions, chopped (1 cup per bag)

6 T. Dijon mustard (1 T. per bag)

6 T. honey (1 T. per bag)

6 tsp. dried thyme (1 tsp. per bag)

6 tsp. ground cinnamon (1 tsp. per bag)

6 tsp. salt (1 tsp. per bag, adjust to taste)

3 tsp. black pepper (½ tsp. per bag)

3 cups apple cider or apple juice (½ cup per bag)

3 cups chicken broth (½ cup per bag)

12 T. olive oil (2 T. per bag)

DIRECTIONS

Follow the instructions on page 156 to fill six freezer bags with equal amounts of the ingredients for this recipe, then freeze for long-term storage. When you're ready to eat, remove one bag from the freezer and simply transfer its frozen contents to your slow cooker. Cook on low for 6 to 8 hours, do not cook on high. To prevent sticking or over-reduction, do not remove the lid during cooking. If a thicker glaze is desired, transfer juices to a saucepan and simmer on the stovetop for 5 to 10 minutes before serving.

Slow-Cooker Beef Bourguignon

This French-inspired classic brings together tender beef, earthy mushrooms, and a rich red wine sauce for a comforting, elegant dish that's simple to prepare and full of flavor. Perfect for family meals or special occasions.

YIELD: Serves 4 to 6 people

INGREDIENTS

6 lbs. beef stew meat, cut into 1-inch cubes (1 lb. or 2 cups per bag)
6 cups mushrooms, quartered (1 cup per bag)
6 medium carrots, peeled and chopped (1 cup per bag)
6 medium parsnips or potatoes, peeled and diced (1 cup per bag)
6 medium yellow onions, chopped (1 cup per bag)
18 garlic cloves, minced (1 T. per bag)
12 slices bacon, diced, or 6 oz. pancetta, diced (2 T. per bag)
6 tsp. dried thyme (1 tsp. per bag)
6 bay leaves (1 per bag)
6 tsp. salt (1 tsp. per bag, adjust to taste)
3 tsp. black pepper (½ tsp. per bag)
3 cups dry red wine (e.g., Pinot Noir or Merlot; ½ cup per bag)
6 cups beef broth (1 cup per bag)
12 T. tomato paste (2 T. per bag)
6 T. Worcestershire sauce (1 T. per bag)
6 T. olive oil (1 T. per bag)

DIRECTIONS

Follow the instructions on page 156 to fill six freezer bags with equal amounts of the ingredients for this recipe, then freeze for long-term storage. When you're ready to eat, remove one bag from the freezer and simply transfer its frozen contents to your slow cooker. Cook on low for 6 to 8 hours, do not cook on high. For best results, stir the mixture once midway through cooking. If a thicker consistency is desired, remove the lid during the last 15 to 30 minutes to allow excess liquid to reduce.

8

Heritage Food Crafts

What we inherit from our ancestors, we must earn anew if we are to possess it.

JOHANN WOLFGANG VON GOETHE

Heritage food crafts are more than just a nostalgic return to traditional skills—they're an inheritance, passed down through generations, requiring our active engagement and commitment to preserve them.

Honoring Tradition and Sustainability

As Johann Wolfgang von Goethe aptly stated, "What we inherit from our ancestors, we must earn anew if we are to possess it." This sentiment beautifully captures the essence of skills like butter making, tincture crafting, and cheese making. These are not static relics of the past but living practices that thrive only when we dedicate ourselves to learning, refining, and incorporating them into our daily lives.

By mastering these time-honored techniques, we honor the legacy of those who came before us while also ensuring this invaluable knowledge is not lost. Each loaf of bread kneaded, each batch of tallow rendered, and each jar of herbal tincture crafted represents a deliberate effort to breathe life into these ancestral skills. These acts remind us that self-reliance and sustainability are not just historical ideals but essential components of a resilient and fulfilling lifestyle.

Foundations of Traditional Food Crafting

In our fast-paced world, where convenience often trumps quality, reclaiming the foundations of traditional food crafting is both empowering and essential. Learning how to make butter, craft vinegar, and corn meat isn't just about connecting to time-honored skills; it's about establishing a clean, healthy foundation for your kitchen and your family. These techniques allow us to create homemade staples free from preservatives and additives, tailored to our tastes and nutritional needs.

In my own kitchen, I make these practices a part of my routine, ensuring I always have high-quality ingredients to work with. There's a deep satisfaction in churning fresh butter, knowing exactly where the cream comes from, or fermenting a batch of vinegar, watching it transform into a tangy elixir enhancing meals and preserved food.

Corning meat at home not only provides clean, chemical-free proteins but creates flavors that far surpass their store-bought counterparts. And at huge cost savings because we can use a variety of less expensive cuts to produce a delicious result. These are the simple, foundational crafts that support my cooking and preserving, giving me tools to create nourishing, delicious meals.

BUTTER MAKING: A SIMPLE, TIME-HONORED CRAFT

While many of us may not have access to a traditional butter churn, modern appliances like a food processor or a KitchenAid mixer make it easy to create fresh, homemade butter in our own kitchen. The process is simple and rewarding, allowing us to control the quality of ingredients and create a versatile kitchen staple.

Whether you're using raw cream from a local farmer or heavy cream from a store, the steps remain straightforward and approachable. With just a little time, you can have fresh butter, ready to enhance your cooking or to be stored for long-term use.

Step-by-Step Guide to Making Butter

INGREDIENTS

2 cups heavy cream
(raw or store-bought, with at least 36% fat content)

Ice-cold water (for rinsing the butter)

Optional: Salt, herbs, or spices for flavored butter

DIRECTIONS

1. Pour 2 cups of heavy cream into your food processor or KitchenAid mixer. For the best result, use cream that's at room temperature. It will churn more quickly and allow the butter to form more easily.
2. Use an "S" shaped blade in your food processor, as it is designed to cut and mix, which helps separate the butterfat from the buttermilk. Use the default speed by selecting its continuous "ON" setting. Avoid pulsing. Turn on the appliance and begin whisking the cream. As it whips, it will first turn into whipped cream.
3. Continue whipping until the cream separates into yellow butterfat (solid) and buttermilk (liquid). This is your cue the butter is ready. The process can take anywhere from 3 to 8 minutes, depending on your appliance. Once this separation happens, stop processing to prevent overworking the butter, which can negatively affect its texture.
4. Once the butterfat and buttermilk separate, pour the mixture into a fine mesh strainer or a chinois (cone-shaped sieve) placed over a bowl. You can collect the buttermilk for later use, because it's great for baking.
5. Transfer the solid butter to a clean bowl and pour ice-cold water over it. Knead the butter with a spatula or your hands to rinse out any remaining buttermilk. Drain the cloudy water and repeat the process until the water runs clear. This step helps prevent spoilage, so take your time and do not rush this process.
6. If desired, mix in a pinch of salt or other flavorings like garlic, fresh herbs, or honey to create flavored butter.
7. Shape the butter into a log or press it into a silicone butter mold. Wrap tightly in wax paper or plastic wrap. You may then refrigerate the butter you intend to use and freeze your individual portions for long-term storage.

Butter Storage Tips

Butter is a remarkably versatile fat when stored correctly. Its longevity depends on the storage method, the environment, and whether it's been salted or unsalted. Proper storage ensures that butter remains fresh, flavorful, and ready for use in a variety of culinary applications. It can last in the refrigerator upwards of 4 months when salted and 2 months unsalted. If you plan to season the butter, it's best to use within 3 weeks when refrigerated.

When freezing butter, be sure each log is tightly wrapped in wax paper, then store them in a freezer-safe bag. The wax paper not only holds the butter's shape but prevents unwanted water and odors from penetrating the butter. Frozen butter can be stored safely for 12 months.

The key factors affecting the longevity of butter are its salt content, its storage conditions, and the quality of its ingredients. Using fresh raw cream from a cow ensures few impurities. Therefore, it will last longer when properly stored. Ensuring you don't have a great deal of light and temperature fluctuation when storing butter in the freezer also helps longevity. This is why I place my butter in the deep freezer, which is opened only rarely. Last, but most importantly, salt inhibits bacterial growth, also greatly increasing the butter's longevity.

Homemade butter is a rewarding addition to your kitchen, bringing unmatched flavor and versatility to your recipes. Whether you use it fresh, freeze it for later, or craft it into ghee, this timeless skill ensures you always have a clean, healthy foundation for your cooking.

What Is Ghee?

Ghee is clarified butter with its roots in South Asian cooking. It's made by simmering butter to remove water and milk solids, leaving behind pure, golden fat with a rich, nutty flavor. Ghee has a higher smoke point than regular butter, making it ideal for high-heat cooking, and it's shelf-stable, meaning it can be stored without refrigeration for extended periods. Because the milk solids are removed, ghee is also suitable for those who are lactose-intolerant or sensitive to dairy proteins.

Making ghee from your homemade butter is a simple process that enhances its flavor and longevity, creating a versatile and nutritious cooking fat.

Step-by-Step Guide to Making Ghee (Clarified Butter)

Ghee transforms your homemade butter into a shelf-stable, multipurpose cooking fat known for enhancing flavors, and it supports your sustainable kitchen practices. Ghee can be used in a variety of ways, from frying eggs to sautéing vegetables, baking, canning, and even adding a spoonful to soups or stews for extra richness. It's an essential addition to your food crafting repertoire—especially if your diet is lactose free.

INGREDIENTS

1 cup homemade butter (or more, depending on your yield)

DIRECTIONS

1. Place the butter in a thick-bottomed saucepan over medium-low heat. Allow it to melt completely and slowly.
2. Once melted, the butter will begin to separate into three layers: foam on top, clarified butter in the middle, and milk solids at the bottom. Reduce the heat to low and let the butter simmer gently. Avoid scorching the butter.
3. As the butter simmers, foam—composed of denatured milk proteins, water vapor, and impurities—forms on the surface. Skim it off with a spoon or ladle and discard.
4. The milk solids at the bottom of the pan will gradually turn golden brown, releasing a nutty aroma. This is how you know your ghee is ready. Be careful not to let the milk solids burn, as this can impart a bitter flavor.
5. Remove the pan from the heat and let it cool slightly. Pour the ghee through a fine mesh strainer, chinois, or cheesecloth into a heatproof jar to separate out the milk solids.
6. Allow the ghee to cool completely, then seal the jar with a lid. Store at room temperature for up to 6 months or in the refrigerator for up to 18 months. I leave mine on the countertop alongside my oils, tallow, and bacon grease so it's within easy reach while I'm cooking and canning.
7. Preserving shelf-stable ghee for long-term storage is simple. Pour freshly made, slightly cooled ghee into jars, leaving a 1-inch headspace.
8. Wipe the rims with a washcloth dipped in vinegar. Place the lid and ring on each jar and hand tighten.
9. Pressure can at 10 PSI or according to your elevation, 75 minutes for pints and half-pints and 90 minutes for quarts.

CRAFTING VINEGAR: A SIMPLE AND HEALTHY ART

Making your own vinegar is a rewarding and straightforward process that transforms simple ingredients like fruit scraps or leftover wine into a versatile kitchen staple. At its core, vinegar is the product of fermentation, a natural process where sugars are converted into alcohol and then into acetic acid by beneficial bacteria. With this age-old practice, you can create a healthier, preservative-free alternative to store-bought vinegar while also reducing food waste.

The fermentation process begins with sugars, broken down by yeast into alcohol. From there, naturally occurring acetic acid bacteria (or a vinegar "mother," if you have one) take over, converting the alcohol into acetic acid. Acetic acid is the component that gives vinegar its tangy bite. A mother of vinegar is a natural, gelatinous film comprised of acetic acid-producing bacteria that forms during the fermentation of liquids. It will look slimy in appearance and take on the color of the liquid in which it is found. This transformation happens over several weeks while the mixture is exposed to air to allow the bacteria to thrive.

What makes homemade vinegar special is its live culture, which is often filtered out of commercial varieties. These live probiotics can support gut health and digestion, adding to the overall wellness benefits.

Turning Fruit Scraps into Vinegar

Fruit remnants or slightly overripe pieces of fruit are perfect for vinegar making. Doing so is not only economical but a sustainable way to reduce food waste while crafting flavorful, homemade vinegar. These ingredients impart unique flavors, allowing you to create vinegars that complement specific dishes or purposes in your kitchen.

Here's a quick breakdown of the many different fruits used to make homemade vinegar:

- **Apples.** Peels, cores, or even bruised apples make a fantastic base for apple cider vinegar.
- **Pears.** As with apple cider vinegar, pear scraps or overripe pears create a light and subtly sweet vinegar.
- **Berries.** Overripe strawberries, blueberries, blackberries, and raspberries can be used for richly flavored berry vinegars.
- **Stone Fruits.** The peels and flesh of peaches, plums, cherries, and apricots add depth and sweetness to vinegar.
- **Citrus Peels.** Lemon, lime, and orange peels (with some pith removed to avoid bitterness) can make unique, tangy vinegars.
- **Pineapple.** The peel and core of a pineapple produce a tropical-flavored vinegar that's excellent in marinades or dressings.

The basic premise of crafting vinegar is the same regardless of the fruit used: Sugars are fermented into alcohol, which is then converted into acetic acid by beneficial bacteria. But slight differences in the process can arise based on the fruit's sugar content, water content, and flavor profile. Crafting vinegar, then, can vary depending on the fruit used.

Key Differences When Crafting Vinegar from Different Fruits

Sugar Content

Fruits with high sugar content, like apples, pears, peaches, and grapes, naturally ferment more easily because the sugars fuel the fermentation process. These may not require additional sweeteners to kick-start fermentation. In contrast, fruits with lower sugar content, like citrus peels and berries, may benefit from adding a small amount of sugar or honey to ensure the fermentation process is robust.

Water Content

Fruits naturally high in water content, like apples, pears, peaches, and pineapple, can often ferment with minimal added liquid, whereas drier fruits, like berries or citrus peels, need added water to create the liquid base necessary for fermentation.

Flavor Development

Mild-flavored fruits, like apples and pears, produce subtle and versatile vinegars that work well for a range of culinary uses. Fruits with stronger flavors, like cherries, plums, or pineapple, yield bold, distinctive vinegars, often used for specific dishes like marinades or fruity dressings. If you wish to use up highly aromatic citrus peels, they'll produce a slightly bitter vinegar perfect for cleaning your home or adding zest to your culinary dishes.

Appearance and Filtering

Some fruits, like berries and cherries, have darker pigments that create a richly colored vinegar, but they may require more straining to remove seeds and pulp. Lighter fruits, like pears or apples, produce clear vinegar with minimal effort in filtering.

Despite these minor variations, vinegar-making steps remain largely the same for any fruit used. Combine the fruit scraps or whole fruits with water, add sugar when needed, and allow the mixture to ferment into alcohol, either naturally or with the help of a vinegar mother or starter. Continue to ferment until the alcohol is converted into acetic acid, then strain, store, and use.

The best part is that this process is adaptable and forgiving. Once you understand the basics, you can experiment with different fruits, blending flavors or adjusting sweetness to suit your preferences. Regardless of the fruit, the result is a healthier, preservative-free vinegar that reflects the unique qualities of its source ingredient.

How to Tell When Alcohol Is Converted into Acetic Acid

Determining when the fermentation process has fully converted all the alcohol into acetic acid requires a combination of sensory observations, visual cues, and timing. One of the most reliable methods is using your senses.

Smelling as fermentation progresses can alert you to a shift from a yeasty or alcoholic aroma to the characteristic tangy aroma of vinegar.

Tasting a small amount can also help you gauge fermentation's progress. If it's sharply acidic and there's no lingering taste of alcohol, the vinegar is likely ready.

Visually, you may notice the formation of a gelatinous film on the surface, known as the "mother of vinegar." This is a natural sign that acetic acid bacteria are actively converting the alcohol. Over time, the liquid may also become clearer as fermentation nears completion. The process typically takes about 3 to 4 weeks, although warmer temperatures can accelerate it, while cooler conditions might slow it down.

Bubbling is another visual indicator, especially in the early stages. During the alcohol fermentation phase, you may see bubbles from carbon dioxide escaping. Once the bubbling stops, it's a sign that the bacteria have converted most of the alcohol into acetic acid.

If you're seeking a more precise method of knowing, testing the pH with your food-grade pH tester can provide confirmation. Fully fermented vinegar usually has a pH between 2.4 and 3.4, which ensures it's acidic enough for culinary use and home canning.

Patience is essential when making vinegar. Allowing it to age slightly beyond when it first tastes tangy ensures deeper flavor development and complete conversion. Once the vinegar smells, tastes, looks, and tests as ready, strain and bottle it to stop fermentation and preserve its quality. This approach balances tradition and science, making the process accessible and satisfying for any home preserver.

THE TIMELESS ART OF CORNING MEAT AND FISH

Corning meat and fish is a centuries-old preservation method dating back to a time when refrigeration was nonexistent and people relied on curing and salting to keep meat from spoiling. The term *corning* derives from the coarse grains of salt, referred to as "corns" of salt, traditionally used in the process. These salt grains acted as both a preservative and a deterrent to bacteria, enabling people to store meat for extended periods, especially during colder months or long journeys.

Today, corning offers a way to elevate inexpensive cuts of beef and pork, as well as firm fish such as salmon or cod, into culinary staples that burst with flavor. Whether you're corning brisket for a traditional corned beef dinner or experimenting with wild game or fish to create something unique, this timeless art bridges history and the modern kitchen with delicious results.

Perfect Cuts and Types of Meat and Fish for Corning

These cuts of meat are perfect for corning and represent a mix of affordability, versatility, and flavor, ensuring delicious results for every budget and preference. Additionally, choosing fish with firm, meaty textures is perfect for corning, providing the best flavor infusion and versatility.

Beef

- Brisket is the traditional choice, rich in flavor and ideal for slow cooking.
- Chuck Roast is economical and flavorful and breaks down beautifully during cooking.
- Bottom Round is leaner but still tender after corning and slow cooking.
- Short Ribs add a unique, meaty richness to corned dishes.

Pork

- Pork Shoulder (Boston Butt) is an affordable cut with excellent marbling, perfect for corning and shredding.
- Pork Loin is a leaner option that works well for slices in sandwiches or dinners.
- Shoulder Roasts are economical, flavorful, and great for slow cooking.
- Pork Belly is an unconventional but indulgent choice for corning.

Wild Game

- Venison (Roast or Shoulder) is a lean meat that takes on the brine beautifully.
- Elk (Rump or Shoulder) has a robust flavor, pairing perfectly with corning spices.
- Bison (Brisket or Round) is another lean and tender meat with a naturally sweet, rich taste.
- Antelope or Moose (Roasts) is great for corning, offering unique flavors depending on the animal's diet.

Fish

- Salmon is rich in flavor, which pairs beautifully with a spiced corning brine.
- Cod is traditionally salted, but it can also be corned for a milder, more aromatic result.
- Mackerel has a bold flavor, allowing it to take on spices well, and it's a fantastic choice for corning.
- Tuna is firm and hardy, so it benefits from corning's ability to infuse depth into its flavor.
- Halibut and Swordfish both possess a sturdy texture, making them excellent candidates for corning.

Tips for Success

By following these steps, you'll create beautifully corned meat and fish bursting with flavor, perfect for meals that honor tradition while showcasing your creativity in the kitchen.

- To determine when it's done curing, slice into the thickest part of the meat after the specified curing time. The color and texture should be a consistent gray throughout, with no raw pink or red untreated center. If the center appears untreated, return the meat to the brine for another 2 to 3 days.
- The use of pink curing salt is optional; however, it does give corned meat its classic rosy-pink color and helps aid in preservation. Without it, the meat will still be delicious but retain its natural grayish hue.

- While traditional pickling spice is commonly used, feel free to customize your spice blend by adding cinnamon sticks, whole dried juniper berries, or dried chilies for unique flavors.
- Once cured, the meat can be kept in the refrigerator for up to 3 to 4 days before cooking, and upwards of 10 days in the refrigerator if vacuum sealed. If you prefer to keep them long-term, freezing corned meats for up to 6 months is an option. After 6 months, they may start losing quality.

Step-by-Step Guide to Corning Meat and Fish

INGREDIENTS

4 to 5 lbs. meat or 2 to 3 lbs. fish fillets/steaks
1 gallon water
1 cup kosher salt
½ cup sugar (white or brown)
1 T. pink curing salt (optional, for traditional color and preservation)
2 T. pickling spice (or a mix of allspice, coriander, mustard seeds, cloves, and bay leaves)
4 garlic cloves, crushed
1 T. black peppercorns

DIRECTIONS

1. Trim excess fat from the meat but leave some fat for flavor and moisture later during cooking. If corning fish fillets or steaks, leave the skin on to give it structure, and remove any pin bones.
2. In a large stockpot, combine water, kosher salt, sugar, pink curing salt (if using), pickling spices, garlic, and black peppercorns. Heat the mixture over medium heat, stirring until the salt and sugar dissolve completely. Remove from heat and let the brine cool to room temperature.
3. Place the meat in a large, nonreactive container (e.g., a glass, plastic, or stainless steel container). Pour the cooled brine over the meat, ensuring it's fully submerged. Use a weight like a plate or small bowl to keep the meat below the surface of the brine.
4. Place the cover on the container and refrigerate. Thinner cuts and pieces of meat should brine for 5 to 7 days, while thicker cuts like whole brisket or shoulders require upwards of 10 to 14 days. Turn the meat every 1 to 2 days to ensure even curing. Fish should brine for 12 to 24 hours.
5. After curing, remove the meat from the brine and rinse it thoroughly under cold running water to remove excess salt and spices.

When you're ready to eat, corned meat is typically simmered or slow-cooked until tender. Cook on low for 8 to 10 hours or on high for 4 to 6 hours. For corned beef, add vegetables like carrots, potatoes, and cabbage to the pot for a traditional meal.

WATER GLASSING FARM-FRESH EGGS

Water glassing eggs is a time-honored method for preserving fresh eggs, ensuring their usability for months without refrigeration. This technique involves submerging unwashed eggs in a solution of water and pickling lime, which creates an alkaline environment that prevents spoilage. Historically, water glassing was a common practice in rural households before refrigeration became widespread, providing a reliable way to store surplus eggs from the spring and summer for use during the colder months.

The Water Matters

When water glassing eggs, the type of water used is critical to the success of the preservation process. If your home water source isn't ideal, such as hard water, chlorinated tap water, or untreated well water, you have two effective options: boiling or buying. Boiling your own water is a practical and cost-effective solution. By bringing water to a rolling boil for 1 to 3 minutes, you can remove chlorine, chloramine, and other chemical treatments, while also eliminating bacteria and pathogens.

If you wish to have a more convenient and foolproof option, purchasing distilled water is an excellent choice. Distilled water is free of minerals, chemicals, and bacteria, ensuring a perfect balance for the lime solution without any risk of interference. It's particularly recommended if your home water supply is hard or contains high levels of impurities.

Storage Notes and Conditions

If an egg cracks inside the water-glassing solution during storage, discard it immediately to prevent spoilage of the entire batch. If the egg leaches into the pickling lime, remove the uncracked eggs from the container, dump the contaminated solution, and rinse out the container. Place the eggs back inside the freshly cleaned container and cover with a fresh pickling lime solution. Uncracked water-glassed eggs can be stored upwards of 12 to 18 months in proper conditions.

After being stored for 6 months, the texture of the eggs changes slightly compared to fresh eggs. The whites may become thinner and less cohesive, while the yolks can become firmer, almost gelatinous, due to the extended storage in the lime solution. This change in texture makes them less ideal for delicate preparations like poaching or frying, where the structural integrity of the egg is essential.

Water-glassed eggs are best suited for baking or scrambling, where their slight textural changes are unnoticeable and their functionality remains intact. They work wonderfully in recipes like cakes, cookies, and bread, providing the same binding and leavening properties as fresh eggs. They're also excellent for incorporating into dishes like omelets or casseroles, where their texture can be fully blended and softened during cooking.

Proper storage conditions are just like your home-canned goods: a temperature between 50°F (10°C) and 70°F (21°C), free from direct and indirect sunlight and with limited to no humidity.

Step-by-Step Guide to Water Glassing Eggs

By following these steps, you can effectively preserve fresh eggs for extended periods, ensuring a steady supply even when hens aren't laying, which is common in the colder months. Eggs remain unwashed to be sure they have their natural protective coating, known as the bloom, intact. In addition to these ingredients, you'll need storage containers with tight-fitting lids, such as a wide-mouth gallon glass jar with a plastic screw lid or a food-grade 3-gallon plastic bucket with a tight-fitting lid.

INGREDIENTS

Food-grade pickling lime (calcium hydroxide), such as Mrs. Wages Pickling Lime
Distilled, treated, or boiled water
Fresh, unwashed eggs

DIRECTIONS

1. In a clean container, mix 1 ounce (2 tablespoons) of pickling lime per quart (4 cups) of water. Stir until the lime is fully dispersed. Please handle pickling lime with care, as it can be caustic. Wear gloves when preparing the solution, and avoid inhaling the powder.
2. Gently place the eggs into a jar or other lidded long-term storage container, then slowly pour the lime solution atop the eggs, being sure the eggs are completely submerged. I'll often stir as I pour to avoid leaving lime in the mixing container.
3. Seal the container with an airtight lid to prevent contamination, then label it with the date and contents.
4. Store the container in a cool, dark place, such as a basement or pantry, where temperatures remain between 50°F (10°C) and 70°F (21°C).
5. When ready to use, remove the desired number of eggs from the solution. Rinse them thoroughly under running water to eliminate any lime residue. After rinsing, use the eggs immediately or store them in the refrigerator and consume within a few days.

CRAFTING HERBAL TINCTURES

Crafting herbal tinctures offers a natural and time-tested way to create remedies for daily wellness. Tinctures are concentrated herbal extracts made by steeping herbs in alcohol or apple cider vinegar, effectively drawing out the plant's beneficial compounds. This simple yet powerful method has been used for centuries to address various health concerns.

To create a tincture, select fresh or dried herbs such as garlic, elderberry, or ginger, renowned for their immune-boosting and healing properties. Chop the herbs finely and place them in a sterilized glass jar, then cover them with high-proof alcohol, ensuring the herbs are completely submerged. Seal the jar tightly and store it in a cool, dark place for 4 to 6 weeks, shaking it gently every few days to encourage extraction.

Once ready, strain the liquid through a fine mesh, or cheesecloth into a clean jar, discarding the herbs. Proper storage is essential, so keep tinctures in amber glass bottles to protect them from light and maintain potency. Label each bottle with the herb name and preparation date.

When using tinctures, follow dosage recommendations carefully, typically 1 to 2 droppers-full diluted in water or tea.

Incorporating these tinctures into your wellness routine can be as simple as adding them to morning drinks or taking them during times of illness or seasonal changes for added support.

Best Types of Alcohol for Tinctures

When making herbal tinctures, the type of alcohol you choose plays a crucial role in extracting the active compounds from the herbs. Vodka is the most-used alcohol due to its neutral flavor and wide availability. High-proof grain alcohol, such as Everclear, is particularly effective for tough, resinous herbs like roots, barks, or seeds.

Brandy and rum are excellent alternatives for tinctures where flavor enhancement is desired. Brandy offers a subtle sweetness and richness, making it ideal for soothing remedies or culinary applications, while rum adds a warming, spiced note that pairs well with herbs like ginger or cinnamon.

Other options include gin and whiskey, which bring unique flavor profiles to tinctures. Gin's herbal and botanical notes complement aromatic herbs such as juniper berries or rosemary, while whiskey's bold, smoky flavor works well with earthy herbs like dandelion root or turmeric. Regardless of the type of alcohol chosen, it should be at least 80-proof (40% alcohol) to ensure proper preservation and extraction.

Selecting the Right Proof for Your Tincture

- **80-Proof (40% Alcohol):** Best for fresh herbs, which contain more water and don't require excessively strong alcohol. Ideal for leaves, flowers, and soft plant parts (such as mint, basil, and chamomile).
- **100-Proof (50% Alcohol):** A balanced choice for most herbs, especially those that are dried. It offers a mix of water and alcohol for broader extraction.
- **190-Proof (95% Alcohol):** Recommended for dried or resinous herbs (such as roots, seeds, or barks), where maximum alcohol-soluble extraction is required. Always dilute 190-proof alcohol with distilled water to achieve a safer and more effective proof (for example, 50 to 75%).

If you're seeking an alcohol-free alternative, apple cider vinegar is an excellent option. Vinegar tinctures, sometimes referred to as herbal vinegar extracts, are particularly appealing for individuals who prefer not to consume alcohol. Apple cider vinegar has a mild, tangy flavor and is effective at extracting water-soluble compounds and some acids and minerals from herbs.

While vinegar isn't as potent as alcohol for extracting certain active compounds, it still creates a valuable remedy with therapeutic benefits. Keep in mind that vinegar tinctures are not as shelf-stable as alcohol-based ones, and that they should be refrigerated, where they will typically last up to a year.

Considerations When Using Alternative Alcohols

1. **Proof.** Regardless of the type, the alcohol should be at least 80-proof (40% alcohol) to ensure proper preservation and extraction of active compounds.
2. **Flavor Impact.** Alcohol like rum, brandy, and whiskey impart their distinct flavors, which may enhance or overpower the herbal taste. So choose them carefully based on the tincture's purpose.
3. **Neutrality.** If you want minimal flavor interference, stick to vodka or a neutral grain alcohol.

While vodka is the most common choice for tinctures due to its neutrality and availability, other types of alcohol and non-alcohol alternatives work well. The type of alcohol selected should align with the herbs you're using and the intended application of the tincture.

Popular Herbal Tinctures for Natural Remedies

- **Elderberry Tincture** is known to boost immunity and help combat colds and flu.
- **Chamomile Tincture** calms anxiety, aids sleep, and soothes digestion.
- **Echinacea Tincture** strengthens the immune system and reduces cold symptoms.
- **Turmeric Tincture** reduces inflammation and supports joint health.
- **Valerian Root Tincture** promotes relaxation and improves sleep quality.
- **Garlic Tincture** supports heart health and fights infections.
- **Ginger Tincture** eases nausea, aids digestion, and reduces inflammation.
- **St. John's Wort Tincture** supports mood regulation and alleviates mild depression.
- **Calendula Tincture** soothes skin irritations and supports wound healing.
- **Peppermint Tincture** relieves headaches, indigestion, and sinus congestion.

Step-by-Step Guide to Creating Herbal Tinctures

INGREDIENTS

1 cup fresh or ½ cup dried herbs of your choice

1 quart-size sterilized glass jar with a tight-fitting lid

2 cups alcohol (80- to 100-proof vodka or other suitable alcohol)

DIRECTIONS

1. Chop fresh herbs finely, or crumble dried herbs, to increase the surface area for extraction.
2. Place the herbs in the sterilized glass jar, leaving enough room for the alcohol to fully submerge them. Pour alcohol over the herbs until they're completely covered, leaving about ½ inch of space at the top.
3. Seal the jar tightly and label it with the herb name and the date. Store the jar in a cool, dark place for 4 to 6 weeks. Shake gently every few days to ensure thorough extraction.
4. After steeping in storage, strain the liquid through a fine mesh, chinois, or cheesecloth into a clean amber or dark glass bottle with a dropper, discarding the herbs. Keep in a cool, dark place to maintain potency.

HERBAL TINCTURE CHART

Typically, tinctures are taken in doses of 1 to 2 droppers-full (approximately 20 to 40 drops) diluted in water or tea, up to 3 times daily. Follow specific guidelines for each type of tincture, for some may also be used in capsules or applied topically.

Herb	Fresh Herb (Cups)	Dried Herb (Cups)	Recommended Proof	Steeping Time
Elderberry	1	0.5	80- to 100-proof	4 to 6 weeks
Chamomile	1	0.5	80- to 100-proof	4 to 6 weeks
Echinacea	1	0.5	100-proof	6 weeks
Turmeric (root)	1	0.5	100-proof	6 weeks
Valerian Root	1	0.5	100- to 190-proof	6 weeks
Garlic	1	N/A	80-proof	4 weeks
Ginger (root)	1	0.5	100-proof	6 weeks
St. John's Wort	1	0.5	80- to 100-proof	4 to 6 weeks
Calendula	1	0.5	80-proof	4 to 6 weeks
Peppermint	1	0.5	80-proof	4 weeks

THE SWEET ART OF HOMEMADE VANILLA EXTRACT

Making your own vanilla extract is like crafting liquid gold for your kitchen. Sure, it takes time—months, in fact—for the rich, complex flavors to fully extract from the vanilla beans, but the payoff is absolutely worth the wait. Homemade vanilla extract is unparalleled in flavor, offering a depth and authenticity store-bought versions rarely achieve. Unlike commercial extracts, which often contain artificial flavors or added sweeteners, your homemade version will be pure, customizable, and brimming with natural, aromatic goodness.

The benefits of making your own vanilla extract extend beyond flavor. It's incredibly cost-effective in the long run, especially if you use vanilla frequently for baking or cooking. You can also control the strength and quality of your extract by selecting premium vanilla beans and your favorite alcohol as the base. Plus, homemade vanilla extract makes for thoughtful and elegant gifts, perfect for holidays, birthdays, or any occasion.

Beans and Booze: Unlocking the Secret to Perfect Vanilla Extract

When it comes to crafting the perfect homemade vanilla extract, choosing the right vanilla beans and alcohol is essential for achieving the desired flavor and quality. There's much debate online about how to craft the "perfect" vanilla, many with strong opinions about everything from the best beans to the ideal alcohol.

The Bean Wars

Madagascar Bourbon vanilla beans, known for their rich, creamy, and slightly sweet profile, have many fans, while Tahitian vanilla bean enthusiasts argue their floral, fruity profile is a fantastic option. Then there's the Mexican vanilla bean lovers who claim their beans' bold, spicy notes reign supreme. Whichever type you choose, look for beans that are plump, moist, and aromatic, as these will yield the most flavorful extract.

Boozy Battles

Vodka is the standard choice, but some vanilla extract makers can't resist experimenting. Whiskey lovers champion the caramel undertones it adds to their vanilla, while rum advocates rave about its warm sweetness. Brandy supporters defend its fruity and spicy flair. Of course, this leads to endless arguments about which alcohol type pairs best with specific beans, but I digress. Choose what alcohol is right for you. At the end of the day, your choice of alcohol depends on how you intend to use your vanilla extract and your personal flavor preferences. But if you're new to vanilla extract making, know that you can't go wrong with vodka.

Alcohol Proof Showdowns

The debate over alcohol proof is another hot topic. Many stick to 80-proof for its balance of water and alcohol extraction, but others argue that 100-proof yields a stronger, more complex extract. Then you'll find the purists, who insist anything less than 190-proof Everclear is a waste of time, even if it leaves your kitchen smelling like a distillery. When in doubt, use nothing less than 80-proof (40% alcohol content).

To Slice or Not to Slice

Whether to split the vanilla beans is another surprisingly polarizing issue. Some say slicing is essential to release the "caviar" inside, while others insist whole beans result in a smoother, purer extract. Some even debate whether you should leave the beans in the bottle indefinitely or strain them out after a few months! Personally, I love to slice my beans open, and I never bother removing or straining them.

Aging Wars

Patience is the name of the game when it comes to making vanilla extract, but not everyone agrees on how long to wait. Some claim 6 months is the sweet spot, while others argue a full year or more is necessary for ultimate flavor. Meanwhile, a few impatient extractors insist that anything more than 3 months is overkill.

While these debates might seem trivial to outsiders, they highlight the personal and customizable art of making vanilla extract. For some, it's a scientific pursuit; for others, a creative hobby. Regardless, we can all agree on one thing: Homemade vanilla extract is infinitely better than store-bought—and well worth the wait!

Step-by-Step Guide to Making Vanilla Extract

INGREDIENTS

12 to 16 Madagascar Bourbon vanilla beans (plump and moist)

1 sterilized (16 oz.) swing top glass bottle with a tight-fitting cap

2 cups (16 oz.) 80-proof vodka

DIRECTIONS

1. Using a sharp knife, carefully slice each vanilla bean lengthwise to expose the flavorful seeds inside.
2. Place prepared vanilla beans into the sterilized glass bottle. Pour the vodka over the beans, ensuring they're completely submerged. Leave about ½ inch of space at the top of the bottle.
3. Place the cap with the gasket onto the lid, and securely close. Label the bottle with the date you started the extract. You may also note the type of beans and alcohol used (e.g., Madagascar beans with vodka). I use a white chalk marker.
4. Store the bottle in a cool, dark place, such as a pantry or cupboard. Shake the jar gently once a week to encourage the extraction process. Allow the beans to steep for at least 6 months for the best flavor, although steeping for up to a year will result in an even richer, deeper extract.
5. When the extract has reached your desired strength, you may use it as-is or strain out the beans and seeds for a sediment-free extract. Transfer the extract to dark glass bottles for long-term storage. Alternatively, you can leave the beans in the bottle to continue infusing, topping off with additional vodka as needed to maintain your supply.

CREATING AND STORING TALLOW, LARD, AND BACON GREASE

Rendering and storing fats like tallow, lard, and bacon grease is a traditional practice standing the test of time, offering both culinary and practical benefits. These animal-based fats are highly versatile, used for cooking, baking, frying, and even for skincare and in household products. Unlike many modern cooking oils, rendered fats have a rich flavor profile and impressive heat stability, making them ideal for high-temperature cooking and pressure canning. Additionally, they're nutrient dense and can be stored for long periods when prepared correctly.

Tallow, derived from beef or lamb fat, is prized for its long shelf life and used in frying or as a base for making soaps and candles. Lard, rendered from pork fat, is celebrated in baking for its ability to create flaky pastries and savory dishes with unparalleled richness. Bacon grease, a by-product of cooking bacon, is a flavorful fat often saved for sautéing vegetables or enhancing dishes like cornbread and gravies.

Proper rendering removes impurities, ensuring a clean, long-lasting fat that can be stored in jars or tins—or even frozen—for extended use. By learning how to render and store these traditional fats, you can reduce waste, elevate your cooking, and connect with a culinary heritage rooted in self-sufficiency.

Step-by-Step Guide to Rendering Tallow and Lard

Tallow is rendered fat from beef or lamb, while lard is rendered fat from pork. Choosing the right fat is crucial for achieving a clean, high-quality product. Ask for leaf fat or kidney fat, located around the internal organs and prized for their mild flavor and smooth texture. Leaf fat is particularly ideal for lard used in baking, while back fat, found just beneath the skin, works well for frying or savory applications.

Procure your fat from trusted sources such as local butchers, farmers markets, or specialty meat suppliers. For the best quality, seek out grass-fed beef or lamb fat for tallow and pasture-raised pork fat for lard. These not only yield healthier results but produce a superior taste and cleaner aroma.

You will need the following equipment:

- Sharp knife or strong kitchen scissors for trimming and chopping the fat
- Slow cooker, stockpot, or electric roaster for melting the fat over low heat
- Heatproof strainer to remove impurities during the rendering process
- Cheesecloth or chinois to use for a final strain to ensure clarity
- Glass jars with tight-fitting lids or any airtight container made of glass, stainless steel, or ceramic for storing rendered tallow or lard

INGREDIENTS

Beef, lamb, or pork fat

DIRECTIONS

1. Begin by trimming off any remaining meat, blood spots, or connective tissue from the fat. These can affect the flavor and shelf life of the rendered product.
2. Chop the fat into small, uniform pieces to ensure even rendering. The ideal size is smaller chunks, roughly 2 to 3 inches in diameter.
3. Place the chopped fat into a slow cooker set on low. This method is excellent for a hands-off approach. If you don't have a slow cooker or roaster, use a heavy-duty stockpot with a thick bottom, setting your stove burners on the lowest heat to slowly melt the fat.
4. Heat the fat gently, stirring occasionally to prevent burning. The fat will gradually melt and separate from any solids. Over time, the solids will float to the top. These are called cracklings. Be patient—this process of rendering can take several hours.
5. Once the fat is fully melted and golden, carefully strain it through a fine-mesh strainer into a large glass container or several glass jars. If desired for added clarity, strain the fat a second time through cheesecloth or a chinois.
6. At room temperature, tallow and lard will solidify into a creamy white consistency.

Cracklings Are Nature's Crispy Little Treasures

When you render tallow or lard, you're left with delicious golden-brown bits floating at the top called cracklings. These crispy, flavorful morsels are the solids that remain after the fat has fully melted, and they're too good to throw away! Cracklings are a prized by-product of fat rendering, cherished for their versatility in the kitchen and irresistible crunch.

How to Save Cracklings

1. When ready to strain the tallow or lard, use a pair of tongs or a slotted spoon to retrieve the cracklings.
2. Spread the cracklings onto a plate lined with paper towels to remove excess grease, similar to how you would spread strips of bacon after frying them.
3. For the best flavor and texture, return the cracklings to a pan after straining and cook over low heat until they're golden and extra crunchy. Just watch them closely to avoid burning.
4. Consume your cracklings once they're cooled or within a few days. You may also store them in an airtight container in the refrigerator for up to 2 weeks or in the freezer for longer storage.

Fun Ways to Use Cracklings

- Season them with salt and pepper and enjoy them as is, like crispy chips.
- Add them to cornbread for a smoky, savory twist.
- Sprinkle them over salads for a crunchy, meaty accent.
- Stir them into sautéed greens or roasted vegetables for extra richness.
- Toss them into soups or stews for added depth and texture.

Capturing, Storing, and Using Bacon Grease

Bacon grease is a versatile kitchen staple with countless culinary benefits. Its rich, smoky flavor enhances dishes, making it perfect for frying eggs, roasting vegetables, or creating flaky biscuits. Whether you strain your grease depends on your preferences and the cut of bacon you use.

When using high-quality bacon, straining the grease can help you achieve a creamy, white result ideal for special recipes. To do this:

1. Drape cheesecloth over a heatproof jar or container. If you prefer convenience, consider purchasing a ceramic bacon grease container with a built-in strainer.
2. After cooking the bacon, carefully pour the warm (not hot) grease through the filter to remove any solids or bits of meat.
3. Once the grease is strained, seal the jar and place it in the refrigerator to keep the grease fresh and ready for special-occasion cooking.

For everyday use or when in a hurry, you can skip straining. Simply pour the grease, bits and all, into a heatproof container and store on a counter or in your refrigerator. The remaining bits add texture and a stronger bacon flavor, particularly delightful in certain recipes.

Benefits of Cooking with Bacon Grease

- **Flavor Enhancement:** Adds a smoky, savory richness to any dish.
- **Versatility:** Perfect for frying, sautéing, roasting, or even as a substitute for butter or oil in recipes.
- **Sustainability:** Reduces waste by repurposing a by-product of cooking.

Whether strained or unstrained, bacon grease is a flavorful way to elevate your cooking while embracing traditional kitchen wisdom.

Replacing Artificial Shortenings with Natural Fats: A Healthier Alternative

Lard is the ultimate natural fat, offering both culinary and health advantages that make it the ideal replacement for artificial shortenings like Crisco. While Crisco and other shortenings were once marketed as modern innovations, they are highly processed products, originally made with partially hydrogenated oils that introduced trans fats into diets. Even after reformulation to comply with FDA regulations, Crisco remains a blend of highly processed oils and additives, devoid of the nutritional benefits found in natural fats.

By contrast, lard is a minimally processed, traditional fat that delivers superior flavor and nutrition. Derived from pork fat, particularly leaf fat around the kidneys, lard is rich in monounsaturated fats, the same heart-healthy fats found in olive oil, and provides a source of vitamin D when sourced from pasture-raised animals. Unlike artificial shortening, which is manufactured through industrial processes known to alter the natural structure of fats, lard is a pure, recognizable ingredient your body can process efficiently.

In the kitchen, lard outshines artificial shortenings in versatility and performance. Its creamy texture and mild flavor make it a baker's dream for flaky pie crusts and tender pastries, while its high smoke point is perfect for frying and sautéing. Rendering your own lard not only improves the quality of your food but aligns with a more wholesome, back-to-basics approach to cooking.

OIL-BASED HERBAL INFUSIONS

Herbal tinctures and herbal infusions are both methods of extracting beneficial compounds from herbs, but they differ significantly in preparation, solvents, concentration, and usage. Tinctures are made by steeping herbs in alcohol for several weeks. Oil-based herbal infusions, often referred to as infused oils, are created by steeping herbs over time in a carrier oil, such as olive oil or coconut oil. This process extracts fat-soluble compounds, creating a product primarily used for topical or culinary purposes.

Common carrier oils for herbal infusions include olive oil, which is moisturizing and rich in antioxidants, and coconut oil, known for its antimicrobial and nourishing properties. These oils serve as excellent mediums for extracting beneficial compounds from herbs like calendula, lavender, rosemary, garlic, and arnica. Choose the highest purity oils for the best results and longest shelf life.

Oil-based herbal infusions are ideal for a variety of uses, from creating soothing balms to drizzling over salads or roasted vegetables.

Step-by-Step Guide to Creating Oil-Based Herbal Infusions

You will need the following equipment:

- Sterilized glass jar with a tight-fitting lid
- Cheesecloth or fine-mesh strainer
- Clean, dark glass container for storage
- Water bather or slow cooker (optional)

INGREDIENTS

1 to 2 cups dried herbs of your choice (e.g., calendula, rosemary, garlic)

2 to 3 cups carrier oil (e.g., olive oil, coconut oil, or another suitable oil)

DIRECTIONS

1. Use dried herbs to prevent introducing moisture that could cause mold or spoilage. Crush or chop the herbs slightly to increase surface area for extraction.
2. Place the dried herbs into the sterilized glass jar. Pour the carrier oil over the herbs until they're completely submerged, leaving about 1 inch of oil above the herbs to ensure full coverage.
3. Seal the jar tightly and place it in a warm, sunny spot for 2 to 6 weeks. Shake the jar gently every few days to encourage extraction. For quicker results, place the jar in a warm water bath or a slow cooker set to low heat for 4 to 6 hours. Ensure the water level remains below the lid to prevent contamination.
4. Once the infusion is complete, strain the oil through a cheesecloth or fine-mesh strainer into a clean container. Discard the herbs.
5. Transfer the strained oil into a clean, dark glass container to protect it from light and preserve its potency. Store it in a cool, dark place. The infused oil will last for 6 to 12 months, depending on the type and purity of oil used, the storage conditions, and the type of container used.

5 Popular Oil-Based Herbal Infusions for Culinary and Medicinal Uses

Garlic-Infused Olive Oil (Culinary)

Garlic-infused olive oil is a delicious and versatile addition to the kitchen. The infusion captures garlic's savory flavor and beneficial properties, making it perfect for drizzling over roasted vegetables, tossing with pasta, and dipping fresh bread. To create this infusion, gently warm olive oil with fresh garlic cloves, then strain and store.

How to use:

- Add to salad dressings for a bold, aromatic flavor.
- Brush on pizza crust or bread before baking.
- Use as a finishing oil for soups or stews.

Calendula-Infused Olive Oil (Medicinal)

Calendula flowers are renowned for their skin-soothing and healing properties. Calendula-infused olive oil is often used to create salves, lotions, or as a stand-alone moisturizer to treat dry skin, minor cuts, or rashes. This infusion is particularly beneficial for sensitive skin and safe for children.

How to use:

- Apply directly to dry or irritated skin for relief.
- Use as a base for homemade salves or balms.
- Add to baths for a moisturizing soak.

Rosemary-Infused Olive Oil (Culinary)

Rosemary-infused olive oil adds a robust, earthy flavor to savory dishes. This infusion is perfect for enhancing meats, roasted potatoes, and dipping sauces. Rosemary also has natural preservative qualities that can extend the oil's shelf life.

How to use:

- Drizzle over grilled meats or vegetables for added flavor.
- Toss with potatoes before roasting for a fragrant finish.
- Use as a marinade base for meats or tofu.

Arnica-Infused Coconut Oil (Medicinal)

Arnica is known for its anti-inflammatory and pain-relieving properties, making it an excellent choice for an oil-based infusion. Arnica-infused coconut oil is used topically to alleviate soreness in muscles, the discomfort of bruises, and joint pain.

How to use:

- Massage onto sore muscles or bruises to reduce inflammation.
- Add to homemade balms for targeted pain relief.
- Apply gently to joints for minor aches and discomfort.

Basil-Infused Olive Oil (Culinary)

Basil-infused olive oil captures the fresh, peppery flavor of basil, making it a staple for Italian cuisine and summer dishes. This oil is perfect for drizzling over caprese salads, mixing into pesto, and finishing a pizza.

How to use:

- Stir into pasta dishes for a burst of fresh flavor.
- Drizzle over bruschetta or flatbreads.
- Use as a dipping oil with balsamic vinegar for bread.

St. John's Wort–Infused Olive Oil (Medicinal)

St. John's Wort–infused olive oil is highly valued for its anti-inflammatory and soothing properties, making it a go-to remedy for skin irritations, minor burns, and muscle pain. This vibrant red oil is created by infusing the flowers of St. John's Wort, known for its therapeutic compounds that support healing and reduce inflammation.

How to use:

- Apply directly to minor burns or sunburns to soothe and promote healing.
- Massage into sore muscles or achy joints for relief.
- Use as a gentle treatment for dry or irritated skin.

Ideal Storage Containers and Conditions for Fats and Oils

Proper storage is essential to maintain the quality, flavor, and shelf life of fats and oils. The right container and environment can protect them from light, heat, oxygen, and moisture, all of which cause spoilage. For solid fats like lard and tallow or liquid oils (infused or pure) such as olive or coconut, following these guidelines will ensure your pantry staples stay fresh and ready to use.

Use the Right Containers:

- Dark amber or green glass jars are ideal for protecting oils from light, which can degrade their quality.
- Stainless steel containers are nonreactive and durable, excellent for both short- and long-term storage.
- Opaque ceramic containers help block light exposure while offering a decorative touch.

Store in Optimal Conditions:

It is best to refrigerate or freeze unrefined or delicate oils. Other fats and oils can be kept in a cool environment (50°F/10°C to 70°F/21°C), such as a pantry or cupboard away from direct sunlight and humidity. Always use lids that tightly seal to limit contact with oxygen.

BASICS FOR HOMEMADE CHEESE MAKING AND CURING NITRATE-FREE BACON

Getting back to basics by crafting your own cheese and curing bacon at home is a delightful way to reconnect with the food you regularly consume. Cheese and bacon are two of the most universally loved staples, and the process of making them from scratch offers a rewarding blend of creativity, tradition, and hands-on learning. Whether you're kneading curds for a creamy ricotta or seasoning pork belly to create nitrate-free bacon, these time-honored techniques transform simple ingredients into gourmet delights.

Best of all, these homemade versions allow you to control every step of the process, ensuring flavors suit your preferences while avoiding unnecessary additives. Let's explore how to make soft cheeses and a beginner-friendly hard cheese, followed by the essentials of curing your own bacon.

Essential Ingredients for Making Soft Cheeses

Before diving into the process, gather these essential ingredients for making soft cheeses at home.

- **Milk:** High-quality whole milk is key, and raw milk works wonderfully if available. Avoid ultra-pasteurized milk, as it won't curdle properly.
- **Cream:** Cream adds richness to cheeses like mascarpone and cream cheese.
- **Acid:** Lemon juice, distilled white vinegar, or citric acid is used to curdle the milk.
- **Rennet:** Liquid or tablet rennet is sometimes used to achieve a firmer curd, particularly for cream cheese or cheeses that benefit from more structure.
- **Salt:** Non-iodized salt enhances flavor and helps preserve the cheese.
- **Cheesecloth or Butter Muslin:** These materials are used to strain curds and separate them from the whey.
- **Thermometer:** Thermometers ensure precise temperatures, critical for consistent results.
- **Cultures:** Some soft cheeses, such as cream cheese, may call for a mesophilic culture to develop specific flavors and textures.

Making Soft Cheeses: Ricotta, Mascarpone, and Cream Cheese

Crafting soft cheeses at home is a simple and rewarding process requiring minimal equipment and just a few steps. Each type of cheese has its unique charm, but they all share the same basic foundation: gently curdling milk, separating the curds from the whey, and adding final touches to perfect the flavor and texture.

Here's a quick overview of the essential steps:

1. Slowly warm milk (and cream if required) in a nonreactive pot over low heat, bringing it to the temperature specified in your recipe (usually 180°F/82°C to 200°F/93°C for ricotta and similar cheeses).
2. Stir in an acid like lemon juice, vinegar, or citric acid to curdle the milk. You'll see curds forming within minutes.
3. Allow the curds to settle undisturbed for 5 to 10 minutes to ensure full separation from the whey.
4. Pour the mixture into a cheesecloth-lined colander or sieve, letting the whey drain off. For firmer cheeses, tie up the cheesecloth and hang it to drain longer.
5. Add salt to taste, or if desired, other seasonings like herbs or spices. For mascarpone and cream cheese, whisk the cheese to achieve a creamy consistency.
6. Transfer the cheese to an airtight container and refrigerate. Soft cheeses are best enjoyed fresh within a few days.

With these simple steps, you can create flavorful, fresh cheeses at home, perfect for spreading on bread, adding to pasta dishes, or elevating your favorite recipes.

Step-by-Step Guide to Making Ricotta

Ricotta is a light, fluffy cheese with a mild flavor, perfect for savory dishes like lasagna or sweet desserts like cannoli. It's a quick and simple recipe that relies on milk and acid with minimal draining time. This recipe makes about 2 to 3 cups, depending on how much whey is grained and the final texture you prefer.

INGREDIENTS

1 gallon whole milk (avoid ultra-pasteurized)

½ cup lemon juice or white vinegar

1 tsp. salt

DIRECTIONS

1. Heat milk to 185°F (85°C) to 200°F (93°C), stirring occasionally to prevent scorching.
2. Remove from heat and add acid slowly while stirring; curds will form immediately.
3. Let mixture rest for 5 to 10 minutes for the curds to fully separate from the whey.
4. Strain through a cheesecloth-lined colander for 15 to 20 minutes for soft ricotta, or longer for a firmer texture.

INGREDIENT TIP: For creamier ricotta, you can add a ½ cup of heavy cream to the milk before heating.

Step-by-Step Guide to Making Mascarpone

Mascarpone is a rich, velvety cheese often used in desserts like tiramisu or as a substitute for cream cheese. Using cream and a gentle acid gives mascarpone its luxuriously smooth finish. This recipe makes about 2 cups because there's very little whey released during the process.

INGREDIENTS

4 cups heavy cream

1 tsp. citric acid or tartaric acid

DIRECTIONS

1. Heat cream to 180°F (82°C), stirring gently to avoid scorching.
2. Remove from heat and add citric or tartaric acid, stirring until the mixture thickens slightly.
3. Allow the mixture to cool for about 10 minutes, then transfer it to a cheesecloth-lined colander with a bowl to capture the liquid.
4. Drain in the refrigerator for 8 to 12 hours until it reaches your desired consistency.

RECIPE TIP: Unlike ricotta, mascarpone relies on cream rather than milk, giving it its signature richness and smooth texture.

Step-by-Step Guide to Making Cream Cheese

Cream cheese is tangy and spreadable, ideal for bagels, cheesecakes, or dips. This recipe uses both rennet and culture for its unique flavor and firmer structure, and makes about 3 to 4 cups depending on its thickness after draining.

INGREDIENTS

4 cups whole milk (avoid ultra-processed)

2 cups heavy cream

1 packet mesophilic culture (or 2 T. plain yogurt as a substitute)

4 drops liquid rennet diluted in ¼ cup water

1 tsp. salt

DIRECTIONS

1. Heat milk and cream to 86°F (30°C), then stir in the mesophilic culture. Let mixture sit for 30 minutes.
2. Add diluted rennet and stir gently. Cover and let the mixture rest for 12 to 18 hours at room temperature until the curds set.
3. Cut the curds into small squares to release the whey, then ladle them into a cheesecloth-lined colander.
4. Let cheese drain for 6 to 12 hours in the refrigerator for a smooth, spreadable consistency.

INGREDIENT TIP: Cream cheese can be seasoned with herbs, garlic, or even honey for a custom flavor profile. After draining and the cream cheese has reached its desired consistency, yet is soft and pliable, place it into a bowl and mix in your desired seasoning. Then shape and chill for long-term use.

Beginner-Friendly Hard Cheeses

Making hard cheeses at home is a rewarding venture for beginners ready to explore the next level of cheese making. While it requires more time, attention, and a few additional tools compared to making soft cheeses, the process is straightforward with the right guidance. Hard cheeses like cheddar, Gouda, or Parmesan develop rich flavors and textures as they age, and there's nothing quite like slicing into a wheel of cheese you made yourself. Starting with beginner-friendly recipes ensures success and builds confidence while creating cheeses perfect for snacking, cooking, or entertaining.

Essential Tools for Hard Cheese

This foundation of tools and ingredients sets beginners up for success, ensuring they have everything needed to create flavorful, beginner-friendly hard cheeses at home.

Tools

- **Cheese Press.** A must-have for shaping and compacting the curds into a dense, uniform wheel. Beginner-friendly presses are available in various sizes.
- **Hard Cheese Mold.** Helps maintain the shape of the cheese during pressing and aging. To help distribute pressure evenly, some molds come with a follower (a flat, solid disc that fits inside the cheese mold between the curds and the weight).
- **Thermometer.** Ensures precise temperature control during key steps like curdling, cooking, and aging.
- **Cheesecloth or Butter Muslin.** Used to wrap the curds before pressing, preventing sticking and aiding whey drainage.
- **Aging Mat or Board.** Provides a clean, breathable surface for aging cheeses.
- **Long-Bladed Curd Knife.** Essential for cutting curds evenly, ensuring proper whey release.
- **Nonreactive Brining Container (like stainless steel or plastic).** Used for soaking the cheese in a salt brine, a key step for hard cheese.
- **Cheese Wax or Coating.** Protects the cheese during aging, preventing moisture loss and mold growth.

The easiest, most confidence-boosting hard cheese for beginners to make at home is farmhouse cheddar. It's a simplified version of traditional cheddar cheese, requiring fewer steps and less aging time while still delivering a delicious tangy flavor and satisfying texture. Farmhouse cheddar is forgiving for beginners, doesn't require a cheese cave, and can be aged for as little as 4 weeks, allowing new cheese makers to enjoy their efforts relatively quickly.

Farmhouse cheddar typically has a pale, creamy white to light yellow color, depending on the type of milk used and whether annatto (a natural coloring agent) is added during the cheese-making process. The color is more muted compared to commercially produced cheddars, as it reflects the natural characteristics of the milk rather than added dyes.

The texture of farmhouse cheddar is firm yet slightly crumbly, with a pleasant creaminess that develops as it ages. When young (around 4 weeks), it's milder in flavor and softer, making it easy to slice for sandwiches or snacking. As it matures, the texture becomes denser and slightly drier, with small cracks or crumbles forming naturally, especially in aged versions. This maturation also intensifies the flavor, adding a tangy sharpness and nuttiness that's characteristic of cheddar.

Step-by-Step Guide to Making Farmhouse Cheddar

This recipe will yield approximately 2 pounds of finished cheese. The overall amount of cheese will depend on the fat content of the milk, how well the whey is drained, and the moisture retention during pressing and aging.

INGREDIENTS

2 gallons whole milk (preferably not ultra-pasteurized)
½ tsp. mesophilic starter culture
½ tsp. liquid calcium chloride (optional, for pasteurized milk)
½ tsp. liquid rennet diluted in ¼ cup cool, nonchlorinated water
2 T. salt (noniodized)

DIRECTIONS

1. Pour milk into a large, nonreactive pot and slowly heat it to 86°F (30°C) over low heat. Stir gently to prevent scorching.
2. Sprinkle the mesophilic starter culture over the milk and let it rehydrate for 2 to 3 minutes. Stir gently for 1 to 2 minutes to mix thoroughly. Let the milk ripen for 30 minutes.
3. If using calcium chloride, stir it into the milk now. Then, add the diluted rennet while stirring gently in an up-and-down motion for 30 seconds. Cover the pot and let the milk sit undisturbed for 30 to 45 minutes, until the curds set and produce a clean break when cut.
4. Using a long curd knife, cut the curds into ½-inch cubes, moving both horizontally and vertically. Let the curds rest for 5 minutes to firm up.
5. Slowly heat the curds to 100°F (38°C) over 30 minutes, increasing the temperature by about 2°F every 5 minutes. Stir gently to prevent curds from matting together. Once at 100°F (38°C), maintain the temperature for 10 minutes while stirring occasionally.
6. Line a colander with cheesecloth and pour in the curds to separate them from the whey. Allow the whey to drain for 5 minutes.

7. Return the curds to a clean pot and mix in the salt evenly.
8. Line a cheese mold with cheesecloth and pack the curds into the mold. Fold the cloth over the top and place the follower on top. Press the cheese lightly (about 10 lbs. of pressure) for 30 minutes.
9. Remove the cheese, unwrap, flip it, and rewrap in the cheesecloth. Press again at 20 lbs. for 12 hours.
10. Remove the cheese from the mold and unwrap it. Place it on an aging mat or wooden cutting board in a cool, dry place to air-dry for 2 to 3 days, flipping it daily until the surface is dry to the touch.
11. Once dry, coat the cheese in cheese wax or a natural cheese coating to protect it during aging.
12. Place the waxed cheese in a cool area (ideally 50°F/10°C to 55°F/13°C with 80% to 85% humidity) and age for at least 4 weeks. Flip the cheese every few days to ensure even aging. For a sharper flavor, age it for 2 to 3 months or longer.
13. Storage: After aging, store the cheese in the refrigerator, wrapped in wax paper or cheese paper. Properly aged farmhouse cheddar can last for months if kept cool and dry.

RECIPE TIP: Save the whey! The leftover whey can be used in baking, soups, or as a protein-packed addition to smoothies.

Where and How to Air Dry Cheese: Ideal Air-Drying Locations

- Kitchen Counter. Ensure it's cool, free of direct sunlight, and away from heat sources. Cover with cheesecloth to keep it clean.
- Pantry or Storage Room. If either of these is a dark, cool space (50°F/10°C to 60°F/16°C) with good airflow, it will work well.
- Refrigerator. Place cheese on a wire rack with space around it for airflow if the ambient temperature is too warm.
- Basement or Cellar. Perfect if it's clean, ventilated, and temperature-stable.

CURING NITRATE-FREE BACON AT HOME

Curing bacon at home is a rewarding way to reconnect with traditional food preservation methods while creating a healthier, more flavorful alternative to store-bought options. Historically, curing meat was essential for preservation before refrigeration, and natural methods using salt, sugar, and smoke were staples in kitchens worldwide.

Today, the process has been refined to balance safety and taste, with nitrate-free options gaining popularity for those seeking a cleaner, preservative-free approach. By using natural ingredients, you can enjoy bacon without the additives and synthetic nitrates often found in commercially produced versions, offering peace of mind and a delicious result.

Techniques for Curing Bacon Using Natural Ingredients

Curing bacon involves drawing out moisture, enhancing flavor, and preserving the meat through a combination of salt, sugar, and optional seasonings. Unlike store-bought bacon, which often contains synthetic nitrates, homemade bacon can be cured safely with natural methods. Salt is the key curing agent, while sugar adds balance and flavor. Optional spices, herbs, and even natural sources of nitrates like celery powder can be included for variety.

Proper Storage Techniques and Shelf Life for Nitrate-Free Bacon

Proper storage is essential for maintaining the quality, flavor, and safety of your nitrate-free bacon after curing. Once cured, bacon should be stored in an airtight container or tightly wrapped in plastic wrap or butcher paper to minimize exposure to air. Vacuum sealing is ideal, as it extends freshness and helps prevent spoilage. Keep the bacon in the coldest part of your refrigerator, typically near the back, where temperatures are most stable.

In the refrigerator, uncooked cured bacon will last 7 to 10 days when properly stored, while frozen bacon can retain its quality for up to 6 months. Although it remains safe to eat beyond this time, you may notice some loss of flavor and texture. Cooked bacon can be refrigerated for 3 to 5 days or frozen for up to 1 month.

For maximum freshness, freeze your bacon immediately after curing if you don't plan to consume it within a week. Before use, always inspect the bacon for signs of spoilage, such as unusual odors, sliminess, or discoloration. By following these techniques, you'll enjoy flavorful, high-quality homemade bacon whenever you need it, whether freshly cured or pulled from the freezer for a special meal.

Step-by-Step Guide to Curing Nitrate-Free Bacon

INGREDIENTS

5 lbs. pork belly
½ cup kosher salt (or another coarse salt)
½ cup sugar (white, brown, or a mix)
2 T. black pepper, coarsely ground
1 T. smoked paprika
1 T. garlic powder
1 T. onion powder
1 tsp. ground cayenne pepper (optional, for a bit of heat)
1 tsp. crushed juniper berries (optional, for a traditional curing flavor)

DIRECTIONS

1. Remove skin from pork belly and discard.
2. In a bowl, combine salt, sugar, and seasonings. Mix thoroughly to create an even blend.
3. Place the pork belly on a clean surface and rub the cure mix evenly over all sides, ensuring full coverage.
4. Place the coated pork belly in a large, resealable plastic bag or wrap it tightly in plastic wrap. Lay it on a tray to catch any drips and refrigerate for 7 days. Flip the pork belly daily to redistribute the cure and ensure even penetration.
5. After 7 days, the pork belly should feel firm to the touch. If it still feels soft, extend the curing time by 1 to 2 days.
6. Remove the pork belly from the bag and rinse off the cure under cold water. Pat it dry with paper towels and place it on a wire rack in the refrigerator for 24 hours to air-dry.
7. For added flavor, smoke the cured pork belly in a smoker at 200°F (93°C) until it reaches an internal temperature of 145°F (63°C). Use wood chips like applewood, hickory, or cherry for a smoky aroma.
8. Once cured (and smoked, if desired), slice the bacon to your preferred thickness. Store it in an airtight container in the refrigerator for up to a week or freeze for longer storage.

9

Cooking and Meal Creation

The preparation of good food is merely another expression of art, one of the joys of civilized living.

DIONE LUCAS

chef

Dione Lucas (1909–1971) was a trailblazing English chef and the first female graduate of Le Cordon Bleu culinary school in Paris. She viewed cooking as an art form, capable of enriching both body and soul, and famously described preparing good food as "one of the joys of civilized living." Her work not only celebrated the importance of technique but highlighted the joy of creating meals that go far beyond satisfying physical hunger. Through her television programs and cookbooks, Lucas introduced French culinary arts to a broader audience, encouraging home cooks to see meal preparation as both a creative outlet and a deeply rewarding activity.

For those of us who preserve food, this philosophy rings especially true. Preserving food is just the first step; the real magic lies in transforming those jars of canned goods or bags of freeze-dried vegetables into flavorful meals that nourish both the body and the spirit. A well-stocked pantry is a canvas, and the meals we create from it become expressions of resourcefulness, creativity, and love.

Incorporating Preserved Foods into Everyday Meals

Preserved foods offer an incredible opportunity to embrace seasonal abundance year-round. However, adapting recipes to incorporate these preserved ingredients often feels daunting to those unfamiliar with their unique properties. One of the most common questions home food preservers ask me is "How do I turn a fresh-ingredient recipe into one that utilizes my stored food resources?"

The key to success is understanding the subtle differences between fresh and preserved ingredients. For instance, home-canned vegetables are already cooked, requiring adjustments in cooking time. Dehydrated foods need to be rehydrated to achieve the proper texture. And freeze-dried ingredients may need balancing with additional moisture or seasonings.

By learning to make these adjustments, you can create vibrant, flavorful meals from your food reserves without feeling restricted by recipes designed solely for fresh ingredients.

Utilizing Your Food Reserves in Meal Creation

Every home cook approaches meal creation differently. Some rely heavily on recipes, while others enjoy improvising, trusting their instincts and experience. Then there are those who view recipes as a starting point for experimentation, adding their own spin to create something unique. Regardless of your cooking style, using preserved foods requires a few key tools and techniques to ensure success.

Conversion Tools and Techniques

Adapting recipes begins with understanding how to measure and prepare preserved foods. Fresh ingredients don't always translate directly to their preserved counterparts, and that's where a conversion chart is invaluable.

Keep in mind, conversions are just a starting point. It's also important to know how to prepare preserved ingredients to match their fresh counterparts as closely as possible.

Here are three practical tips:

- **Rehydrate.** Soak dehydrated ingredients in warm water or broth for 15 to 30 minutes before using them. For extra flavor, rehydrate in a seasoned liquid.
- **Drain and Rinse.** Learn when to drain and rinse home-canned foods if you want to reduce salt or liquid content.
- **Adjust Texture.** Freeze-dried ingredients can soften quickly in liquid, so add them just before serving if you want to retain some of the food's texture.

I've created a Comprehensive Fresh to Preserved Conversion Chart (pages 211–215) so you can easily convert any fresh-ingredient recipe to confidently use your preserved food resources. Feel free to scale the chart measurements up or down to create the desired yield. In addition to the chart, here are some general rules of thumb you can follow to help you convert easily and swiftly.

DRIED BEANS AND LEGUMES

Home-Canned: 1 pint = 2 cups cooked beans (drained).

Dehydrated: Shrinks to one half of the original volume when cooked; 1 cup cooked beans = ½ cup dehydrated cooked beans.

Freeze-Dried: Retains size and volume; 1 cup cooked beans = 1 cup freeze-dried beans.

VEGETABLES

Home-Canned: A half-pint jar typically holds 1 cup of cooked/processed vegetables.

Dehydrated: Dehydrated vegetables shrink significantly, typically reducing to about a quarter of their original volume.

Freeze-Dried: Freeze-dried vegetables retain their original size and shape but lose moisture, so 1 cup freeze-dried = 1 cup fresh when rehydrated.

FRUITS

Home-Canned: 1 pint = 2 cups for most fruits.

Dehydrated: Typically shrinks to one quarter to one third of the original volume, depending on water content.

Freeze-Dried: Retains size and volume, with moisture removed.

MEAT AND POULTRY

Home-Canned: 1 pint = 2 cups for most meats and poultry (diced or ground).

Dehydrated: Typically shrinks to one half of the original volume; 1 cup fresh = ½ cup dehydrated. Ground meat often dehydrates at a 1:1 ratio.

Freeze-Dried: Retains size and volume; 1 cup fresh = 1 cup freeze-dried.

FISH

Home-Canned: 1 pint = 2 cups for most fish (fillets or small whole fish).

Dehydrated: Typically shrinks to one third to one half of the original volume; 1 cup fresh = ⅓ to ½ cup dehydrated.

Freeze-Dried: Retains size and volume; 1 cup fresh = 1 cup freeze-dried.

SHRIMP

Home-Canned: 1 pint = 2 cups cooked shrimp (peeled).

Dehydrated: Shrinks to one half of the original volume; 1 cup fresh cooked = ½ cup dehydrated.

Freeze-Dried: Retains size and volume; 1 cup fresh = 1 cup freeze-dried.

While there may be some nuances depending on the fresh ingredient, these rules of thumb will help you immensely when cooking with your preserved resources.

COMPREHENSIVE FRESH TO PRESERVED CONVERSION CHART

Category	Fresh Ingredient	Home-Canned Equivalent	Dehydrated Equivalent	Freeze-Dried Equivalent
DRIED BEANS AND LEGUMES				
	1 cup cooked beans	½ pint canned beans	½ cup dehydrated cooked beans	1 cup freeze-dried cooked beans
	1 lb. cooked beans	1 pint canned beans	1¼ cups dehydrated cooked beans	2 cups freeze-dried cooked beans
	1 cup dry lentils	1 pint canned lentils	1 cup dehydrated cooked lentils	1 cup freeze-dried cooked lentils
VEGETABLES				
	1 cup fresh asparagus	½ pint canned asparagus	¼ cup dehydrated asparagus	1 cup freeze-dried asparagus

COMPREHENSIVE FRESH TO PRESERVED CONVERSION CHART, (CONT'D)

Category	Fresh Ingredient	Home-Canned Equivalent	Dehydrated Equivalent	Freeze-Dried Equivalent
VEGETABLES				
	1 cup fresh broccoli	½ pint canned broccoli	½ cup dehydrated broccoli	1 cup freeze-dried broccoli
	1 lb. fresh carrots	1 quart canned carrots	2½ cups dehydrated carrots	4 cups freeze-dried carrots
	1 cup celery (diced)	½ pint canned celery	¼ cup dehydrated celery	1 cup freeze-dried celery
	1 cup fresh corn kernels	½ pint canned corn kernels	½ cup dehydrated corn kernels	1 cup freeze-dried corn kernels
	1 cup fresh green beans	½ pint canned green beans	½ cup dehydrated green beans	1 cup freeze-dried green beans
	1 cup fresh hot or sweet peppers	½ pint canned peppers	¾ cup dehydrated peppers	1 cup freeze-dried hot peppers
	1 cup fresh mushrooms	1 pint drained, canned mushrooms	1½ cups dehydrated mushrooms	1 cup freeze-dried mushrooms
	1 cup fresh okra	½ pint canned okra	½ cup dehydrated okra	1 cup freeze-dried okra
	1 cup onions (diced)	½ pint canned onions	⅓ cup dehydrated onions	1 cup freeze-dried onions
	1 lb. fresh peas	1 pint canned peas	¾ cup dehydrated peas	2 cups freeze-dried peas
	1 cup fresh parsnips (diced)	1 pint canned parsnips, drained	¾ cup dehydrated parsnips	1 cup freeze-dried parsnips
	1 lb. fresh potatoes (cubed)	1 quart canned potatoes	2½ cups dehydrated potatoes	4 cups freeze-dried potatoes
	1 cup fresh pumpkin (diced)	1 pint canned pumpkin, drained	¾ cup dehydrated pumpkin	1 cup freeze-dried pumpkin
	1 cup fresh spinach or collard greens	½ cup canned spinach/collards	¼ cup dehydrated greens	1 cup freeze-dried greens

Category	Fresh Ingredient	Home-Canned Equivalent	Dehydrated Equivalent	Freeze-Dried Equivalent
VEGETABLES				
	1 cup fresh sweet potatoes (diced)	1 pint canned sweet potatoes, drained	¾ cup dehydrated sweet potatoes	1 cup freeze-dried sweet potatoes
	1 cup fresh tomatoes (diced)	½ pint canned tomatoes	¼ cup dehydrated tomatoes	1 cup freeze-dried tomatoes
	1 lb. fresh tomatoes (diced)	1 pint canned tomatoes	½ cup dehydrated tomatoes	2 cups freeze-dried tomatoes
	1 cup fresh turnips (diced)	½ pint canned turnips	¼ cup dehydrated turnips	1 cup freeze-dried turnips
	1 cup fresh winter squash (diced)	1 pint canned winter squash, drained	¾ cup dehydrated winter squash	1 cup freeze-dried winter squash
	1 cup fresh zucchini (diced)	1 pint canned zucchini	½ cup dehydrated zucchini	1 cup freeze-dried zucchini
FRUITS				
	1 cup fresh apples (diced)	½ pint canned apples	¼ cup dehydrated apples	1 cup freeze-dried apples
	1 cup fresh apricots (diced)	½ pint canned apricots	⅓ cup dehydrated apricots	1 cup freeze-dried apricots
	1 cup fresh bananas (sliced)	Not Applicable	⅓ cup dehydrated bananas	1 cup freeze-dried bananas
	4 cups fresh whole berries	1 pint canned whole berries, drained	1 cup dehydrated whole berries	4 cups freeze-dried whole berries
	1 cup fresh cherries	1 pint canned cherries	½ cup dehydrated cherries	1 cup freeze-dried cherries
	1 cup fresh citrus slices	Not Applicable	1 cup dehydrated citrus slices	1 cup freeze-dried citrus slices
	1 cup fresh crabapples	½ pint canned crabapples	¼ cup dehydrated crab apples	1 cup freeze-dried crabapples

COMPREHENSIVE FRESH TO PRESERVED CONVERSION CHART, (CONT'D)

Category	Fresh Ingredient	Home-Canned Equivalent	Dehydrated Equivalent	Freeze-Dried Equivalent
FRUITS				
	1 cup fresh whole figs	½ pint canned figs	½ cup dehydrated figs	1 cup freeze-dried figs
	1 cup fresh grapefruit (segmented)	½ pint canned grapefruit	½ cup dehydrated grapefruit	1 cup freeze-dried grapefruit
	1 cup fresh grapes	½ pint canned grapes	½ cup dehydrated grapes (raisins)	1 cup freeze-dried grapes
	1 cup fresh guavas (diced)	½ pint canned guavas	⅓ cup dehydrated guavas	1 cup freeze-dried guavas
	1 cup fresh mangoes (diced)	½ pint canned mangoes	⅓ cup dehydrated mangoes	1 cup freeze-dried mangoes
	1 cup fresh nectarines (segmented)	½ pint canned nectarines	¼ cup dehydrated nectarines	1 cup freeze-dried nectarines
	1 cup fresh papayas (diced)	½ pint canned papayas	⅓ cup dehydrated papayas	1 cup freeze-dried papayas
	1 cup fresh peaches (sliced)	½ pint canned peaches	½ cup dehydrated peaches	1 cup freeze-dried peaches
	1 cup fresh pears (sliced)	½ pint canned pears	½ cup dehydrated pears	1 cup freeze-dried pears
	1 cup fresh pineapple (chunks)	½ pint canned pineapple	½ cup dehydrated pineapple	1 cup freeze-dried pineapple
	1 cup fresh plums (diced)	½ pint canned plums	⅓ cup dehydrated plums	1 cup freeze-dried plums
	1 cup fresh rhubarb (diced)	½ pint canned rhubarb	⅓ cup dehydrated rhubarb	1 cup freeze-dried rhubarb
	1 cup fresh whole strawberries	½ pint canned strawberries	¼ cup dehydrated strawberries	1 cup freeze-dried strawberries

Category	Fresh Ingredient	Home-Canned Equivalent	Dehydrated Equivalent	Freeze-Dried Equivalent
POULTRY				
	1 lb. boneless skinless breasts	1 pint canned poultry	1 cup dehydrated poultry	2 cups freeze-dried poultry
	1 lb. boneless skinless thighs	1 pint canned poultry	1 cup dehydrated poultry	2 cups freeze-dried poultry
	1 lb. ground poultry	1 pint canned ground poultry	2 cups dehydrated ground poultry	2 cups freeze-dried ground poultry
PORK				
	1 lb. pork (cubed)	1 pint canned pork	1 cup dehydrated pork	2 cups freeze-dried pork
	1 lb. ground pork	1 pint canned pork	2 cups dehydrated ground pork	2 cups freeze-dried pork
	1 cup bacon (crumbles)	Not Applicable	½ cup dehydrated bacon crumbles	1 cup freeze-dried bacon crumbles
	1 lb. diced ham (cooked or raw)	1 pint canned ham	⅓ cup dehydrated ham	2 cups freeze-dried ham
BEEF				
	1 lb. beef (cubed)	1 pint canned beef	1 cup dehydrated beef	2 cups freeze-dried beef
	1 lb. ground beef	1 pint canned beef	2 cups dehydrated ground beef	2 cups freeze-dried beef
FISH				
	1 lb. fish fillets	1 pint canned fish	2 to 3 dehydrated fish fillets	2 to 3 freeze-dried fish fillets
	1 lb. smelt, sardines, or other small fish	1 pint canned	1 cup dehydrated small fish	2 cups freeze-dried small fish
	1 lb. shrimp	1 pint canned	½ cup dehydrated shrimp	2 cups freeze-dried shrimp

How to Adjust a Fresh-Ingredient Recipe

Adapting a fresh-ingredient recipe starts with understanding its structure. Most recipes include a balance of flavors and textures that rely on fresh ingredients. To modify a recipe, follow these steps:

1. Identify which ingredients can be replaced with preserved versions. Consider both flavor and texture. For instance, swap out canned or freeze-dried tomatoes for fresh tomatoes. Another example would be using home-canned boneless, skinless chicken breasts instead of cooking raw chicken breasts.
2. Prepare your preserved ingredients. For canned items, drain and rinse as needed. Rehydrate dehydrated and freeze-dried ingredients to their original state or increase the recipe's overall liquid content to compensate for rehydration. Adjust seasoning, as preserved foods often concentrate flavors, meaning less is more.
3. Modify cooking times to compensate for using pre-cooked ingredients that only need to be heated through rather than raw ingredients that need to be cooked. For example, home-canned vegetables are pre-cooked and require less time in the recipe, whereas rehydrated items may need longer cooking to achieve the desired texture.
4. Canned and rehydrated ingredients often add extra moisture, so you may need to reduce the liquid content from the recipe.

An example would be creating a fresh chicken-and-vegetable soup recipe that calls for raw chicken, fresh carrots, and fresh celery. Using preserved foods, you could substitute canned chicken for the raw chicken, canned or dehydrated carrots for the fresh carrots, and freeze-dried celery for the fresh celery. Rehydrate the vegetables before adding them to reduce the cooking time. Consider adding the drained, canned chicken last to avoid overcooking the chicken and vegetables.

Step-by-Step Guide to Adjusting a Fresh-Ingredient Recipe

Using a common and popular recipe like beef stew, let's dive into how we'll substitute our preserved foods for fresh ingredients to produce a delicious outcome. Here is the fresh-ingredient recipe.

Step 1: Find Areas to Incorporate Preserved Foods

We start by reviewing the list of fresh ingredients to see what can be substituted with our preserved resources.

- Beef stew meat (2 pounds)
    - Home-canned stew meat, drained
    - Freeze-dried stew meat, rehydrated
- Vegetables: Onions, potatoes, carrots, celery, and peas
    - Canned, dehydrated, freeze-dried, and frozen options may all come into play.
- Fresh Herbs
- Cornstarch

Traditional Beef Stew Example

INGREDIENTS

3 T. all-purpose flour
½ tsp. garlic powder
½ tsp. salt, plus more to taste
½ tsp. black pepper, plus more to taste
2 lbs. stewing beef, trimmed and cubed
3 T. olive oil
1 onion, chopped (1 cup)
½ cup red wine, optional
6 cups beef broth
1lb. potatoes, peeled and cubed (4 cups)
4 carrots, cut into 1-inch pieces (2 cups)
4 celery ribs, cut into 1-inch pieces (1 cup)
6 oz. tomato paste
1 sprig fresh rosemary
3 T. cornstarch
2 T. water
1 cup peas

DIRECTIONS

1. Combine flour, garlic powder, salt, and pepper in a gallon bag. Toss beef in flour mixture, shaking to coat evenly.
2. Heat olive oil in a large Dutch oven or stockpot. Working in batches, brown the beef on all sides and remove from heat. Add the onion and cook until translucent.
3. Slowly add the red wine (if using) to the Dutch oven and deglaze the pan, scraping up any brown bits from the bottom. Slowly add the beef broth and mix well.
4. Add the potatoes, carrots, celery, tomato paste, and sprig of rosemary. Reduce heat to medium low, cover, and simmer 1 hour or until beef is tender (up to 90 minutes). Mix infrequently to blend flavors.
5. Mix the cornstarch and water to create a slurry. Slowly add the slurry to the boiling stew to reach desired consistency. Stir in peas and simmer 5 to 10 minutes before serving. Season with salt and pepper to taste.

Step 2: Compare the Conversion Chart with the Fresh Ingredients You've Identified

Using the Comprehensive Fresh to Preserved Conversion Chart on pages 211–215, you know you'll need the following preserved amounts to create this recipe:

- You need 1 quart of home-canned beef stew meat, drained, to yield 4 cups raw. Or you need 4 cups freeze-dried beef stew meat to yield 4 cups raw once rehydrated.
- Vegetables:
  - 1 cup onion: Because you're deglazing the pan after cooking, keep in mind that if you choose a higher water content option (frozen or canned), it will take a bit longer to cook out the water.
  - Potatoes, carrots, celery, and peas: There's no wrong answer, because each of the three preserved options will work perfectly, including frozen vegetables.
- If fresh herbs aren't available, you can use 1 teaspoon of dried herbs to accomplish the same result.
- Cornstarch is just one of many thickeners. You can also use dehydrated or freeze-dried potato flakes or flour.

Step 3: Review the Recipe Instructions for Adjustments

Now let's review the instructions to see where we'll amend the steps to produce the desired outcome without compromising flavor and texture.

- Home-canned meat is a pre-cooked substitute that will decrease the cooking time. We must be careful the pre-cooked meat doesn't shred apart during cooking. The adjustment is adding the drained home-canned stew beef toward the end of the cooking process.
- Notice how the peas are reserved for last to avoid over cooking? It's the same if using home-canned peas, whereas if you opted for frozen, they could be cooked with the other vegetables. If using freeze-dried or dehydrated peas, adding an additional cup of stock or water to the stew will compensate for the moisture they'll absorb when cooking and rehydrating.
- Fresh herbs are great—if you have them handy. Using concentrated dried herbs is a suitable solution, but less is required compared to fresh. And they can be added at the same time as the vegetables without having to remember to remove and discard the sprig of fresh.
- Thickening agents can be store-bought or home preserved, and they can also be natural ingredients without having to create a slurry. Or you can simply mash several cubes of potatoes within the stew itself to create a creamy, thick texture.

This simple three-step process makes using your preserved foods convenient. Over time, you'll never look at a recipe the same way. It will become second nature for you to swap in your home-canned, freeze-dried, and stored pantry items.

SIMPLE RECIPES INCORPORATING FRESH AND PRESERVED INGREDIENTS

Breakfast Recipes

Spiced Apple and Oatmeal Bake with Dehydrated Apples and Home-Canned Cinnamon Syrup

This hearty, comforting breakfast is perfect for chilly mornings, combining pantry staples and preserved ingredients with fresh flavors. This dish can be prepared the night before for an easy, ready-to-bake breakfast. Serve warm, topped with a dollop of yogurt and sprinkled granola.

INGREDIENTS

½ cup dehydrated apple slices
1 cup water
2 cups rolled oats
1 tsp. ground cinnamon
½ tsp. ground nutmeg
½ tsp. ground ginger
¼ tsp. salt
½ cup chopped walnuts or pecans
¼ cup dehydrated grapes (raisins)
2 cups milk
½ cup home-canned cinnamon syrup (or maple syrup)
2 large water-glassed eggs
1 tsp. vanilla extract
2 T. melted homemade butter or oil

DIRECTIONS

1. Preheat the oven to 350°F (175°C) and lightly grease a 9 × 9-inch baking dish.
2. Place the dehydrated apple slices in a bowl and cover them with the 1 cup of water. Let them sit for 10 minutes or until softened. Reserve the soaking water.
3. In a large mixing bowl, stir together the oats, cinnamon, nutmeg, ginger, salt, nuts and raisins.
4. In a separate bowl, whisk together the milk, reserved apple soaking water, cinnamon or maple syrup, eggs, vanilla, and butter or oil.
5. Add the wet ingredients to the dry ingredients, stirring until combined. Fold in the rehydrated apple slices.
6. Pour the mixture into the prepared baking dish. Smooth the top of the mixture with a spatula. Bake for 35 to 40 minutes, or until the top is golden and pricks clean with a knife in the center.
7. Let the oatmeal bake cool for 5 to 10 minutes before serving. Drizzle with additional syrup, if desired.

RECIPE TIP: This recipe also works wonderfully with a pint of home-canned sweet cherries or blueberries, drained.

Garden Veggie Frittata with Freeze-Dried Spinach, Home-Canned Bell Peppers, and Fresh Eggs

A vibrant, protein-packed dish combining fresh eggs, pantry staples, and preserved vegetables for an energized start to your day. Serve with a side of fresh fruit and toast.

INGREDIENTS

6 large eggs

½ cup milk

¼ tsp. salt

¼ tsp. black pepper

½ tsp. dried oregano

¼ tsp. smoked paprika

¼ cup freeze-dried spinach

1 T. homemade butter or tallow

½ cup home-canned bell peppers, drained and chopped

¼ cup fresh cherry tomatoes, halved

¼ cup shredded cheddar or mozzarella cheese

DIRECTIONS

1. Preheat the oven to 375°F (190°C).
2. In a medium bowl, whisk together the eggs, milk, salt, pepper, oregano, and paprika until fully combined.
3. Place the freeze-dried spinach in a small bowl and cover it with warm water to rehydrate. Let it sit for 5 minutes, then drain well.
4. Heat the butter or tallow in an oven-safe skillet over medium heat. Once melted, add the rehydrated spinach, bell peppers, and cherry tomatoes. Sauté for 2 to 3 minutes, stirring occasionally.
5. Pour the egg mixture into the skillet over the vegetables. Tilt the skillet gently to ensure the eggs are evenly distributed.
6. Sprinkle the shredded cheese on top. Let the frittata cook on the stovetop for 2 to 3 minutes, just until the edges begin to set. Then transfer the skillet to the oven and bake for 10 to 12 minutes, or until the frittata is fully set in the center and lightly golden on top.
7. Remove the frittata from the oven and let it cool for 5 minutes. Slice into wedges and serve warm.

Lunch Recipes

Mediterranean Couscous Salad with Home-Canned Chickpeas, Dehydrated Tomatoes, and Fresh Herbs

A refreshing, nutrient-packed salad featuring a mix of pantry staples and garden-fresh flavors. It is the perfect side dish for a light lunch, and whips up in a jiffy.

INGREDIENTS

1 cup couscous
1 cup boiling water or vegetable broth
2 T. extra virgin olive oil
1 T. lemon juice
1 tsp. homemade apple cider vinegar
1 clove garlic, minced
¼ tsp. salt
¼ tsp. black pepper
¼ cup dehydrated diced tomatoes
½ cup home-canned chickpeas, drained and rinsed
½ cup chopped fresh parsley
¼ cup chopped fresh mint
¼ cup diced cucumber
¼ cup diced red onion
¼ cup crumbled homemade farmhouse cheddar cheese

DIRECTIONS

1. Place the couscous in a heatproof bowl. Pour the boiling water or vegetable broth over the couscous, cover, and let it sit for 5 minutes. Fluff with a fork and set aside to cool slightly.
2. In a small bowl, whisk together the olive oil, lemon juice, apple cider vinegar, garlic, salt, and pepper to create the dressing.
3. Rehydrate the dehydrated tomatoes by soaking them in warm water for 5 to 10 minutes. Drain and set aside.
4. In a large mixing bowl, combine the couscous, rehydrated tomatoes, chickpeas, parsley, mint, cucumber, onion, and cheese.
5. Pour the dressing over the couscous mixture and toss until everything is evenly coated.
6. Let the salad rest for 10 to 15 minutes to allow the flavors to meld. Serve at room temperature or chilled.

RECIPE TIP: If you haven't made farmhouse cheddar yet, you may substitute store-bought cheddar or use feta or aged Gouda.

Hearty Black Bean and Sweet Potato Soup with Home-Canned Black Beans and Freeze-Dried Sweet Potatoes

This comforting, nutrient-packed soup balances the earthiness of black beans with the natural sweetness of fresh sweet potatoes. It's an easy, satisfying lunch or dinner option that comes together with pantry staples and preserved ingredients. Serve alongside a buttered slice of peasant bread.

INGREDIENTS

1 T. tallow or homemade butter

1 small onion, diced

2 cloves garlic, minced

1 tsp. ground cumin

½ tsp. smoked paprika

¼ tsp. ground coriander

½ tsp. salt (adjust to taste)

¼ tsp. black pepper

1 quart home-canned vegetable broth (or chicken broth)

1 pint home-canned diced tomatoes

2 cups freeze-dried sweet potatoes

2 cups home-canned black beans, drained and rinsed

1 tsp. fresh lime juice

¼ cup chopped fresh cilantro (optional, for garnish)

DIRECTIONS

1. Heat the tallow or butter in a large stockpot over medium heat. Add the onion and sauté for 3 to 4 minutes, until softened. Add the garlic and cook for an additional minute, stirring frequently.
2. Stir in the cumin, paprika, coriander, salt, and pepper. Cook for 1 minute to toast the spices and release their aroma.
3. Pour in the vegetable or chicken broth and tomatoes. Bring the mixture to a boil, then reduce the heat to a simmer. Add the sweet potatoes, then cover the pot and let the soup cook for 15 to 20 minutes, or until the sweet potatoes are tender.
4. Add the black beans to the pot and stir to combine. Simmer for an additional 5 minutes to heat through.
5. Remove the soup from the heat and stir in the lime juice. Adjust seasonings as needed. Serve warm, garnished with fresh cilantro, if desired.

RECIPE TIP: If you don't have freeze-dried sweet potatoes for this recipe, not to worry. Use 2 cups fresh or 1 pint home-canned, drained. Add the home-canned sweet potatoes the same time you add the home-canned black beans.

Dinner Recipes

Savory Lemon Herb Chicken with Home-Canned Chicken, Dehydrated Lemon Slices, and Freeze-Dried Zucchini

A bright and comforting dish that pairs tender, home-canned chicken with vegetables and fragrant herbs. This one-pan meal is quick, flavorful, and perfect for busy evenings. Serve this hot over rice, quinoa, or couscous with a fresh side salad for a complete meal.

INGREDIENTS

2 T. tallow
1 medium onion, sliced
2 cloves garlic, minced
1 cup frozen green beans
1 cup diced freeze-dried zucchini
1 quart home-canned chicken breasts with its broth
1 tsp. dried thyme
1 tsp. dried parsley, plus more for serving
½ tsp. paprika
½ tsp. salt (adjust to taste)
¼ tsp. black pepper
10 dehydrated lemon slices
1 cup cherry tomatoes, halved
1 T. fresh lemon juice

DIRECTIONS

1. Heat the tallow in a large skillet over medium heat. Add the onion and sauté for 3 to 4 minutes, until softened. Stir in the garlic and cook for an additional minute.
2. Add the green beans and zucchini to the skillet. Sauté for 2 to 3 minutes, stirring occasionally, allowing the vegetables to start softening.
3. Push the vegetables to the side of the skillet, exposing the center of the pan. Add the chicken with its broth to the center. Sprinkle the thyme, parsley, paprika, salt, and pepper evenly over the chicken and vegetables.
4. Arrange the lemon slices and cherry tomatoes on top of the chicken and vegetables and bring to a gentle simmer. Cover with a lid and cook on low heat for 7 to 10 minutes, allowing the lemon slices to rehydrate and the vegetables to become tender.
5. Remove the lid, stir gently to combine all ingredients, and adjust seasoning if needed. Stir in the fresh lemon juice for a final burst of citrus flavor. Serve warm; garnish with additional parsley and drizzle a tablespoon or two of broth from the skillet on each serving.

Pasta Primavera with Freeze-Dried Zucchini, Home-Canned Tomato Sauce, and Homemade Ricotta

This light and flavorful pasta dish pairs the convenience of preserved ingredients with the freshness of homemade ricotta cheese, creating a vibrant and creamy primavera, perfect for any season. Serve this dish as a main course or even as a side to roasted chicken or seafood.

INGREDIENTS

1 lb. pasta (penne, bowtie, or spaghetti)
2 T. tallow or olive oil
2 cloves garlic, minced
1 cup freeze-dried zucchini, rehydrated and drained
½ cup freeze-dried bell peppers, rehydrated and drained
1 pint home-canned tomato sauce
½ tsp. dried basil
½ tsp. dried oregano
¼ tsp. red pepper flakes (optional)
½ tsp. salt (adjust to taste)
¼ tsp. black pepper
½ cup homemade ricotta cheese
½ cup freshly grated Parmesan cheese
2 T. fresh parsley or basil, chopped (for garnish)

DIRECTIONS

1. Cook the pasta in a large pot of salted boiling water until al dente. Reserve ½ cup of pasta water before draining.
2. While the pasta cooks, heat the tallow or olive oil in a large skillet over medium heat. Add the garlic and sauté for 1 to 2 minutes until fragrant.
3. Add the zucchini and bell peppers to the skillet. Sauté for 3 to 4 minutes, stirring occasionally, until softened.
4. Stir in the tomato sauce, basil, oregano, red pepper flakes (if using), salt, and pepper. Simmer for 5 minutes to combine the flavors.
5. Add the drained pasta to the skillet, tossing to coat it evenly in the sauce. If the sauce is too thick, add the reserved pasta water, 1 to 2 tablespoons at a time, until the desired consistency is reached.
6. Remove the skillet from the heat and gently fold in the ricotta cheese. Adjust seasonings as needed.
7. Serve warm, topped with Parmesan and garnished with the parsley or basil.

RECIPE TIP: If you have not yet made the homemade ricotta, you may substitute store-bought ricotta or another soft cheese like mascarpone.

Dessert Recipes

Berry Crumble with Freeze-Dried Blueberries, Home-Canned Strawberry Jam, and Pantry Oats

A simple yet irresistible dessert that blends the sweetness of preserved berries with the texture of freeze-dried fruit and a buttery oat topping. Perfect for any occasion, this crumble is easy to assemble and packed with flavor. Serve this dessert warm with a scoop of vanilla bean ice cream or a dollop of whipped cream on top.

INGREDIENTS

For the Filling:

2 cups freeze-dried blueberries, rehydrated and drained

½ cup home-canned strawberry jam

1 T. cornstarch

1 tsp. lemon juice

¼ tsp. cinnamon

For the Crumble Topping:

1 cup old-fashioned oats

½ cup all-purpose flour

½ cup brown sugar

½ tsp. cinnamon

¼ tsp. salt

½ cup homemade butter, melted

DIRECTIONS

1. Preheat the oven to 375°F (190°C) and lightly grease a 9 × 9-inch baking dish.
2. In a medium bowl, combine the blueberries, strawberry jam, cornstarch, lemon juice, and cinnamon. Mix well to coat the berries evenly and set aside.
3. In a separate bowl, prepare the crumble topping by mixing the oats, flour, brown sugar, cinnamon, and salt. Pour in the melted butter and stir until the mixture forms a crumbly texture.
4. Spread the berry mixture evenly into the prepared baking dish. Sprinkle the crumble topping evenly over the berries.
5. Bake in the preheated oven for 30 to 35 minutes, or until the topping is golden brown and the berry filling is bubbling around the edges.
6. Remove from the oven and let the crumble cool for 10 minutes before serving.

RECIPE TIP: Feel free to substitute one pint of drained, home-canned blueberries for the freeze-dried blueberries.

Chocolate-Cherry Bread Pudding with Dehydrated Cherries and Home-Canned Vanilla Custard Sauce

This decadent dessert combines rich chocolate, tart cherries, and a creamy vanilla custard sauce for the ultimate indulgence. The dehydrated cherries rehydrate beautifully, adding bursts of flavor to the warm, comforting bread pudding.

INGREDIENTS

For the Bread Pudding:

6 cups cubed day-old peasant bread

1 cup dehydrated cherries, rehydrated and drained

½ cup semi-sweet chocolate chips

1½ cups whole milk

1 cup heavy cream

½ cup granulated sugar

½ cup brown sugar

4 large water-glassed eggs

2 tsp. homemade vanilla extract

For the Topping:

½ cup semi-sweet chocolate chips

2 T. homemade butter

For the Vanilla Custard Sauce:

1 pint home-canned vanilla custard sauce

DIRECTIONS

1. Preheat the oven to 350°F (175°C) and lightly grease a 9 × 13-inch baking dish.
2. Place the cubed bread in a large mixing bowl. Add the cherries and chocolate chips, tossing to distribute evenly.
3. In a separate bowl, whisk together the milk, cream, granulated sugar, brown sugar, eggs, and vanilla. Pour the custard mixture over the bread and gently fold to coat all pieces. Let it sit for 10 minutes to allow the bread to absorb the liquid.
4. Transfer the bread mixture to the prepared baking dish, spreading it evenly. Bake in the preheated oven for 40 to 45 minutes, or until the pudding is set and golden on top.
5. While the bread pudding bakes, prepare the chocolate topping by melting the chocolate chips and butter together in a small saucepan over low heat. Stir until smooth and set aside.
6. Heat the home-canned vanilla custard sauce in a separate small saucepan until warmed through.
7. Remove the bread pudding from the oven and drizzle the melted chocolate over the top. Serve warm, with a generous pour of the warmed vanilla custard sauce.

RECIPE TIP: If you don't have home-canned vanilla custard sauce, you can quickly create homemade custard. Combine 1 cup milk, 1 cup heavy cream, ⅓ cup sugar, 1 tsp. vanilla extract, and 4 large egg yolks in a saucepan. Whisk over medium heat until the sauce thickens slightly, about 5 to 7 minutes. Strain and serve warm or chilled.

10

Embracing Seasonal Living

To every thing there is a season, and a time to every purpose under the heaven.

ECCLESIASTES 3:1 (KJV)

Eccesiastes 3:1 tells us, "To every thing there is a season, and a time to every purpose under the heaven" (KJV). This verse is a timeless reminder that life has natural rhythms, and that by aligning ourselves with the changing seasons, we can better navigate life's challenges. This includes securing food for ourselves and our families. Reflecting on the journey of food security presented in this book, consider how each chapter equips you with practical tools and knowledge to weather hardships, reduce dependency on fluctuating food markets, and build a sustainable, balanced approach to nourishment and preparedness.

Finding Balance and Security in Every Season

Through presenting practical methods like gardening, food preservation, and creative meal planning, this book helps you reduce dependency on external food sources, making the most of what you have available. It emphasizes ways to stretch your budget, reduce waste, and store food efficiently so you can build reserves that sustain you during leaner times.

Each chapter offers tools to help manage rising food costs and create personal food security by building a well-rounded food supply to sustain your household through every season. By reflecting on these lessons and putting them into practice, you're not just preparing for the future; you're reclaiming control over your personal food security, ensuring you and your family have the nourishment you need, no matter the challenges ahead.

Holistic Nourishment Through Seasonal Living

True nourishment goes beyond filling your pantry or preparing meals; it's about addressing both the physical and emotional aspects of sustaining yourself and your family. A holistic approach to food security considers how the food you grow, preserve, and eat impacts your well-being on every level. By engaging in seasonal living, you reduce stress, promote self-sufficiency, and find joy in the process.

Gardening offers a sense of accomplishment and connection to nature. Preserving food instills confidence as you see the tangible results of your efforts, and cooking with ingredients you've stored fosters pride and creativity. Even in times of hardship, this approach reminds us that small, consistent actions create stability.

Joy comes from knowing you've prepared for uncertain times. But we're also to be joyful in the process itself. The satisfaction of stocking your pantry and knowing where your food and all its ingredients come from is priceless, not only for your budget but for your overall health.

Practical Ways to Make This Book Work for You

- **Grow Your Connection to Food.** Use the gardening and planting chapters to cultivate your own food, deepening your relationship with the earth and the cycles of nature.
- **Celebrate the Seasons.** Follow the preservation methods to capture the flavors of each season, creating a pantry filled with vibrant, nourishing ingredients.
- **Cook with Love and Creativity.** Turn your preserved foods into flavorful meals with the recipes and tips provided, infusing every dish with care and inspiration.
- **Embrace Tradition.** Learn heritage food crafts to connect with the time-honored practices of past generations, keeping their wisdom alive in your kitchen.
- **Build Community.** Share recipes, trade canned goods, or host seasonal gatherings to strengthen bonds with friends, family, and neighbors.
- **Foster Resilience.** Use its storage and preservation techniques to prepare for uncertain times, creating a sense of security and peace of mind.
- **Spark Curiosity and Growth.** Experiment with new preservation methods, ingredients, or recipes, allowing yourself to learn and grow along the way.
- **Find Joy in the Process.** Slow down and savor the steps, from planting and harvesting to cooking and sharing, discovering fulfillment at every stage.
- **Create a Legacy.** Pass down the skills you've learned to the next generation, ensuring that the knowledge and values of seasonal living endure.
- **Reflect and Reconnect.** Let this book be a source of inspiration as you pause to reflect on your journey, reconnecting with the purpose behind every action.

Living Off the Land: Embracing God's Bounty with Purpose and Joy

Living off the land is a practical and rewarding way to reconnect with the earth and sustain yourself as God intended. And living off the land and knowing where your food comes from are powerful ways to reclaim control over your health and well-being. It connects you to the cycles of nature, teaching you to appreciate the time and effort it takes to cultivate, harvest, and preserve the bounty of the earth. This is something many of us forgot once food became convenient and eating meals became "fast."

The joy in this process comes from witnessing the fruits of your labor, from the first sprout in the garden to having a fully stocked pantry. Even those with limited space or resources can take small steps, like growing herbs in pots or joining a community garden. Embracing the bounty of the land also teaches gratitude. And valuing the land's abundance and using it wisely honors God's creation, giving us purpose while providing sustenance.

Finding joy in the process of seasonal living doesn't require unlimited time or financial resources. It starts with small, intentional steps that build over time. Even with limited means, choosing one area to focus on—like dehydrating fruits and vegetables—can lay a strong foundation for food security. A single dehydrator tray of apple slices or zucchini chips represents progress toward creating a reserve of nutritious, shelf-stable food.

Each small success brings satisfaction, and over time, these efforts add up, creating a sense of accomplishment and peace of mind, even in challenging seasons. Starting small allows you to enjoy the process without feeling overwhelmed, making it a sustainable and joyful way to secure your future.

Building Community Through Seasonal Living

Seasonal living and eating aren't just personal journeys; they're pathways to fostering community and strengthening bonds with those around us. Whether it's trading seeds in spring, hosting a harvest meal in autumn, or preserving summer's abundance with others, continue to create opportunities for connection and collaboration. These shared experiences remind us food has the power to unite, transcending differences and building relationships rooted in trust, care, and tradition.

While this book equips you to grow, preserve, and prepare food for your own family, it also encourages you to extend those skills outward, creating a network of shared knowledge and support. Perhaps it's teaching a neighbor how to can tomatoes, swapping jars of pickled vegetables with a friend, or forming a local group to trade recipes and tips. These acts strengthen not only individual food security but collective resilience, fostering a community that can thrive together.

By embracing seasonal living and eating as a communal experience, we honor the traditions of our ancestors who relied on one another to weather life's challenges. In today's fast-paced world, building these connections offers a grounding reminder that we are stronger together.

Resources for Continued Learning and Growth

The journey toward sustainable living and food security does not end here; it's a lifelong pursuit of learning, experimenting, and growing. Whether you're diving deeper into canning, mastering dehydrating techniques, or expanding your garden, abundant resources are available to guide you. All my books offer step-by-step instructions, innovative recipes, and practical tips to help you incorporate home canning into your daily life.

For those interested in broadening their skills, *The Dehydrator Bible* by Jennifer MacKenzie, Jay Nutt, and Don Mercer is an excellent resource, offering techniques and recipes for dehydrating fruits, vegetables, meats, and more. Platforms such as Pinterest and YouTube offer endless inspiration and tutorials. Explore The Canning Diva's social media groups and my online Canning University dedicated to food preservation.

Local organizations, such as agricultural extensions, gardening clubs, and community centers often host workshops and classes on topics like gardening, composting, and preserving. Farmers markets are also valuable hubs for connecting with others who share your passion for seasonal living. Many markets feature booths run by master gardeners or food preservation experts who can provide tailored advice. Libraries and bookstores are treasure troves of additional reading, offering books on everything from permaculture to traditional cooking techniques.

Tips for Inspiring Others While Sharing Your Journey

One of the most rewarding aspects of seasonal living is sharing your journey with others. By connecting with family, friends, and your community, you not only spread the joy of sustainable practices but inspire others to embark on their own path toward food security and seasonal living. Here are some tips to help you share your experiences in meaningful ways:

- Invite loved ones to a harvest dinner or canning day. Share meals made with your preserved foods or teach others how to preserve their own. These gatherings create lasting memories and introduce people to the joys of seasonal living.
- Use social media, a personal blog, or even a scrapbook to document your journey. Share photos of your garden, pantry, or favorite recipes, and provide tips for others who may want to try similar projects. Be sure to tag @CanningDiva when you do so I can celebrate with you!
- Home-canned jams, pickles, and spice blends make thoughtful and personal gifts. Include a handwritten note about the process or the story behind the ingredients to make the gift even more special.
- Form a local club or group focused on gardening, food preservation, or seasonal

cooking. Whether it's a monthly meetup or an online group, these spaces allow you to exchange ideas, share resources, and foster a sense of community.

- Offer to teach a neighbor how to plant a garden or host a workshop on pressure canning. Sharing your skills helps others grow while reinforcing your own knowledge.
- Work with schools, libraries, or community centers to organize classes, seed swaps, or garden projects. Collaborating with local organizations can help you reach more people and make a bigger impact.
- Lead by example. Simply living your values can inspire others, and when people see the joy and fulfillment those values bring you, they'll be more curious to learn and adopt similar practices.
- Share books, websites, or tools that have helped you on your journey. Whether it's this book or others like it, offering accessible resources can empower others to take their first steps.

By sharing your journey, you create ripples of inspiration that can transform lives. Your passion and knowledge can ignite a movement toward healthier, more-connected living, helping others discover the profound joy of seasonal living from seed to table.

APPENDIX

Recommended Resources

Below is a list of valuable books to help you expand your knowledge of seasonal living, food preservation, and sustainable practices. Each title has been carefully chosen for its practical insights and timeless wisdom.

The Canning Diva Presents Meals in a Jar
by Diane Devereaux, The Canning Diva® (Ten Peaks Press, 2024)

The Complete Guide to Pressure Canning
by Diane Devereaux, The Canning Diva® (Callisto, 2018)

The Beginner's Guide to Canning
by Diane Devereaux, The Canning Diva® (Callisto, 2020)

Canning Full Circle
by Diane Devereaux, The Canning Diva® (Patoka Pr, 2023)

The Grace-Filled Homestead
by Lana Stenner (Ten Peaks Press, 2022)

The Grace-Filled Homestead Cookbook
by Lana Stenner (Ten Peaks Press, 2023)

The Accidental Homesteader
by Kathi Lipp (Ten Peaks Press, 2023)

The Beekeeper's Bible
by Richard A. Jones and Sharon Sweeney-Lynch (Stewart, Tabori and Chang, 2011)

The Encyclopedia of Country Living
by Carla Emery (Sasquatch Books, anniversary edition, 2019)

The Dehydrator Bible
by Jennifer MacKenzie, Jay Nutt, and Don Mercer (Robert Rose, updated edition, 2025)

Root Cellaring
by Mike Bubel and Nancy Bubel (Storey Publishing, LLC, 2nd edition, 1991)

Ball Complete Book of Home Preserving
by Judi Kingry and Lauren Devine, Editors (Robert Rose, new and updated edition, 2024)

Fermented Vegetables
by Kirsten K. Shockey and Christopher Shockey (Storey Publishing, LLC, 10th anniversary edition, 2024)

The Self-Sufficient Backyard
by Ron and Johanna Melchiore (Capital Printing Co; standard edition, 2020)

The Complete Guide to Your New Root Cellar
by Julie Fryer (Atlantic Publishing Group Inc., illustrated edition, 2011)

Midwest Medicinal Plants
by Lisa M. Rose (Timber Press, 2017)

How to Cure & Preserve Beef, Pork, Poultry, Fish & Wild Game
by Nick Romano (Valley Dreams Press, 2021)

Raised-Bed Gardening for Beginners
by Tammy Wylie (Rockridge Press, 2019)

INDEX

Recipes

Step-By-Step Guides

About the Author

Diane Devereaux, The Canning Diva®, is an internationally recognized food preservation expert, author, television presenter, instructor, and mother of two. Since 2012, Diane has been sharing her lifelong passion for canning and food preservation, translating over 30 years of experience into practical solutions for the busy lives of families across the globe. She recently became a Floridian and is enjoying the splendors of sunshine and a long growing season.

Diane earned her bachelor's degree in international business from Davenport University and later plunged into a career in disaster management, where she applied her knowledge of food preservation, survival, and sustainability to those in crisis. Her deep-rooted experience in home canning, combined with her background in preparedness, led her to create The Canning Diva®—a brand that blends her love of gardening and preserving with her commitment to self-reliance and practical education.

A staunch advocate for the individual's rights to know what's in the food they eat, Diane proudly supports honest and transparent food labeling. This belief fuels her year-round dedication to gardening and preserving foods at home, ensuring a healthy lifestyle for herself and her loved ones. Through everything she creates, writes, and shares, her mission is to keep the time-honored traditions of food preservation and heritage food crafts alive and thriving, teaching these invaluable skills to households across the world.

WWW.CANNINGDIVA.COM